Making America Competitive

MAKING AMERICA COMPETITIVE

Policies for a Global Future

Marcia Lynn Whicker
and
Raymond A. Moore

PRAEGER

New York
Westport, Connecticut
London

Library of Congress Cataloging-in-Publication Data

Whicker, Marcia Lynn.
    Making America competitive : policies for a global future / Marcia
Lynn Whicker and Raymond A. Moore.
        p.   cm.
    Bibliography: p.
    Includes index.
    ISBN 0–275–93056–4
    1. United States—Economic policy—1981-   . 2. Economic forecasting—
United States.   3. Industry and State—United States.
4. Competition, International.   I. Moore, Raymond A.   II. Title.
HC106.8.W49   1988
338.973—dc19   88–5889

Library of Congress Catalog Card Number: 88–5889
ISBN: 0–275–93056–4

First published in 1988

Praeger Publishers, One Madison Avenue, New York, NY 10010
A division of Greenwood Press, Inc.

Printed in the United States of America

The paper used in this book complies with the Permanent
Paper Standard issued by the National Information Standards
Organization (Z39.48—1984).

10   9   8   7   6   5   4   3   2   1

CONTENTS

PREFACE

As the United States prepared for the election of a new president in 1988 and the inauguration of a new administration in 1989, a wise and experienced journalist observed, "We know that for the rest of the 1980s and the beginning of the 1990s the politics of the world will be dominated by the dialogue between the President of the United States and General Secretary Gorbachev of the Soviet Union, and we know something else, or think we do: that something important is happening in the Soviet Union as it approaches the 70th anniversary of its revolution" (Reston 1987). James Reston's precient observations highlight what is a major thrust of this book.

How can the United States of America organize (or reorganize) to compete successfully with its fellow superpower in the decades ahead when this competition is under new and dynamic leadership? How can we compete successfully with not only our political allies, but our major economic competitors—Japan and Western Europe, especially West Germany—as well?

Certainly, the Soviet Union is here to stay as a formidable rival for the foreseeable future. This rivalry will continue to express itself in the political, economic, ideological, cultural, technological, and scientific arenas—in the "correlation of forces" as communists label it. As if this were not challenge enough, the modernization of leadership in the Soviet government makes that competition all the more intense. The result is that the United States is being challenged as never before on the world stage.

While the Soviet rivalry, and its attendant problem of deterring nuclear war, must be at the forefront of any consideration of America's global policies, there are obviously others of nearly equal importance that sharpen the need for the United States to maintain and improve its competitive position.

High on this list is the double problem of "the twin towers" of continuing high levels of domestic and foreign trade deficits. Both had risen to dangerous heights by 1987 (budget deficits were $221 billion in 1986 and $155 billion in

1987, and trade deficits were $156.2 billion in 1986 and $171 billion in 1987) and threaten not only the internal economic stability of the United States, but also the financial well-being of Japan, West Germany, Great Britain, France, Australia, and Canada. Indeed, many believe they threaten the entire international economy.

The unprecedented drop of 508 points on the New York Stock Exchange on the Black Monday of October 19, 1987 was thought to have been greatly influenced by the existence of the "twin towers" and the inability of the U.S. government to effectively manage its economy in a way that would alleviate these problems. This perception at home and abroad, combined with attendant creeping interest and inflation rates, a declining dollar, and $8 trillion debt twice the size of the gross national product, low rates of productivity, a declining manufacturing sector, and Persian Gulf jitters—all contributed to market losses of over $1 trillion and resounding reverberations in the stock markets of London, Tokyo, Sydney, Hong Kong, Toronto, Paris, and Bonn.

The inability of the Reagan administration and the Congress to get the deficits under control while Japan and West Germany, the world's two other largest economies, ran up large trade surpluses, further contributed to the widespread conviction, at home and abroad, that the United States was ignoring the budget deficit and pushing down the dollar even further (it had dropped 40 percent since 1985 against the yen, the mark, and the pound) as a way to get rid of the trade deficit.

Black Monday and its consequences abroad only highlighted the general problem that, while the United States was increasingly dependent on foreign investments to cover its deficits, such a strategy itself was dependent on the continued viability of the American economy and the capacity of the U.S. government to manage the economy in a way that would convince investors and foreign governments that it was stable, sound, and safe. Uncertainty about the United States on these counts and others, including protectionism and foreign policy adventurism, has created the gravest problems for the United States, as well as for its trading partners and allies.

How America responds to these challenges and many others will largely determine its future into the twenty-first century. The failure to meet them, and meet them well, will put into great jeopardy not only the standard of living of the American people, but also their economic and political security.

This book addresses the ways in which America can begin to respond constructively to these challenges in areas of trade, education, health, housing, employment, technology, energy, investment, and foreign policy.

We will draw upon economic theory, political philosophy, specific policy expertise, plus the creativity and innovativeness of the authors to address the crucial question of how the United States can become more competitive in international markets to stimulate economic growth and maintain American living standards.

The book has two themes. First, the role of the government in a changing world is evolutionary. Views of the policymakers regarding what is appropriate for both the United States and foreign governments must also evolve in order to adopt policies that will promote international competitiveness.

Second, previously hostile attitudes between the three giants of the U.S. economy—management, labor, and government—must be replaced by cooperative ones if the United States is to compete abroad in foreign markets. Cooperation at home is increasingly necessary to ensure competitiveness abroad. Furthermore, competitiveness abroad is the key, not only to the trade deficit and continued U.S. prosperity, but also to the maintenance, and even improvement, of the U.S. posture vis-à-vis the Soviet Union. Unless we do better—much better—we face the real danger of a slow demise in our quality of life at home and a slow decline in our power position abroad. The future presents dangers as well as opportunities to determine the worth of the American system. It will test the capacity of the American people to demand adequate solutions and the ability of its leadership to deliver them.

The authors wish to thank Ola Linville Whicker, for indexing this book, and Ruth Moore, for careful editing and thoughtful suggestions.

Making America Competitive

MAINTAINING THE LEADING EDGE

AMERICA AT A CROSSROAD

The United States is currently at a crossroad. This situation is not unique, since the country has experienced several major decision points where the future of the nation and its very existence have hung in the balance. Major decision points may be symbolized by a single dramatic event that captures the essence of the dilemma being confronted or by a series of smaller, less dramatic actions, which nonetheless collectively alter the country's course.

The first major crossroad, of course, was the American Revolution, which determined whether or not the nation-state would be born at all. Next came the Philadelphia Convention, which hammered out, through a long hot summer, the details of the U.S. Constitution along with the framework and structure of the government and the basis for a bold new experiment in democracy. The events surrounding the acquisition of huge land masses, including the Louisiana Purchase and the eventual dominance of the fledgling state over previously French and Spanish territories, was another significant point. This was made even more important to the nation's expansion and long-term position by the willingness of its citizens to stream to the frontier and open up those lands through the backbreaking, painstaking reality of living in an empty, often harsh, and unforgiving wilderness.

Thundering on the horizon was the issue of slavery—an issue ignored at America's creation but inescapable half a century later, festering and rupturing into a civil war that pitted brother against brother, father against son, and threatened to split "the more perfect union" asunder. Survival was bloody and brutal but the nation, amid great anguish and loss, did survive to rush headlong into yet another decision point: how would the United States treat the hordes of people—some seeking a chance for their children to live a better life, some fleeing oppression, hunger, starvation, and sometimes death—who clamored to come to American shores? In the 1880s and early 1900s, the country opened its arms and allowed the world to send us its tired, its poor, and its huddled masses. These became labor for massive public works projects, the building of necessary infrastructure, and the development of industries that would eventually achieve economic preeminence.

The Great Depression of the 1930s posed yet another crossroad—the United States could continue to stagnate in the throes of falling prices, foreclosures, bank closings, high underemployment, devastating unemployment, and a shortage of money that economists call a "liquidity trap" —or it could abandon old ways of doing things, old philosophies, and outmoded ideas, and embrace untried methods, new institutions, and new roles for major economic actors who held hope of economic recovery and greater long-term economic stabilization. Under the incisive leadership of Franklin Roosevelt, the country chose the latter. Whether the New Deal programs or subsequent war spending finally shook off the last vestiges of economic depression is still debated, but the New Deal did shake the premise that unfettered markets and no government intervention always produced the maximum collective good.

World War II shook the United States from its previous isolationist posture in international affairs, a posture so pervasive that the United States has rejected the opportunity to join Woodrow Wilson's League of Nations after World War I, dooming that organization to insignificance and ultimate failure. More than anything else, this war and its aftermath showed that the United States had ascended to a new and dominant role in international politics. Gaining victory for the Allies in Europe, ending the Pacific War with the nuclear attack on Nagasaki and Hiroshima, and rebuilding the German and European economies through the Marshall Plan, the United States became a dominant actor on the world scene—a defender of freedom and democracy. Gone were the days of innocence when the United States could sit by, protected by large expanses of ocean and friendly neighbors, watching the machinations and intrigue of international affairs from afar. With the outbreak of the cold war, the United States found itself in worldwide political, military, economic, and psychological competition with the Soviet Union, clashing in troublespot after troublespot around the world. That competition continues today, more than 40 years after the collapse of the WW II alliance.

Now another major crossroad looms on the immediate horizon: the issue of developing an economy capable of competing in the new international trade wars. Just at the shift from a national politics to an international politics was not totally voluntary and was not without pain, the shift from a national economy to a global economy is being stimulated by factors beyond U.S. control. Yet the choice of whether or not to resist the shift, or to embrace the opportunity to become a significant player in international economics, as it has been in international politics, is within the nation's control. Just as at other crossroads, the option selected will affect the country's character, future, quality of life, and standard of living for decades to come. Great creativity is required to draw a successful blueprint for such a momentous, significant, and arduous endeavor. If those unaware of history are doomed to repeat it, what can we learn from the great ideas and economic philosophers of the past?

WISDOM FROM THE PAST

Mark Twain once remarked that nothing was certain but death and taxes, yet implicit in that remark is awareness of the constancy of a third factor: change itself. Across time, little remains unchanged. Typically, things get better or they get worse. Rarely do people, events, circumstances, conditions, environments, and governments remain the same. Even on those rare occasions when a phenomenon does appear to be relatively stable, the entire environment is evolving, growing, declining, or decaying, so that one constant factor is change itself.

Great ideas focus upon the concept of change. Great theorists try to explain it. The entire thrust of the social sciences, relative newcomers to scientific explanation when compared with the physical and biological sciences, has been to explain the nature of social, economic, and political change, as well as to examine the consequences of change on the lives of humans. Theories that are dynamic and explain change are usually embraced as being superior to those that examine impacts and relationships at a given point in time. Indeed, the very nature of scientific explanation requires the incorporation of time into research to progress beyond tests for correlation and to begin to address issues of causation. Typically, theories that include change, such as Darwin's theory of evolution, come to dominate competing theories that do not, such as religious-oriented creationism.

What have economic theorists said about change that might guide the United States as it moves into its third century? Beginning with Adam Smith in his classic work in 1776, *The Wealth of Nations*, which laid the basis for classical theory, economists have not lacked for willingness to theorize changes in economic phenomena (Smith 1937). Smith was the first to articulate coherently the concepts and laws of supply and demand, arguing that these forces guided both producers' decisions about how much to produce and consumers' decisions about how much to buy, as surely as if they were an "invisible hand" determining market interactions. In the concepts' simplist form, an increase in demand drove prices up, serving as a cue to producers, who were impelled by the profit motive to increase the quantity of goods produced. This in turn lowered prices again. Low prices became an incentive to consumers, also economically driven, to increase buying, thereby contributing to scarcity of the goods in question and increasing prices. Through such behavior, both profit- and income-maximizing, market equilibrium was obtained.

Despite Smith's brilliant insight into the impact of economic behavior and shifts in supply and demand upon markets, the price of goods, and the quantities produced, his theory remained essentially static, devoid of any notion of evolution. Smith's ideas were modeled upon the deterministic principles of Newtonian physics, which had achieved scientific eminence the century before and which reigned as the dominant form of scientific theory. In Newton's world, the trajectory of an object was always and inevitably certain, based upon position and its derivatives, speed and acceleration. A falling body always experienced the same gravitational pull, and force was always equal to mass times acceleration. Similarly, in Smith's world, falling prices always signaled cutbacks in quantities produced and declining wages, while rising prices preceded increases in the quantities produced, employment, and wages. In Newton's world, most changes were instantaneous. In Smith's world, change was either instantaneous or obscure. Rather, classical economists following Smith focused mostly upon predicting and explaining what changes would occur, rather than the length of time they would take, and on proving that ultimately, supply would equal demand and market equilibrium would be achieved.

Closely following Adam Smith (1937), Thomas Robert Malthus and David Ricardo (Sraffa 1962) rapidly earned the title of "the dismal science" for economics by predicting not inevitable growth and happy equilibrium, but inevitable decline and class conflict. Malthus (1863) argued that population growth was exponential and would outstrip the slower growth in resources, while Ricardo (Sraffa 1962) contended that landlords were the unique beneficiaries of the capitalist system and their dominance would ultimately wreak havoc and hardship on other classes, including the rising industrial class.

While both Malthus and Ricardo attempted to explore change in a limited fashion, it was not until the appearance of Karl Marx that the issues of economic evolution and distribution were firmly bound together. Yet while Smith and his followers may have erred on the side of explaining output growth and productivity at the expense of explaining distribution, Marx perhaps erred in the reverse direction, focusing upon class conflict and economic distribution at the expense of explaining productivity. The opposition of Marx's message to supporters of unfettered capitalism, plus his conclusions that ultimately economic maldistribution would create revolt among the proletariat and the eventual dominance of the working class, have obscured one of his major insights as an economic theoretician: namely, that economies are systems that evolve through various discernable and definable stages, much as biological organisms progress through the stages of life. Implicit in Marx's theory was the idea that economic principles operable at one stage may be less applicable or inoperable at another stage as economic conditions change. Marx (1961) wrote in the nineteenth century at the same time that the idea of evolution was being introduced into the biological sciences by Charles Darwin and his remarkable treatise on the origin of the species, and Marx's notion of evolution ran contrary to the equilibrium posited by the classical economists. Classical economists conceived of equilibrium as a state in which conditions would remain at rest and constant unless disturbed by some force or event exogenous to the economic system; in short, change was a anomaly, introduced only by external forces. In contrast, the concept of evolution included the idea that change was the natural and ordinary state of events.

Of course, change is not without distributional and ideological consequences. It is not without reason that Marx's theory of evolutionary change was embraced by those ill-served by and unhappy with the economic status quo, while those benefiting from the distributional implications of existing economic institutions embraced a theory of equilibrium supporting and justifying the extant arrangements. Nor was Marx's cause helped by the fact that many of his economic predictions proved inaccurate: revolution by workers, when it occurred, took place in agrarian, not industrialized nations; and the stage to which capitalistic countries evolved proved to be welfare capitalism rather than the total collapse of free enterprise. Marx's writings were not particularly helpful in describing the later evolutionary stages of advanced economic systems. Noting only that the state would disappear and the workers would rule, it was hardly a detailed blueprint of a future complex system. He chose instead to devote much of his energy to his theory of surplus value, which described the mechanics of capitalistic decline. Hence, his works have often been treated as polemical rather than theoretical. Despite Marx's predictive failures, his views of economies as evolutionary systems remain an important contribution and a significant point of departure from the viewpoint of the Newtonian world.

John Maynard Keynes (1936), at once the policy radical and the theoretical savior of capitalism, did embrace time as important in economic phenomena. On one occasion, responding to criticisms that his theory called for unnecessary government intervention into markets because it emphasized and responded to short-run factors, Keynes observed that in the long run we were all dead. Noting the scant correlation in the past between the time frame of government budgets and the length of the average business cycle, Keynes proposed countercyclical government fiscal policy to stabilize the economy, holding down inflation during periods of boom and bolstering the economy with needed dollars to stimulate production. This policy induced purchasing and reduced unemployment during periods of recession or deeper troughs of depression. With government acting as a rudder to guide the economy along a stable track, the disadvantages of the extremes of the business cycle could be avoided.

Keynesian philosophy was conservative in that it included the notion of propping up the capitalist system with government injections and modifications, rather than predicting and encouraging its total demise as had Marx. However, it was radical in that it proposed deficit spending in times of recession to stimulate production, an anathema to political and economic traditionalists who had lived by the policy bible of balanced budgets. From this and the subsequent action of politicians in the years after his theory became the justification for altered practices, Keynes was wrongly accused of promoting budget deficits indefinitely without regard for the government's ability to pay its bills. What he actually proposed, however, was to lengthen the cycle in which the budget would be balanced to free it from the arbitrary tenets of the fiscal calendar. The calendar of Washington and its concomitant Congress timetables did not coincide particularly well with real-world economic pressures more congruent with the business cycle, a length of time typically consisting of several years. Keynes fully expected, and indeed advocated, that the budget deficits accrued during recession years would be offset by the budget surpluses accumulating during boom years. What he did not anticipate, and what John Kenneth Galbraith (1959) later observed to be the case, was that the surpluses never materialized, not because economic conditions prevented their accumulation, but because political pressures resulted in their being spent immediately, either to create new programs or to increase funding levels for existing programs. To supporters of Keynes, the economic theory was right, but the political will was lacking; the intervention of politics into economics made the application of Keynesian theory a one-sided affair.

Milton Friedman, a modern-day disciple of Adam Smith, rejected much of Keynesian philosophy and advocated a return to unfettered markets as necessary to achieve economic freedom (Friedman 1962). An avid opponent of Keynesian countercyclical policy, Friedman developed a competing theory of monetarism, which contended that changes in the money supply were the only systematic factor influencing the overall level of private spending and economic activity. Friedman argued that government intervention was undesirable, and that the only action necessary to ensure stability was an increase in the money supply by the central bank at a rate approximately equal to the growth of the whole economy. Federal Reserve interventions to stabilize interest rates through manipulation of the discount rate or reserve requirements or through open-market operations were invariably incorrect in Friedman's world, always constituting too little or too much correction too late. Yet Friedman's world did not become the American world. While Keynesian philosophy became the policy norm in the United States, Friedman's philosophy remained intellectually intriguing enough to earn him a Nobel Prize. It also remained largely unadopted, perhaps reflecting its throwback to an all but disappeared past.

Opposed to Friedman in his views on the role of government in a modern mixed economy, as well as just about everything else, was John Kenneth Galbraith, an advocate of New Deal programs and of war price controls to stem inflation during World War II. To Galbraith, economics was as much a belief system as a scientific inquiry—a peculiar arena where policy outcomes were determined as much by circumstance as by theory. Meshing both Newtonian deterministic views and evolutionary ideas of change, Galbraith (1967) attacked the classical competitive model as unrealistic and not descriptive of the U.S. economy, while espousing a theory of countervailing powers. Not unlike the principle in physics that each force generates an equal and opposite counterforce, Galbraith contended that economic power, reflected by economic concentration, stimulated countervailing and offsetting concentration in other areas. Thus, the growth of large business corporations led to the growth of large unions. Chain stores for distribution were the response to growing concentration among producers. Large government grew partially in response to large corporations.

Galbraith saw these changes as inevitable, and attempts to revert through antitrust legislation and other means to the free competition implicit in the assumptions of classical economics as futile. Galbraith showed how, in contrast to the classical assumption that consumers predominantly influence producers through consumer buying decisions, producers equally influence consumers through advertising and salesmanship. Unlike the antiseptic classical world where principles cranked out outcomes in a mechanical fashion, Galbraith's was peopled with institutions and economic actors who experienced emotions and weaknesses. Like Leontiff who preceded him, Galbraith gravitated toward state planning and viewed the uncontrolled arms race and economic inequality as the most important problems not addressed by either economic theory or the political system.

Perhaps no economist has embraced the notion of evolutionary change as the natural state of events as much as Kenneth Boulding (1981a, 1981b). Largely ignored by his follow economists, Boulding (1981b) perceived the economy as an environment in which competing goods and producers would find niches favorable to their financial survival, much like organisms find physical niches favorable to their continued existence in the real environment. While in biological systems, the relationship between the total stock (population) and production (births) or consumption (deaths) is mediated through food shortages, housing shortages, predation, maternal care, material limitations, and a number of other factors, he contended that economic systems were mediated primarily through price, with other considerations such as storage, spoilage, anticipation of prices, etc., having a secondary impact.

Boulding viewed the employed and the unemployed both as species, each with an economic niche. In addition, he held that centrally planned economies had less unemployment and inflation than capitalist economies because when the state is the only employer, workers have greatly reduced power to raise wages, and decision makers setting employment policies do not suffer directly from bad judgments. While eschewing economic libertarianism, Boulding remained a supporter of a mixed economy, contending that full employment is bought at the cost of large inefficiencies and exploitations. Boulding's analogy comparing economic systems with biological organisms represented a major departure from classical economics, but his attempts to develop an evolutionary theory of economics fell far short of prediction. Perhaps his greatest contribution remains the recognition that no policy can be successful unless it acknowledges the constant drift of evolutionary change.

Of the voices of economic theorists from the past, conservatives then have favored the classical theory that emphasizes equilibrium and ignores the time required for adjustments to achieve it. Liberals, on the other hand, have favored a more evolutionary approach to economic theorizing, which includes natural transitions through increasingly mature stages and regards various forms of government intervention and even planning as the natural successor to laissez-faire capitalism. Somewhere between these two extremes lies reality.

THE ECONOMIC PHYSICIANS

In general, economic theory lags behind economic reality. Only after markets were operating did Smith correctly articulate their mechanics, and the problems of maldistribution generated by the industrial revolution occurred before Marx sought to explain them. Similarly, Keynes did not develop his governmental correctives for business booms and busts until after business cycles were a well-recognized phenomenon. Hence, many of the early theorists, while laying the foundation for understanding economies as price sensitive and evolving, did not grapple with the issue of competing in a global economy since the production system they observed was oriented toward large, homogeneous, seemingly un-ending domestic markets. More recent economists, some achieving public ac-claim, have focused to a greater extent than their predecessors upon specific policies that addressed U.S. economic decline from failing to compete effec-tively. Such decline is a reality for recent economists, while it was only a remote speculation for theorists of earlier years.

More than any other modern economist, Lester Thurow, the intellectual heir to the philosophy espoused by Galbraith, has dealt with major problems con-fronting the U.S. economy, including an economy that no longer performs, energy, inflation, slow economic growth, environmental problems, spreading rules and regulations, and direct redistribution issues. To solve most of these problems, Thurow (1980, 1983, 1985, 1987) argues that distributional concerns must be confronted head on; however, the probability of doing so in a democracy is small.

Each group and each individual, in striving to achieve group or personal economic security, is willing to use government for those ends and yet is de-rogatory of the attempts of other groups and individuals to do the same. The collective impact of autonomous drives toward economic security is to slow the rate of economic growth for all. Guarantees of economic security require col-lective action and decision making and therefore coercion, but individuals are inconsistent, supporting coercive collective actions that raise their own standards of living and opposing those that do not. By the late 1970s, however, over ten percent of the gross national product (GNP) was redistributed by government from one private individual to another. Yet generally when confronted with zero-sum choices in which the relative well-being of one group is improved at the expense of another, benign neglect has been the preferred option in the past. In international competition, Thurow advocates the use of strategic coordination to improve U.S. relative market position, increased investment in public and private education, and the creation of an incentive structure in which the labor force has a direct investment in improving productivity.

Thurow sees a strong relationship between economic supremacy and education, contending that when the United States was overtaking Great Britain as the world's economic leader between 1860 and 1900, it had one of the most skilled and educated labor forces in the world. Now U.S. educational standards and performance rank close to the bottom of the industrial world. Upgrading the educational system is a necessity if the nation is to compete globally, as is the attainment of substantial increases in both public and private investment and savings. Movement toward a bonus system would not only provide incentives to increase productivity, but also would stimulate savings, since unpredictable lump-sum payments are easier to save than weekly or monthly wages. Thurow makes a case for the adoption of a national industrial policy and for increased government spending on research and development through a public investment bank to fill a gap currently left open by U.S. private investment bankers.

If Thurow is the intellectual successor to Galbraith, Arthur Laffer is the bearer of Friedman's mantle, arguing for a decrease in government interference in the economy and a reduction in the size of government (Lekachman 1982). The father of "supply-side" economics, Laffer is said to have first scribbled out his famous Laffer's Curve depicting a curvilinear relationship between tax revenues collected by the government and tax rates on a napkin in a restaurant where he was engaging in animated debate on the topic. Laffer contended that two levels of taxation, one with a high rate and another with a low rate, would both yield the same tax revenues. Arguing that the United States was employing the high rate, he advocated a sharp reduction in nominal tax rates despite high inflation, a policy ultimately followed by the Reagan administration.

Despite such a drastic reduction in tax rates, tax revenues were not supposed to decrease, since productivity would be stimulated by the increase in private monies as a result of tax decreases, which were presumed to be invested in new plants and equipment. Rising productivity would stimulate economic activity, expanding the tax base and allowing tax revenues to remain constant. The great American experiment embracing supply-side economics in the early years of the Reagan administration, however, failed to hold down deficits, with red ink accumulating in unprecedented numbers. Nor was the adoption of supply-side economics without redistributional concerns. Conveniently, tax cuts rewarded the constituency loyal to the Reagan administration, since typically businesses and higher-income individuals have higher marginal tax rates and larger tax bills. Inflation did fall to a near post-World War II low, but its decline was attributed as much to the crack in the Organization of Petroleum Exporting Countries (OPEC) cartel, which flooded world markets with cheap oil, as it was to supply-side theories. When David Stockman, the financial "enfant terrible" of the Reagan administration left, he began issuing invectives against the deficits, supply-side tax cuts piled up instead of official memos, and the favored theory fell from political grace.

Although not an economist, Alvin Toffler has dealt with the future, providing some tantalizing glimpses of what it might hold. Toffler observed (1970) that the place of life is accelerating and that obsolescence is increasingly the norm as the nation turns into a throw-away society. Having moved through agricultural and industrial eras of production, the country is now into the third major productive era in which most workers manipulate, generate, and massage information (Toffler 1980). Society is becoming demassified and increasingly modular, with individuals becoming more autonomous than in earlier eras of mass production. In an industrial society, processes were linear and sequential, whereas in the information era, they become simultaneous and parallel. The potential for diversity increases and organizations will become increasingly ad hoc, convening to achieve a particular task and then disbanding or being reconfigured. Corporations will be redefined as multi-purpose organizations with many bottom lines.

According to Toffler, new operating rules will end the exception that work should occur for most of the labor force between nine and five, and will focus upon decentralization and matrix organizations. The intellectual lines between producers and consumers will become blurred, along with their roles, leading to the rise of a new economic creature, the "prosumer," who will be more active in economic decision making than the preceding passive consumer. Transnational corporations will become more numerous, bigger, and more powerful, controlling more of the world's economic growth than in the past.

Robert B. Reich, a Harvard economist, agrees with Toffler that diversity and heterogeneity in production will replace earlier periods of mass homogeneous production. Reich (1983) traces America's recent relative decline to changes in world markets and the poor showing of the United States in exporting. Similar to Toffler's ad hoc organizations, Reich advocates flexible-system processes in which a great deal of training occurs on the job because the precise skills needed cannot be anticipated and communicated in advance, and because greater coordination among workers must become an integral part of mastering specific skills.

Earlier production systems were oriented toward mass, homogeneous, standardized, high-volume production. By contrast, new production systems will involve precision, custom, and technology-driven products. Dependent upon high-level skills rather than standardized production, these three product groups are sheltered from low-wage competition. Developing countries cannot easily make products that require precision engineering, testing, and maintenance. Tailor-made custom products are also sheltered since they are made in relatively small batches in close coordination with their customers, and rapidly changing technologies make technology-driven products more dependent upon innovation than mass production. All three of these product categories, which Reich predicts will be emphasized in U.S. manufacturing in the future, depend on the skills of employees and are often developed within teams. For all three, the business functions of research, design, engineering, purchasing, manufacturing, distribution, marketing, and sales, which are traditionally separate from each other, must be highly integrated to respond to new opportunities.

According to Reich, government facilitated the movement to high-volume mass-production systems earlier and now must facilitate the movement toward more flexible production systems, especially by heavy investment in people, the nation's most valuable resource. Rejecting both liberal faith in a welfare state disconnected from American economic development and the conservative philosophy of reducing social expenditures in order to have more resources for business investment, he argues that labor, business, and government must work together with the long term, not just the short term, in mind. Reich contends that social justice is not a luxury, but a necessity for prosperity.

With the exception of supply-side proponents, these more recent economic physicians with prescriptions for the ailing American economy hold several common views. In contrast to supply siders, who in the Reagan administration proposed and enacted cuts in national expenditures for education, all of these economists see dramatic improvements in educational performance made possible by additional national investment in that area as being essential to the United States' continued economic development and ability to compete in global markets. All of them see an end to the previously unquestioned dominance of mass, homogeneous, high-volume production systems in manufacturing, and the development of more specialized, flexible, and sometimes temporary production systems in their place. All of them see a need to increase spending for research and development, and to take a long-run rather than a short-run view. Unlike supply siders who adhere to a trickle-down theory of income distribution (i.e., who contend that wide-scale progressive redistribution is unnecessary since wealth will trickle down across income classes, ultimately benefiting the lower brackets), Thurow and Reich confront distributional issues directly, arguing that competitiveness cannot be purchased by penalizing the poor. Finally, except for supply-siders, most of these forecasters see an expanded role for government, in which it works more closely with industry to facilitate exports and international competitiveness for U.S. firms.

THE ROLE OF GOVERNMENT IN THE ECONOMY AND SOCIETY

Some consensus on the role of government in formulating policies to make the United States competitive in global markets is crucial, as well as some degree of agreement on what those policies should be. Yet not only do conservatives tend to favor equilibrium notions and analyses while liberals favor the concept of economic evolution, but also disagreement over the appropriate role of government in the economy and society is a major ideological distinction between those positioned on the right side of the political spectrum and those positioned on the left. Conservatives favor a smaller government fulfilling fewer functions, while liberals do not fear a larger government even if they do not actively embrace it. A great deal of the new field of public choice theory—an area of inquiry with largely a conservative bias, which attempts to use microeconomic market concepts to analyze government and problems of collective goods and decision making—is oriented toward proving that government is too big. Yet the heat of these long-standing debates over the desirable size of government often obscures the observation that not only does the size of government traditionally become larger, regardless of the political ideology of the country or its specific political system, but also the very demands and needs that government is required to meet are transformed.

Nation-states progress through a developmental sequence in the same manner as individuals, confronting a hierarchy of goals for government similar to the hierarchy of needs for individuals originally posited by Abraham Maslow (1970), so that the role of government in the economy and in society changes across time. Maslow contended that human beings are motivated by a five-level hierarchy of needs, consisting of: (1) physiological; (2) safety; (3) affiliative; (4) esteem; and (5) self-actualization needs. Satisfaction of a need (sometimes called a "drive") is an end in itself, requiring no further justification. Needs in an individual cannot be observed directly, but rather must be inferred from the observation of individual behavior.

Physiological needs include hunger, thirst, and sex. Safety needs are quite extensive: security, stability, dependency, and protection. Social or affiliative needs include the desire for love, affection, and "belongingness." Achievement and prestige are two of the esteem needs. Two subcategories or esteem needs are self-esteem (the desire for confidence, competence, mastery, adequacy, achievement, independence, and freedom) and esteem from other people, including prestige, recognition, acceptance, attention, status, reputation, and appreciation. Self-actualization needs include drives for creativity, for knowledge and understanding, and aesthetic needs.

According to the need hierarchy, concern over unsatisfied lower-level needs dominates concern over unsatisfied higher-level needs. Thus, unsatisfied physiological needs dominate the satisfaction of the remaining four need levels; unsatisfied safety needs dominate the satisfaction of affiliative, esteem, and self-actualization needs, and so forth. Gratified needs no longer motivate individual behavior. The satisfaction of needs frequently or infrequently in childhood, according to Maslow, determines basic personality traits. Permanent frustration of needs creates psychopathy.

In both phylogenetic (group) and ontogenic (individual) development, higher needs appear later. As the individual grows, he or she progresses through the need hierarchy. Infants are preoccupied with physiological and safety needs. Young children are usually preoccupied with safety and affiliative needs. Older children find affiliative and esteem needs dominant. Only at the start of adolescence do self-actualization needs become evident.

Like Marx and Boulding especially, Maslow's hierarchy of individual needs emphasizes evolution, an idea he derived from reading William Graham Sumner's *Folkways*. Sumner (1906) argued that the mores of folkways of a society evolve in such a way as to accommodate basic biological needs and environmental contingencies, similar to the process of natural selection proposed by Darwin. A corollary thesis of cultural relativity proposed that, while biological necessities are constant across societies, the nature and pattern of environmental contingencies will vary across societies. Consequently, different societies will evolve different patterns or folkways for dealing with the same biological exigencies, just as nations evolve different economic systems for dealing with questions of production and distribution. Yet many conceptual schemes for nation-states and their governments have failed to encompass this evolutionary diversity.

A government's needs hierarchy (GNH) which is parallel to Maslow's needs hierarchy for individuals, may be constructed for nations and their economies. Each level represents the needs and behavior of government at the particular level of national advancement or development. Functions, such as education or health care, may occur at more than one level but with different emphases, foci, and intensities. In the following discussion, five stages of governmental need are identified.

Ideally, a country can be readily classified as falling within a unique and mutually exclusive stage of the government needs hierarchy. In reality, the stages may not always be mutually exclusive nor strictly sequential, particularly when a country is in transition from a lower level to a higher level. Much as Toffler described movement from industrial to information societies as waves, movement from one stage on the GNH to the next may also be wave-like. The beginning of a higher level may become apparent before the vestiges of the immediately preceding stage have receded. Nor is movement always linearly progressive. Revolutions, revolts, and other jolts to a political and economic system may cause a country to regress down the hierarchy, just as an individual facing adversity may regress in Maslow's terms.

GNH Level I: Developing a Minimum Economic Infrastructure

The first level of the government needs hierarchy corresponds to Maslow's category of individual physiological needs. This level of development for nation-states is primitive. National governments are preoccupied with developing an economic infrastructure sufficient to provide a minimum living standard for at least some citizens, by providing an environment in which most of the population has minimal nutritional and shelter needs satisfied.

Nations in level 1 development may provide direct subsidies or incentives for the creation of a transportation network adequate to transport agricultural and some commercial products. In most countries, maintaining dirt farm-to-market roads is essential to feeding a majority of the population, especially as urban growth progresses. Eventually, nations expand to include a network of highways, as well as providing for railroads. Countries bordering oceans or large bodies of water or rivers develop ports to facilitate the transportation of food products and people by barge and ship.

A second level 1 activity is monetarizing the economy to facilitate commercial exchange. This task involves, at a minimum, establishing a national currency and ensuring its integrity. Some nations opt to meet this task through the establishment of a national banking system controlled and run by the state, while others provide a regulatory climate that allows private interests to facilitate banking, financial, and exchange services necessary for commercial activities. Related to these financial activities is the need to develop a national mail system so that financial exchanges and commerce can function across longer distances.

A third level 1 activity is creating an environment for jobs and a minimum level of employment through one of several policies. One strategy to generate employment is to provide tax subsidies or loans as incentives for private-sector agricultural and industrial development sufficient to hire large numbers of workers. A second policy is to redistribute land, so that employment levels in the agricultural sector are maintained, even with urban growth. A third employment policy is to form state-owned agricultural and industrial entities that employ a substantial portion of the labor force. Nor are these strategies mutually exclusive, since countries can, with differing emphases, use all three.

Most countries in the modern era, even emerging nations, are well advanced in developing a minimum economic infrastructure. Those countries are more likely to be working on one or more higher levels within the GNH. Many of the former colonial possessions in Africa inherited some degree of economic infrastructure from their colonizers. Failure to develop an economic infrastructure to meet minimum nutritional and housing needs for a substantial portion of the population can lead to upheaval and chaos. However, adequate handling of this level allows a nation to develop some sense of national cohesion and to advance through the GNH.

While the United States is clearly at the top of the GNH, not the bottom, recognizing the primary concerns of other nations and tailoring export policy to meet those needs is a desirable strategy for restoring American competitiveness in global markets. Level 1 countries must often import a great deal of their agricultural equipment, and most of their industrial and manufactured consumer goods. Skillful recognition of an importing country's position on the GNH not only helps to identify the type of economic goods most likely to be successful as imports, but also keys U.S. business and political executives into the major concerns of officials in the importing country with whom our exporters must deal.

GNH Level 2: Providing for Internal and External Security

At the second level of the government needs hierarchy, countries focus on providing adequate internal security to maintain their hegemony, as well as obtaining adequate external security to guarantee sovereignty. This level of governmental development parallels Maslow's second level in the individual needs hierarchy, in which the person is preoccupied with ensuring physical safety and integrity from external and potentially violent threats.

Internal security is the ability to protect citizens and their private property, and to ensure the survival of the government and existing political elites. Activities include the creation of a legal framework, an infrastructure to provide for leadership succession, a police force, and eventually other safety forces, such as fire departments and agencies to deal with national disasters. Internal security also may be applied to minimal health guarantees, such as preventing epidemics of infectious diseases, creating basic sanitary conditions, safeguarding the purity of the water supply, and developing basic health care and emergency medical services.

External security is the ability to protect national territory from invasion by foreign powers and the population from violence by intruders. External security includes the ability of the national government to make decisions without undue external influence. Governments promote external security in two basic ways. One way is the creation of a military force potentially including an army, navy, and air force. A second way is via foreign relations, through the development of non-aggression agreements with neighbors and mutual defense agreements with other countries.

Nations at this level are especially interested in purchasing arms and weapons in the international marketplace. Often they do not yet have the industry capacity to support a domestic arms industry, and must secure all their weapons through importing. Some U.S. foreign policymakers have criticized foreign governments of various development countries for investing very heavily in arms when their own people continue to have a relatively low standard of living and many unmet needs.

Increasing the total stock of weapons in the world may do little in the long run to abate various arms races, not only between the United States and the Soviet Union, but also between various hostile or warring nations, such as Iran and Iraq, and India and Pakistan. Yet the GNH indicates that governments ignore the maintenance of internal order and security from external threats at their own peril, and that further progress to higher levels in the GNH will not occur until these basic security needs are met. Perhaps the construction of stronger international controls through some form of world government would lower the level of weapons required to meet perceptions of adequately fulfilling security needs. Nor are all safety needs military, since countries at this level are also potential purchasers of medical supplies, services, and training—an area on which the United States currently spends 11 percent of its own GNP. Other potential U.S. exports for countries at this level involve the construction of basic sewer, water, and sanitation systems.

GNH Level 3: Creating Political and Social Cohesion

The third level of the government needs hierarchy for nations corresponding to Maslow's affiliative needs for individuals is the creation of political and social cohesion. Countries at level 3 develop a national political culture. Governments at this level are interested in creating political consensus and harmony, and are also concerned with education and mass literacy. A sense of polity is promoted both through the socialization process integral to education, and through the creation of a literate population capable of using and understanding the mass media. With education, citizens more readily comprehend government initiatives, communications, and policies. Understanding enhances loyalty and system support.

Governments at level 3 may subsidize or directly provide primary schooling to achieve their educational goals. Education is also essential to economic advancement beyond a basic agrarian society, since many urban jobs require minimum reading skills, and a semiliterate labor force enhances industrial growth. Capital intensification and the adoption of new technologies are crucial for productivity increases and require an educated labor force.

At level 3, nations strive to create citizen access to government. Activities may range from efforts to increase the basis of political support for the existing elites to developing a process of open elections. Falling between these two participation extremes is the co-optation or incorporation of new people into the existing political hierarchy. In many countries, the incorporation of previously excluded elites occurs through the civil service and the military, which attract the bright and capable youth of less privileged classes, as well as the youth of traditional elites.

Another method that governments use to broaden their base of support beyond the traditional elite, but still short of universal inclusion, is to encourage a single national political party to work closely with the official government hierarchy. Access to government may also include the formation of independent or semi-independent interest groups, such as trade unions and business federations.

Countries at level 3 have the beginnings of an urban middle class and have started to industrialize. These countries import machinery, equipment, and some consumer goods. Also, they continue to build up their infrastructures, especially schools. Often eager for education to advance economically, American educational materials are not particularly suited to their needs. However, typically lacking universities and advanced technical schools, level 3 countries do send a steady stream of students to U.S. universities and technical institutes, funded both privately by their parents and by their government.

GNH Level 4: Establishing Mobility and Status Mechanisms

At level 4, nations develop laws and mechanisms to promote a more advanced level of economic well-being for citizens, including the establishment of universal secondary education and broad access to domestic technical schools. Broader access to higher education creates a more highly trained labor force with more white-collar workers and more service-sector personnel. Societal stratification may be exacerbated in level 4, as highly educated and better paid workers in newer technical areas rise in number, with a consequent gap between their economic well-being and status and the financial and social status of less skilled workers in labor-intensive, less capitalized industries. The working class becomes bifurcated into the very skilled and the very unskilled, while status lines between management and skilled white-collar technical workers blur in distinction. Any of the highly industrialized Western countries, including the United States and Great Britain, have experienced these shifts.

To prevent social discord arising from status differentials, many countries develop social programs oriented toward eradicating poverty and including access to better housing, employment training, and income support. More extensive programs attempt income equalization, while less comprehensive programs establish a minimum-level safety net to prevent the poor from falling into total destitution. In the United States, categorical welfare programs have filled this function on a somewhat ad hoc basis. Other countries have approached the issue more systematically through guaranteed income programs based on economic need rather than fitting into an appropriate category.

Racial and ethnic discrimination undercuts governmental objectives at level 4, creating social cleavage and tension. Discrimination prevents individuals from achieving status, mobility, and their personal economic goals otherwise obtainable on merit. Nations at this level may establish active civil rights laws and policies, such as universal franchise, anti-discrimination laws in employment and housing, and affirmative action programs.

Countries at this level have begun to experience a sufficient level of economic well-being to be interested in a whole variety of consumer goods, including consumer durables. Products exported to level 4 countries must be not only functional, but also attractive and appropriately advertised and marketed. Having lost their image for superior quality, U.S. products successfully sold in level 4 countries may draw upon the status appeal that certain American products still convey.

GNH Level 5: Enhancing the Quality of Life

The fifth and highest level of Maslow's hierarchy of individual needs was self-actualization, in which individuals expressed their abilities for creativity, understanding, and aesthetics. In the governmental needs hierarchy, the fifth and analogous level is likewise focused on higher-level concerns to enhance the quality of life. Having progressed through earlier stages in which more basic economic concerns were often directly or indirectly dominant, governments at level 5 can afford to focus on policies that increase citizens' mental and social well-being.

One major governmental activity at level 5 involves the extension of health care well beyond the traditional public health concerns to universal access for nearly all citizens through socialized health care or national health insurance. The extension of health care may also include governmental responsibility for environmental quality and for product safety. Government-sponsored programs to change lifestyles and behavior patterns in order to enhance health may occur. Mental health is often promoted by government-subsidized or sponsored counseling services.

Countries at level 5 become involved in the care of children. Some countries, including many in Europe, provide child allowances for parents, consisting of cash payments at the birth of a child. While the United States does not provide direct cash payments, it allows greater tax deductions based on family size, which increase as the number of dependents increases. Other child care activities include the provision of an income floor for children and/or families with dependent children. Many nations offer maternal and child health services, either based on need or universally to all mothers and infants. Key to this stage of development are government incentives to provide child care services, either directly through state-operated child care centers, or indirectly through incentive programs for privately run centers.

Level 5 government benefits include legal services, ranging from the services of a public defender for indigents unable to retain private legal counsel to offices providing the gamut of legal services for the poor. Behind the push to make access to legal representation universal is a heightened commitment to human rights and the extension of civil rights to previously excluded or partially covered political and ethnic minorities, and to the economically disadvantaged.

Government support of the arts is an additional level 5 activity. While governments have been involved with artistic projects at earlier GNH levels, at level 5 more extensive artistic efforts are launched to reach a greater number of citizens. Government-sponsored or subsidized programs acquaint citizens who have never been exposed to the fine and performing arts to various arts ranging from paintings, theater productions, films, sculpture, and native crafts to dance productions, symphonies, operas, orchestras, and other types of concerts. Governments may also support artists and organizations employing artists through direct subsidies and other means. Sometimes this involves providing artistic training for promising youths who would otherwise not be able to afford an artistic education. Often these two objectives interact, for by supporting organization such as art guilds, symphonies, national dance companies, and national theater companies, artists receive support while simultaneously exposing a greater number of citizens to their work.

Nations typically move up the governmental needs hierarchy as economic growth and development take place. Plainly, the United States has progressed from levels 2 and 3 at the birth of the country to levels 4 and 5. Normal movement is sequential so that national progress from one level to the next consecutive or adjacent one, and levels can be omitted or skipped only under duress or special circumstances. Forward movement occurs only after the needs at the current level have been satisfied to an acceptable degree. The level at which a government is located depends in large part on its stage of economic development, but this may be moderated by the attitude of the dominant elites controlling the government and by the degree of centralization or decentralization in the political structure. Highly centralized structures facilitate forward movement, while highly decentralized structures do not. Nor is movement always unidirectional. Just as nations progress up the hierarchy, they may also slip backwards under deteriorated and adverse conditions.

The realization that governments evolve in both size and function largely in accordance with the GNH renders useless debates over the desirability or undesirability of U.S. government intervention in the domestic economy. As the nation becomes wealthier and more advanced economically, government will grow and provide additional functions to improve the quality of life. More appropriate are concerns about the effectiveness with which government addresses the tasks at its current and lower levels on the needs hierarchy, and whether it is making the necessary preparations to move forward.

In short, there is no one ideal size for government. While big is not always good, small is not always best. As an instrument designed to implement the common will and achieve common objectives, government is a tool, not unlike any other, which may be used wisely and appropriately or poorly and inappropriately. In the past, American foreign policy and trade, and export policy in particular, have failed to reflect the necessity of this diversity and to tailor policies to take advantage of it, rather than enforce conformity with U.S. expectations— an impossibility given the huge range in levels of the GNH on which other nations are operating. To become competitive in global markets, Americans must cease regarding their own government as their enemy, to be pruned, cut, and slashed regardless of the impact of cutbacks, and must view it instead as a significant tool to be manipulated, managed, and massaged, to improve the standard of living at home and to penetrate increasingly competitive markets abroad.

2

THE TRADE DEFICIT

More than any other economic indicator, the mounting U.S. trade deficits of the mid–1980s are simultaneously symbols and products of declining American competitiveness. The statistics are staggering, but two in particular show the decline in the position of the United States in the world economy. By 1986, the trade deficit was $170 billion annually. The United States had shifted from being a major creditor internationally to being the largest debtor nation in the world. International debt, no longer just a third world problem, had come home to roost in the eaves of an economy that used to think of itself as the most efficient and productive capitalistic system in the world.

Robert Samuelson, a columnist on economic affairs for *Newsweek*, has contested the popular view that large trade deficits indicate a decline in U.S. competitiveness, arguing that competitiveness is a broad concept encompassing more than just economic well-being, and that no other country is more emulated abroad (Samuelson 1986). According to Samuelson, the willingness of foreigners to invest billions of dollars in the United States indicates confidence in U.S. stability and prosperity. Rather, the trade deficit has been exacerbated by changes that have hurt U.S. exports and have increased imports, including fast economic growth at home, slow growth abroad, a strong dollar, and the third world debt crisis.

However, projections for Japanese investment in the United States for 1987 predicted a slowdown to $115 billion, a decline from the $132 billion invested the previous year caused by a weaker dollar and relatively low U.S. interest rates. Samuelson has also acknowledged that current institutional changes could hurt competitiveness, especially deterioration in the quality of education. However, he contends that some of the U.S. superiority in trade and technology after World War II was artificial, since the war destroyed our most significant economic competitors and these circumstances cannot be easily recreated, if at all. Forces that contributed to the relative international economic decline of the United States after this period and facilitated the growth of new competitors, such as the spread of technology, modern education, and multi-national companies to Japan and the developing world, cannot be reversed. Nor does Samuelson think that the government can easily change something as sweeping as productivity—a concept and phenomenon that involves all aspects of the economy from management, education, technology, and labor relations to popular attitudes and government. He is concerned that the concept of competitiveness may become a disguise for special interest lobbying.

Others are less sanguine about the implications of the massive trade deficits for U.S. competitiveness. Falling behind, according to Thurow, is what enormous trade deficits are all about. The economic position of the United States today is similar to that of Great Britain around 1900, when it faced a world full of technologically equal if not superior competitors. If the United States does not alter its institutions to compete more effectively, it will fall to a position of economic inferiority, just as Great Britain did before it. Nor is halting economic progress in the rest of the world the solution. Living in a rich world is preferred to living in a poor world. Furthermore, the United States needs wealthy trading partners with healthy economies and incomes to purchase American goods. Somewhat cynically, but perhaps aptly, Thurow (1985) contends that the United States may need the moral equivalent of defeat to prompt it to undertake the painful efforts necessary to reconstruct old institutions and to create new ones—both necessary tasks for economic revitalization. It was the psychological impact of defeat in World War II that prompted Japan and Germany to embark on those very difficult efforts, departures that led to the current successful trajectories of economic indicators for those countries. While in general few would dispute the notion that major changes are needed to reduce trade deficits and restore competitiveness, significant disagreement exists over how to proceed.

PROTECTIONISM

Perhaps nothing is more controversial in discussions of trade deficits than the issue of protectionism, or imposing import restrictions on the flow of foreign goods and services into the United States to reduce their availability and to encourage citizens to buy American-made items instead. Buying American rather than foreign products initially sounds like a good idea and has been proposed and pushed by specific industries fearful of losing profits and labor unions fearful of losing jobs. Like quotas and tariffs, programs to buy American goods and domestic content bills are also protectionist in nature.

Advocates of protectionist legislation are typically more vocal in periods of economic decline and mounting trade deficits. Declining sunset industries involved in heavy manufacturing are particularly prone to make protectionist arguments, contending that the United States should reject the doctrine of free trade and recognize that the U.S. industrial base is the strategic core of the free world's defenses. If America is not strong, the defense of liberty is jeopardized. The cry is for fair trade, not free trade.

Despite the impassioned and patriotic sound of such protectionist prose, contemporary U.S. presidents have adamantly opposed trade barriers, although significant pressure exists for both formal and informal restrictions on imports. Perhaps presidential opposition to protectionist legislation and support for free trade rests on the fact that U.S. consumers pay heavy costs for import restrictions. In the short run, with restrictions, American pay higher prices for domestically produced goods than they would for foreign goods of the same or better quality. While a few U.S. jobs may be temporarily saved if U.S. consumers have restricted access to foreign products, these jobs are bought at the cost of lowered living standards brought about by paying more for equivalent or inferior products.

In the long run, without the pressure of foreign competition, American industry may become complacent, failing to adopt new cost-saving and quality-improving technologies. This complacency further reduces product choice and the quality of life for the consumer. One notable example of the lack of responsiveness of U.S. producers to growing consumer demand was the failure of U.S. auto manufacturers to develop reliable fuel-efficient small cars until foreign competition threatened to overtake and dominate that growing market.

Trade barriers do not occur in a political vacuum, since nations that find their entry into U.S. markets restrained are often compelled to retaliate, blocking the sale of U.S. products in foreign markets. Trade wars result, with U.S. exports, a growing share of all American economic activity, suffering.

Trade barriers clash headlong with an important principle of international economics called "comparative advantage." Economists have theorized that the total world experiences greater growth and prosperity if free trade is the norm. Under comparative advantage, world output is maximized if each country specializes in the manufacture of products that it produces most efficiently, and then trades with other countries to secure the goods that it needs but does not produce domestically. For comparative advantage to work, the goods in which a country specializes do not have to be produced more efficiently than they could be produced in other countries; rather they should be produced more efficiently than other products that same country might produce.

To provide evidence that the theory of comparative advantage works, economists point to the post-World War II period, in which the General Agreement on Trade and Tariffs (GATT) led to a world-wide reduction in trade barriers until the thrust for protectionist legislation in the late 1970s and 1980s. That same time period saw the greatest sustained long-term economic growth and prosperity occurring in modern times.

Thurow (1985) advocates at least two strategies for competing abroad that are manifestations of the theory of comparative advantage. One is to allow trading partners to sell their goods and services to Americans, both to allow trading partners to generate the foreign exchange necessary to buy American goods and to reduce the incentive for others to impose retaliatory quotas and tariffs on U.S.

imports into their countries. Thurow also argues that if Americans want to maintain a high standard of living, we must take advantage of international specialization and concentrate on producing the things that we produce best.

Interestingly, rarely are the business leaders who lobby for protectionist trade legislation, which impedes the flow into the country of consumer imports, willing to be subjected to the equivalent for manufacturers and corporations, that is, legislative restrictions on the flow of capital, jobs, and plants from the country. In the past, American firms have often moved manufacturing plants abroad, especially in labor-intensive industries, to take advantage of lower labor costs and wages in poorer countries. In decisions about whether to locate American-owned plants in the United States or in foreign countries, profits have won over patriotism.

Theoretically, advocates of protectionism do not embrace the notion of evolutionary economic systems, which necessarily change across time and compete successfully for their niches in the larger world economy, or die. The thrust of protectionism is to hold back the hands of time, maintaining old industries at high if not any, costs. Yet clearly the composition and dominant sectors of a nation's economy change as the nation becomes more wealthy. Poor countries with few resources tend to be agrarian. As countries modernize, they develop industrial bases, typically emphasizing heavy manufacturing, machine development and acquisition, and the development of an infrastructure initially, then moving into an emphasis on manufacturing consumer durables and more specialized consumer goods.

Countries that continue to grow move into a service or information economy, in which the majority of the labor force either manipulates information or provides some sort of service, rather than being directly employed in manufacturing. The United States is well advanced in the service stage of economic development, with the vast majority of the U.S. labor force in 1986—more than 76 million workers—in the service sector, compared to 25 million in goods-producing jobs and 3 million in agriculture. Of the $2.3 trillion in private services generated in the U.S. economy in 1985, 27 percent came from finance, insurance, and real estate; 16 percent from retail business; 12 percent from wholesale trade; 12 percent from transportation and utilities; and 5 percent from communications.

While not inevitable, since regression or stagnation as well as progression may occur, these developmental trends have occurred in enough countries so that the pattern has become apparent. Protectionist legislation is one of several attempts to fix a nation at a particular point in time, halting the natural flow of labor-intensive manufacturing to less developed countries. To retain manufacturing requires the adoption of new technologies and capital intensification, not protectionist legislation producing stagnation and resistance to innovation.

If applied long enough, protectionist legislation may result in nothing worth protecting. Yet businessmen live in the short run of quarterly and monthly reports and annual bottom lines, not the ideal theoretical long run, so the pressures for protectionism in the political arena are immense. Yet the misguided adoption of such legislation cannot erase the fact that, while many American industrialists were not watching, the nature of economic competition changed. The key to success now is developing products and services that can compete in world markets. Trade barriers are throwbacks to the old game of business in which only domestic markets mattered. Their strongest proponents are those who would gain most from their imposition. Protectionism is maintained at the expense of the American consumer and of forcing American industry to toughen up for its upcoming task: winning at the world game.

TRADE ISSUES

While there are many trade issues, trade will most likely be the issue on the U.S. agenda in both the immediate and near future. Without trade and effective exporting, the U.S. economy cannot maintain its relative standing and the American standard of living. In 1982 and 1983, a world recession brought about a drop in global trade and brought home our increased dependence on trade. However, the emphasis on trade is less than two decades old. Trade constituted only 6 percent of U.S. GNP in 1973, but by 1983 it had doubled to 12 percent. According to former U.S. Trade Representative William Brock III, by 1983 four out of five new jobs in manufacturing were created by international trade and one out of every three acres planted by U.S. farmers was producing crops for exports. At that time, $2 trillion of goods and services were being traded, and Brock saw the potential for trade and export growth as unlimited.

Growing Trade Deficits

The growing trade deficits of the 1980s are even more ominous for U.S. competitiveness. Especially troublesome was the role that the declining quality of American products was playing. Shoddy workmanship and poor merchandising too often affected our efforts to export successfully. Job losses resulted from lower exports and higher imports. Despite a dramatic reduction in inflation during the Reagan years, the unemployment rate remained stubbornly stuck between 6 and 7 percent. Alfred E. Eckes, the chairman of the U.S. International Trade Commission, a nonpartisan government advisory agency, has estimated that each $1 billion change in the trade deficit affected at least 25,000 jobs. Employment fell by 39 percent in the U.S. auto industry between 1979 and 1982, 19 percent in shoe manufacturing, and 17 percent in the apparel industry— industries that have lobbied for trade protection. Yet a study by C. Fred Bergsten and William R. Cline estimated that U.S. consumers paid $92,000 in 1982 dollars for each job saved that way (Thompson 1984, pp. 1–4).

In the past, increases in agricultural exports, which rose from $7.3 billion in 1970 to $43.3 billion in 1981, helped to offset increasing imports. However, weak worldwide economic conditions and a strong dollar contributed to a decline in agricultural exports in the mid–1980s. The United States also chose to intermingle foreign and trade policies, embargoing grain sales to the Soviet Union in 1980 to punish that superpower for its invasion of Afghanistan. The Soviet Union quickly found alternative suppliers, however, and many analysts feel that the U.S. embargo created an image of the nation as unreliable, diverting foreign buyers to other more reliable grain suppliers, particularly Argentina and Canada. Favorable weather conditions in grain-exporting countries created a worldwide surplus, pushing prices down on the international market and further contributing to a decline in the value of U.S. agricultural exports.

The General Agreement on Trade and Tariffs

Despite the current pressure to institute trade restrictions for both economic and foreign policy reasons, the United States has traditionally been a world leader in the movement to reduce lower trade barriers. After World War II, it was in large part U.S. effort that encouraged 23 nations to sign the General Agreement on Trade and Tariffs (GATT) in 1947. The GATT, a multinational effort to mediate differences in trade patterns among participating nations, embodied the policy of the 1934 U.S. Trade Agreements Act, which established presidential authority to lower U.S. tariffs in exchange for reciprocal concessions from other countries. GATT became a worldwide organizational device for lowering legal barriers to international trade, which had reached an all-time high during the Great Depression of the 1930s, a period when many countries, out of desperation to try anything to lower unemployment, grasped at protectionist legislation as a potential solution.

In response to both GATT and rising economic conditions throughout the world, the volume of international trade grew at exceptional rates during the next three decades, increasing at rates greater than either population growth or production increases. A sixfold increase in the volume of world trade and a twentyfold increase in its value occurred between 1950 and 1980. By the mid–1980s, 88 countries were members of GATT. Under its principle of most-favored-nation status, if any member nations negotiate a reciprocal trade concession between or among themselves, that same trade concession is automatically extended to all GATT members.

GATT has been characterized as economic disarmament, but has it been successful? Many analysts feel that with respect to industrial products, the answer is yes. Since its creation, several multinational trade negotiations (MTN) have occurred among member nations. As a result of these negotiations, tariffs declined from an average of 25 percent for influential members of GATT at the end of World War II to about 5 percent. The United States was a major winner in these tariff reductions since during the economically productive and prosperous decades of the 1950s and 1960s, the United States produced about one-fourth of the world market in manufactured goods. By the end of the 1970s, this advantage had eroded somewhat as U.S. market share fell to about 17 percent.

However, GATT has its problems. It has never been highly supported by developing countries, which prefer an international trade organization where decisions would be made by simple or two-thirds majorities. In GATT, power depends on a country's ability to grant trade concessions, which is a function of market size, making the United States, the European community, and Japan the major GATT actors. (The Soviet Union and the People's Republic of China are not GATT members, although some smaller socialist countries belong.) Many developing countries have small markets with limited ability to grant trade concessions, but there is a large number of countries in the developing category. The disaffection of developing nations is indicated by the fact that only 59 percent of the 122 members of the Group of 77, the developing nations' caucus in international affairs, are GATT members. Further, in 1964, developing countries were able to vote in block in the United Nations to establish a potentially competing body, the Untied Nations Conference on Trade and Development (UNCTAD), which does operate under one-state, one-vote, majority-rule decision making. The UNCTAD, however, has remained secondary and has never rivaled GATT's rule-making authority.

Nor has GATT been as successful in reducing trade barriers to services and other nonindustrial products as in the reductions it achieved for industrial products. Many agricultural products were excluded from most GATT agreements, as were most services such as banking, consulting, insurance, and shipping until the 1980s.

Voluntary Export Restrictions

Yet another gap in GATT has been its inability to reduce nontariff barriers to trade, since GATT has primarily been a vehicle for reducing tariffs. While economic theory holds that in the long run, world output will be increased through unrestrained international trade, in the short run, huge unanticipated influxes of competing imports could create substantial dislocation in the domestic economy, with rapidly rising unemployment. Most Western nations, including the United States, have become committed to some version of a modern welfare state where rapid increases in unemployment are costly if not politically intolerable.

The result has been voluntary export restrictions (VERs) and orderly marketing agreements (OMAs), which are attempts by countries to secure voluntary agreements from competing countries to limit exchange, a device used in recent years to limit Japanese auto imports to the United States. In 1986, in the face of a $58.6 billion trade surplus with the United States and fearful of a flare-up of U.S. protectionist sentiments, Tokyo agreed to continue a program of voluntary export quotas on cars shipped to the United States. The 1987 ceiling of 2.3 million cars remained the same as the previous two years. Since VERs and OMAs are bilaterally negotiated restrictions on imports, not exports, they technically do not violate GATT agreements, but they do contravene the GATT thrust toward liberalization of world trade—a thrust that the recent protectionist trend threatens to undermine.

Automobiles have not been the only area in which the U.S. government has aggressively sought to limit imports through bilaterally negotiated agreements. Ideologically oriented to free trade, in practice, the Reagan administration did much to stifle it. Since 1982, the Reagan administration negotiated 18 different agreements with steel-producing countries to limit their exports to the United States. In 1986, the administration pressured Japan and Taiwan into limiting machine-tool exports to the United States for five years. West Germany and Switzerland refused to agree to similar arrangements, but were then confronted with quotas that rolled back their level of U.S. imports to 1981 levels.

Other bilateral agreements negotiated in 1986 limited textile exports to the United States from Taiwan, Hong Kong, Japan, and South Korea to a growth rate of 1 percent a year or less. The cumulative impact of VERs has been considerable, since according to the estimate of Michael Aho, a senior economist at the Council on Foreign Relations, the percentage of U.S. imports subject to some form of government limitation grew from 25 percent in 1981 to 40 percent in 1986, with pressure building for even more limitations (Russell 1987).

Antidumping Legislation

The GATT rules, under Article XVI, specify when countervailing duties may be imposed by the country receiving imports because of unfair export subsidies supplied by the government in the producing country. According to section XVI(2), export subsidies should not cause harmful effects on other nations. Section XVI(3) specifies that export subsidies should not be used to gain more than an equitable share of the world market, while section XVI(4), an anti-dumping provision, prohibits the use of export subsidies to sell goods for less than the price charged in the home market.

Despite these GATT restrictions, many countries practiced dumping in the 1970s. In 1979, the United States transferred dumping enforcement from the Department of Treasury, which was not as active in this area, to the Department of Commerce, which was more active in pursuing the interests of American businesses in court. Countering Article XVI in spirit is Article XIX, which allows government assistance to an industry in decline internationally. Article XIX allows an importing country to raise tariffs because of unforeseen circumstances harming a domestic producer, such as the Japanese dominance of the U.S. motorcycle market, a development that has caused serious injury to domestic producers. In these circumstances, the burden is on the exporting country to prove that the safeguards imposed by the importing country contradict the provisions of GATT. If the exporting country fails to make a sufficient case, the importing country may impose higher tariffs or quantitative restrictions. If the importing country fails to make a convincing case of injury, it is required to compensate the exporting country.

Antidumping duties may be imposed under the 1921 Antidumping Act and the 1979 Trade Act when imports are sold in the Untied States at less than their fair-market value, a price less than that at which they are sold in the country of origin. Firms experiencing such competition may initiate a petition with the International Trade Commission for relief. Sections 337 of the Tariff Act and section 301 of the 1974 and 1979 Trade Acts also impose all the restrictions against unfair trade practices listed in the Sherman, Clayton, Federal Trade Commission, and Robinson-Patman Acts on imports as well. Despite these legal protections, many American businessowners feel that they have not been sufficiently enforced.

Trade Adjustment Assistance

As part of the Trade Expansion Act of 1962, consideration was given to industries confronting GATT-induced lowered tariffs. Industries threatened by increased export competition brought about by tariff reductions were protected by "peril points." Peril points were predetermined by the U.S. Tariff Commission and were tariff levels below which duties could not be set by U.S. negotiators without congressional approval. These peril points were based on potential material injury to the industry in question and constrained U.S. negotiators. Affected industries could either attempt to obtain special protection through escape clause action or receive adjustment assistance in the form of low interest loans, free technical advice, and tax allowances for losses resulting from trade liberalization. Affected workers could receive extended unemployment compensation, retraining for new occupations, and relocation allowances to assist a worker's family in moving to locales where employment was available.

Trade assistance to dislocated workers and businesses is viewed by many as an alternative to increasing protectionism. In the 1962 legislation, however, the procedure for establishing that the major cause of material injury was an increase in imports resulting from trade liberalization was lengthy and complex. The first group of workers did not receive trade adjustment assistance (TAA) until 1969. The Trade Act of 1974 liberalized both the criteria for eligibility and the size of TAA benefits, so that it became necessary to demonstrate only that increasing imports contributed "importantly" to material injury, not that imports were a "major" cause of injury. Two years later, more than 500,000 workers had applied for TAA, four times more than had applied the previous 12 years under more strict eligibility requirements. Between 1975 and 1981, worker payments, predominantly concentrated in import-sensitive industries such as automobiles, steel, apparel, textiles, and shoes, totaled $2.7 billion. Additionally, more monies were spent for worker training and relocation, and about $250 million was provided to firms. The Reagan administration cut trade assistance in 1981, reducing benefits and tightening requirements, so that imports had to be a "substantial" cause of injury instead of just a contributing cause.

The Strength of the Dollar

The U.S. maintenance of an appropriate value of the dollar on international money markets is a perpetual problem plaguing exporters and affecting the whole economy. Economists have applied their neoclassical concept of equilibrium to international currency exchanges as well as to supply and demand for goods within any particular economy. Ideally, a nation tries to discover the rate of exchange that roughly balances out all the supplies and demands for its currency so that it has a stable "equilibrium" relationship between its own currency and those of other countries. Overvalued or too high exchange rates may lead to unemployment. Undervalued or too low exchange rates may lead to inflation.

Nor are exchange rates neutral in their impact on exporting and importing. When the value of the dollar is falling, fewer units of foreign currency are needed to exchange for the same amount of dollars, so U.S. exports cost foreign buyers less of their own currency and become comparatively less expensive. At the same time, imports to the United States become more expensive to U.S. buyers who need more dollars to purchase them. With the growth in exports and decline in imports, unemployment may fall, but the increase in the price of imports may contribute to an increase in inflation.

Central banks, including the Federal Reserve, may attempt to manipulate the value of their currencies by buying and selling them in international markets. Heilbroner and Thurow (1981) note that a government is always able to lower the price of its currency more easily than raise the price, since it can sell unlimited quantities of its own money on the foreign-exchange market, but has a limited power to buy its own money. This power is most effective in stemming short-term speculation, but is rarely effective in reversing decreasing prices resulting from major worldwide currency and capital flows.

Throughout the early 1980s, many observers felt that a strong dollar hurt U.S. exports and contributed to growing and massive trade deficits. Many companies began to clamor for a weaker dollar, and the administration began a policy of "talking it down." By 1985, amid wide recognition that the dollar was grossly overvalued, it began a long decline, eventually prompting some other countries and certain sectors within the United States, particularly those reliant upon imports, to clamor to have the dollar stabilized. By early 1987, the finance ministers from six countries (the United States, Japan, West Germany, France, Britain, and Canada) issued a joint statement concluding that the 23-month decline in the dollar had gone far enough and calling for stability in currency markets. Federal Reserve Chairman Paul Volcker warned that a continued drop in the dollar could cause a severe recession in the United States (Volcker, 1987).

While overvalued or undervalued currencies induce economic dislocations and hardships, rapid swings in exchange rates inject great uncertainty into the export process. Initially, when world-wide flexible exchange rates were first adopted in 1971, economists were confident that gradual adjustments induced by constant market forces would prevent large fluctuations in exchange rates between major countries over short periods of time, as well as fundamentally overvalued or undervalued currencies. Yet both evils subsequently arose.

Thurow, among others, has called for more active management of the dollar's value in international markets, arguing that without such action, the United States could lower the value of the dollar internationally by selling dollars on the foreign-exchange market, but would control the value of the dollar and the domestic money supply at home by buying dollars (i.e., selling bonds) in domestic money markets. Managing the value of the dollar in the foreign-exchange market to manage growth of exports is the intellectual and policy equivalent of using fiscal policy to manage domestic economic growth. As the United States becomes more active in global markets, can more active management of the value of the dollar and U.S. exporting be far behind?

THE MECHANICS OF EXPORTING

Grand theory aside, the mechanics of exporting are far more complicated than producing and marketing for domestic markets. Exporting involves the following multistep process, which may initially appear overwhelming to new and smaller firms just venturing into foreign markets for the first time.

Export Education and Counseling

A firm must first acquire information about trade and investment opportunities abroad, foreign markets, financing, and insurance from the Foreign Credit Association (FCA), the tax advantages of exporting, international trade exhibitions, export documentation requirements, economic facts about targeted foreign countries, export licensing, and import requirements. Currently, the U.S. Department of Commerce can inform prospective exporters about these matters through 47 local district offices scattered throughout the country. Most of these offices have a business library with the latest reports on statistical data published by the Commerce Department. District offices also have lists of contacts of people experienced in exporting who serve on District Export Councils.

The Business Counseling Section of the International Section of the International Trade Administration, a Commerce Department agency, provides counseling to prospective and current exporters. Abroad, the U.S. Foreign Commercial Service (FCS), created in 1980 to represent U.S. trade and investment interests overseas, has 124 locations in 65 countries and can provide coordination with programs in the Export-Import Bank and the Overseas Private Investment Corporation, which offers political risk insurance as well. Some state-government development agencies and state departments of commerce provide further assistance to new exporters. Finally, more than 250 large commercial banks in the United States have international banking departments capable of offering certain types of financial expertise. Industry trade associations and the U.S. Department of State country desks are additional sources of information.

Selecting Markets Abroad

Currently, the U.S. government provides the fledgling exporter with some information useful in selecting an export market, although more information from various sources might be made available. The Bureau of Census publishes the *Foreign Trade Report*, which includes statistical records of all merchandise shipped from the United States to foreign countries, including both the quantity and dollar value of exports to each country per month. Other reports include international economic indicators, international demographic data, and market-share reports. *Overseas Business Reports* provides details on marketing strategies for individual countries. *Foreign Economic Trends* (FET) reports are prepared by U.S. embassies and consulates and provide country-by-country data on business conditions. *Global Market Surveys* (GMS) are product specific, whereas occasional country market-sector surveys focus on a single sector in a single country. For a nominal annual subscription fee, TOPS (Trade Opportunities Program) provides computer matches of firms with business opportunities. The New Product Information Service (NPIS) provides worldwide publicity for U.S. products available for immediate export through publication of *Commercial News USA* (CN). Private marketing research firms also offer services to help firms new to exporting develop an exporting strategy.

Developing an Export Marketing Strategy

Successful market strategies identify export objectives, specific tactics to be used by the exporting firm, activity schedules, and resource allocations among scheduled activities. Experts advocate written strategies, since the advantages and disadvantages of written plans become more apparent than those expressed orally, and written plans are less easily forgotten and easier to communicate.

Considerations here include deciding if there is something unique about the product to be exported that will increase the probability of sales, and assessing the quality of the export product compared to the competition abroad. Once known for quality abroad, American products have slipped in image, if not reality, to where the current image is the reverse—one of inferior quality compared with competitive items. The degree of customer service needed should also be factored into decisions about an export strategy, as well as whether or not production capacity can serve both domestic and foreign demand, unless the exporter wishes to focus exclusively upon foreign markets.

Organizing and Export Operation

After defining an export policy and setting realistic goals, exporting plans should develop an organizational plan to achieve the goals. This includes assigning tasks and responsibilities, determining export training needs, evaluating production and distribution methods, and gearing up production and distribution resources for international operations.

Direct or Indirect Selling

Exporting may use one of two basic sales approaches. With direct selling, a bilateral relationship is established between the U.S. manufacturer and the foreign customer, with the U.S. manufacturer responsible for shipping products overseas. With indirect selling, a second U.S. firm acts as a sales intermediary interacting between the U.S. manufacturer and the foreign customer. The intermediary usually assumes responsibility for shipping the U.S. exports overseas. Since with indirect selling the marketing and distribution abroad is handled by others, this method of exporting requires the smallest allocation of resources.

Several types of firms may serve as intermediaries with indirect selling. Commission agents are "finders" for foreign firms that want to buy U.S. products. Country-controlled buying agents are foreign government agencies or quasi-government agencies that fulfill the same function. Export management companies (EMCs) are firms that purchase U.S. goods for resale in foreign markets. Export merchants purchase products directly from the manufacturer and sell them overseas through their own contacts. Export agents act similarly to a manufacturer's representative, but the risk of loss is retained by the manufacturer.

Export trading companies (ETCs) were made possible by federal legislation in 1982, to enhance the practicality of exporting by small- and medium-sized firms. Under the law, manufacturers in the same industry may establish joint exporting ventures without violating antitrust regulations, if they have been given antitrust certification, or preclearance. The purpose of the ETC legislation was to create a legal device that could provide to smaller firms export expertise and resources beyond what they otherwise could afford. Export trading companies could be called upon to finance suppliers' production, if an order was unusually large or had to be specially made to meet foreign specifications.

Direct selling may involve several methods as well. Sales representatives or agents are the equivalent of domestic manufacturer's representatives. Foreign distributors are merchants who buy their own account with the manufacturer and resell products abroad, maintaining an inventory and facilities for servicing operations. The foreign retailer is the equivalent of the domestic retailer—the last link between the production and distribution process and the consumer. Finally, some countries have state-controlled trading companies.

Modifying the Export Product

Products may have to be modified for export. Many countries use both the metric system for sizing and different electrical systems. Freight charges are often based on both volume and weight, which may enhance the rationale for disassembling products for shipping. Exporters also need to develop strategies for dealing with breakage, moisture, and pilferage.

Pricing, Quotations, and Terms of Sale

A variety of factors affect price quotations, including personnel and equipment costs needed to establish an export operation, marketing research and credit checks, shipping and insurance costs, business travel, international postage, and cable and telephone rates. Prices are also affected by product modifications and special packaging, overseas advertising and promotion efforts, translation costs, fees charged by consultants and freight forwarders, commissions, and training charges. Exporters may choose between several terms of sale and, to protect themselves, may state that prices are subject to change without notice.

Communicating Overseas

Translations may be necessary, depending upon the part of the world selected as an export market target, and foreign retailers may want assistance with advertising materials. Cultural norms vary widely, and acceptable advertising practices in the United States may be offensive in other countries—something to be checked before beginning an advertising campaign abroad.

Shipping and Documentation

Except for U.S. territories and in most cases, Canada, all items require an export license. Validated export licenses are required for products with potential defense and military uses or those that affect national security, which in the past has included both oil-processing and computer equipment. For some products, collective documentation is available, including commercial invoices, certificates of origin, inspection certificates, plant health inspection certificates, bills of lading, dock and warehouse receipts, certificates of manufacture, and insurance certificates. Prospective exporters need to consider if shipping costs will be too high to make the product competitive.

Government Export Regulations and Tax Incentives

Government regulations include antidiversion and antiboycott clauses, as well as the Federal Corrupt Practices Act of 1977, which makes certain payments to foreign officials and parties illegal. Tax incentives have included selective relief from customs duties: domestic international sales corporations (DISCs), which help defer taxes; and free-port and free-trade zones, which eliminate customs checks. Enacted in 1972, legislation enacting DISCs were appended to sections 991 and 997 of the IRS Code. One-half of all DISC earnings were tax deferred and not subject to interest payments for late payment of corporate income taxes.

GATT considered DISCs an illegal subsidy and a violation of sections XVI(1) and XVI(4) of its provisions. The Carter administration agreed to submit legislation to revise DISC so that it would conform with GATT. The legislation converted DISCs to foreign sales corporations (FSCs) was actually submitted by the Reagan administration and passed in 1984.

Financing Exports

Options include commercial banks, factoring houses that also make collections, EMCs, and the Export-Import Bank, which makes direct loans for projects requiring long-term financing. The Small Business Administration in the past has provided some export assistance.

Generally, exporting is a cash-intensive business, since working capital requirements may be higher than those for domestic enterprises because accounts receivable, an important current asset, will possibly be older than for a purely domestic concern. Large accounts payable would normally finance large accounts receivable, with the two types of payments roughly coinciding. In exporting, longer transportation times and various foreign business practices may extend the normal time in which payments from the importer would be received by the exporter for the exporter's accounts. Cash squeezes could develop, if similar time extensions are not by the exporter's creditors for accounts payable due to the creditors, or if working capital is not somehow secured. Sometimes exporters may insist upon letters-of-credit or receivable factoring to mitigate this cash squeeze. Since these inconvenience the importer, some believe their use impedes buying American products abroad.

Export trading companies may be able to raise cash through either debt or equity, depending upon the nature of the investors in the ETC. Here profit margins of ETCs are considered a distribution cost by the exporting manufacturer, and the higher the markup, the higher the price of the final product and the less competitive it is. At least some of the success of Japanese ETCs is that their markups are usually less than 2 percent before taxes. Low ETC markups are made possible by deriving external sources of funding, and by a high sales-to-capital ratio, with sales possibly exceeding capital ten to twenty times.

Larger banks may possess both export credit and financing experience, as well as overseas contacts and offices, and are another potential source of capital. Although bank holding companies are limited in the amount of equity and they can invest in an ETC, they may extend both short- and long-term credit through their subsidiaries and by purchasing receivables.

Different Customs Abroad

While in the United States commission rates, market coverage, and profit margins are central features of contracts between manufacturers and distributors or agents, abroad, termination clauses are often more important and may be closely regulated by law. Laws in other countries developed to protect local commercial representatives may require that contracts be drafted in the local language, that local law govern the contract even if it specifies otherwise, that local courts be used for settling disputes, and that contract clauses calling for litigation or arbitration elsewhere are unenforceable.

Terminating a relationship with an agent or distributor is typically straightforward in the United States but can be difficult and expensive abroad, where the principle of termination exists only for narrowly defined "just cause," such as acts of negligence, breach of contract, conduct damaging to the U.S. exporter, or conviction of a serious criminal offense. Months of notice may be required, creating a period when the agent is not particularly effective in his sales and distribution role, and some local laws require cash payments to the terminated representative. Forewarning U.S. exporters of their heightened risk and vulnerability from various local laws and customs is essential to effective exporting.

A DEPARTMENT OF INTERNATIONAL TRADE

Given the complexities of marketing in foreign and often unfamiliar markets, does the U.S. government do enough to facilitate exporting for American producers? Japan, among others, has created a separate Ministry of Trade to emphasize, promote, facilitate, and coordinate exporting. While considerable expertise is offered to U.S. exporters through the U.S. Department of Commerce, especially the International Trade Administration, centralization of trade-related activities into a Department of International Trade (DOIT) has considerable advantages. In addition to providing raw data to prospective exporters on current flows of volumes and prices of goods internationally, DOIT could conduct market surveys of countries throughout the world, identifying the level on the government needs hierarchy at which the each country is located. Considering each country's GNH level, natural resources, and domestic capacity, DOIT could project likely imports for each country for both its public and private sectors.

Just as the Department of Defense has established defense bases around the world, the Department of International Trade could establish major trade centers, which house major trade shows for various U.S. industries and services, and serve as training centers and information bureaus for Americans conducting business abroad. A Department of International Trade could explore the possibility of developing new products for export and facilitate projects that may require many enterprises, such as the sale of an entire health or educational system or other major infrastructure.

At home, DOIT could provide intensive seminars in languages and culture on a user-charge basis for business personnel planning to venture into exporting for the first time, or planning to move into a new market with a different language and culture. These seminars could be abbreviated versions of the intensive language schools currently offered to some military personnel who are to be stationed abroad. A DOIT could collect and distribute information on export financing and fund sources. Its forecasting models, again on a user-charge basis, could provide exporters with sensitivity analyses that predict the implications of fluctuations in currency exchange rates, payment delays, hidden agent costs, lower pricing by competitors, etc., on the exporter's specific firm. Rather than waiting for charges of dumping or other trade violations to be brought by firms in the United States, DOIT could monitor importer compliance to GATT and bilateral agreements. DOIT could provide exporters with comparative statistics on their competitors' expenditures and costs, including comparisons of relative expenditures on capital costs, labor costs, and research and development. Finally, through direct loans to exporters with exporting goals compatible with market surveys conducted by DOIT and indirect loan guarantees to banks, the department could provide exporters with an additional source of working capital needed to ease the cash crunch of conducting business abroad. In the past, loan guarantees have been offered to prop up failing U.S. businesses, but DOIT could target businesses that it projects for export success.

EXPORTING IN THE FUTURE

By the mid–1980s, President Reagan had moved the issue of international trade higher up on his agenda for the nation. Confronted in 1986 with the largest trade deficit the nation had experienced to that date, the tone of the administration turned more bellicose, even though the content of the rhetoric still embraced the concept of free trade. In one showdown in early 1987, Spain joined the European Economic Community (EEC), and the EEC effectively cut off $400 million of U.S. grain exports to that country when it joined. Unless it was compensated, the United States threatened to raise the tariffs on EEC exports such as British gin, French cognac, and Dutch cheese by as much as 200 percent. A compromise was worked out at the last minute, which avoided adding additional flame to the growing international trade wars. However, at the same time, U.S. negotiating teams trying to gain increased access for U.S. firms to Japanese markets for supercomputers, semiconductors, and civil engineering services, achieved mixed success at best. Looming on the political agenda in 1984, although subsequently defeated, was a strict provision proposed by Representative and Democratic presidential aspirant Richard Gephardt of Missouri, which would have created Gramm-Rudman-style reduction targets for trade deficits. Gephardt's provision called for automatic trade restrictions on countries with highly protected markets that run large surpluses with the United States. Gephardt's proposal would have removed all presidential discretion in dealing with bilateral trade difficulties further, reflecting congressional impatience with the trade problem and concern over whether or not the administration would be forced to compromise. While Gephardt's proposals struck at some of the more superficial surface problems with exporting, they did not address the long-term problem of making America competitive in global markets in the next decades and beyond into the twenty-first century.

A set of changes—including management of the dollar in foreign-exchange markets, adherence to free trade whenever possible, and the creation of a Department of International Trade to promote exports—may contribute to reducing the trade deficit, but even these alone are insufficient to ensure competitiveness. Long-term competitiveness is a function of the basic structure of U.S. institutions and the economy. While other nations have forged partnerships between their basic institutions of management, labor, and government, in the United States these three giants continue to regard each other adversarially, while the problem of conquering the global economy cries out for greater cooperation between the three. Nothing less than revitalization of basic educational institutions and the creation of an industrial policy that forges a partnership between management, labor, and government will work. Founded on beliefs of individualism and institutional distrust, such partnerships do not come easily to Americans. Yet the truth is that achieving international competitiveness abroad may indeed require heightened cooperation at home.

3

THE FEDERAL DEFICIT AND DEBT

THE SIZE OF THE FEDERAL DEFICIT AND DEBT

Can a country continue indefinitely to mortgage its future to engage in profligate spending in the present, indebting future generations with debts they cannot pay for benefits they never received? Can a country, unlike corporations, individuals, or even states, continue to spend beyond its means? Does not the impact of massive federal deficits inhibit economic growth and worsen the balance of trade, perhaps irreparably? Most Americans believe the answer to each of these questions is yes. Yet time and again various efforts to eliminate deficit spending fall short and federal deficits persist. This is the dilemma of U.S. politics. Nor is there a single culprit. The responsibility for this problem is widespread, resting with not only the impulses of politicians and bureaucrats, but private-sector and interest group demands as well.

Among the evils attributed to large deficits are high interest rates, enlarged trade deficits, and reduced economic growth and standards of living. Yet despite these harmful aspects of federal deficits, imbalances in revenues and expenditures have grown substantially in recent years. By the middle of the Reagan years, federal deficits exceeded $220 billion. In 1987, the last year in which the United States experienced a budget surplus was 1969. In the 58 years between 1929 and 1986, surpluses were accumulated in only ten, with deficits accumulated in the other 48 years.

In addition to deficits included in the budget, a growth in off-budget expenditures—outlays for agencies not included in the overall budget—has pushed deficits even higher than budget figures suggest. Between 1941 and 1945, deficits totaled $170 billion, identical to the total increase in deficits, including off-budget outlays. Between 1945 and 1984, on-budget deficits grew by $988 billion, but total deficits including off-budget outlays grew by over $111 trillion. Nor was the rate of increase in deficits slowing, since the increase during the first term of the Reagan administration, between 1980 and 1984, exceeds the increase for the entire preceding 35-year post-war period. Between 1945 and 1980, on-budget deficits grew by $448 billion and total deficits by $513 billion. However, between 1980 and 1984, on-budget deficits increased $539 billion and total deficits by $600 billion (Eisner 1986).

During the 1980s, federal budget deficits not only escalated in absolute size, but also as a share of GNP. In 1980, deficits constituted 2.8 percent of GNP. A brief drop to 2.6 percent of GNP in 1982 was followed by a sharp increase to 4.1 percent in 1983, and an even sharper increase to 6.3 percent in 1983. A drop to 5 percent in 1984 was followed by slightly higher figures for 1985 (5.4 percent) and 1986 (5.3 percent).

The growth in federal deficits has escalated the national debt. When the stock market crashed in 1929, setting off the worst economic depression of this century, total federal debt was $17 billion. In 1941, when the country plunged into World War II, debt had tripled to $48 billion. Fighting World War II increased the national debt far more quickly than did fighting the economic depression that preceded it. By the end of the war, in 1946, debt had grown over five times the size that it was at the beginning, increasing to $271 billion. The Korean War and the decade of the 1950s saw comparatively modest increases, so that 15 years later, when John F. Kennedy assumed the presidency in 1960, national debt had increased only by $20 billion to $290 billion. Another $20 billion was added during that youthful president's short tenure in the nation's highest office. In 1963 when Kennedy was struck down by an assassin's bullet, federal debt totaled $310 billion. Fighting both the war on poverty and the Vietnam War during the Johnson administration added $59 billion more: the total was raised to $370 billion in 1968 when Johnson, beseiged by antiwar protestors, announced that he would not run again. In 1969, national debt amazingly decreased by almost $3 billion, but the upward trajectory was resumed by 1970 ($382 billion).

During the Nixon era, another $100 billion was added to the federal debt, so that by the time Nixon was forced from office in disgrace for the Watergate cover-up in 1974, national debt totaled $486 billion. Gerald Ford was president just two short years, but during his time in the Oval Office, federal debt increased 36 percent totalling $646 billion in 1976. An additional $268 billion pushed aggregate figures to $914 when Carter stepped down from office in 1980. President Reagan oversaw the passing of the $1 trillion mark in 1981. During the next five years, as a result of escalating annual deficits during the Reagan years, federal debt more than doubled, approaching $2.1 trillion in 1986, and was expected to reach $2.5 trillion two years later. By the mid–1980s, without a change in policy, estimates for total debt by the end of the decade predicted that the federal debt held by the public as a percent of GNP would increase from 35 to 46 percent (Bell and Thurow 1985).

As federal debt mounts, so do interest payments on the debt. The Congressional Budget Office projected that in 1987, net interest totaled $168 billion, or 15 percent of the budget and 3.64 percent of GNP. This represented an increase from $108 billion in 1984, or 12.7 percent of the federal budget and 3.03 percent of GNP (Bell and Thurow 1985). These figures, plus growing public concern over federal deficits and debt, provided a political backdrop for the debates on Gramm-Rudman-Hollings limitations in 1985.

THE APPROPRIATE ROLE FOR GOVERNMENT

Some pundits, including Robert Samuelson (1985), have contended that balancing the budget is not so difficult, but rather requires a rethinking of what is the proper use of government power and what isn't. The root of the problem, Samuelson argues, is confusion over the appropriate role of government, a role that has become so broadened that we now use government to support almost anything worthy. Asserting that government has no role in sponsoring local operas or other artistic entertainment, he argues that the functions of government should be limited to national security activities that benefit society as a whole but may not be funded privately, such as environmental regulation and protecting those most vulnerable to private markets. Faulting individual benefits as a main source of mounting deficits, Samuelson argues that most Americans would not be discomfited by the severe cutbacks in those benefit programs that eliminating deficits would require. His solutions include increasing user fees; eliminating programs without a compelling national need, including farm programs and subsidies for exports, culture, and Amtrak; increasing copayments for Medicare recipients; and imposing an additional gasoline tax.

Big deficits and big federal debt are most likely to occur concomitantly with big government. Philosophically one of the major ideological differences between liberals and conservatives is their attitude toward an expansion in the role of government. With long roots in eighteenth-century liberal thinking, the precursors of modern liberals adhered to the teachings of John Locke and Rousseau, and brought the then-unique perspective to politics that individual rights and individualism were preeminent and took precedence over group duties. Locke advanced the idea of a social contract—that the individual had a right to barter with any government he helped create to limit the impact of government upon individuals. Implied in the social contract was the notion that the government existed only by the mutual consent of the individual and the government. Fearful of abuses perpetuated in the past by the blending of religion and government authority into disfavored treatment and exclusion for those not embracing the government-sanctioned religion at best, and sometimes repressive theocracies at worst, classic liberals wished to limit government's role and authority. While still emphasizing individual rights and freedoms, modern liberals have shifted to accepting, if not embracing, an enlarged role for government to intervene for the individual against other repressive nongovernmental forces, such as market imperfections, business decisions, and repressive social institutions and customs, including that of racial segregation.

By contrast, modern conservatives have their ideological roots in the thinking of Edmund Burke, also and eighteenth-century philosopher. Unlike John Locke and Jean Jacques Rousseau, Burke (1949) saw society as a whole as the basis and justification for government. Classic conservatives contended that government existed to allow society to meet necessary tasks and envisioned a limited role for government in society. Government was not to be an agent of redistribution or social changes. Social classes existed, according to the classic conservative view, to meet different needs, and efforts to reduce class differences were not only futile, but also undesirable since needs for menial or less rewarding work would go unmet if government altered the role of lower and working classes. Classic conservatism emphasized maintenance of the status quo and small government—aspects that modern conservatives have retained.

Both liberals and conservatives have some claim to the legacy of Adam Smith, the first to clearly articulate the laws of markets and of supply and demand. Smith's emphasis upon individual rights within markets, including individual property rights (a relatively new concept at the time) was clearly a basis of classic liberalism. In essence, Smith (1776) was arguing for a system that provided individuals with the potential for owning the means of production and the ability to make their own livelihood. Massive industrialization and the changes it was to bring—large factories, separation of the laboring class from the owners, and in turn, the owners from the managers of large industrial enterprises—were to lie ahead.

Clearly Smith did not see society as one big organic whole with different classes fulfilling different functions, but rather as a collection of autonomous economic entities (individuals and firms), each pursuing its own self-interest and guided only in purchasing and production decisions not by monopolistic state charters but by market-determined prices. This process produced the greatest total output with products distributed to those who desired them most, hence achieving the greatest good for the greatest number. It is Smith's emphasis on unfettered markets and small government unwilling or incapable of government intervention into those markets, or both, that has become a cornerstone of modern conservatism.

Smith did not deal much with questions of distribution, focusing mostly upon how production decisions are made and assuming that market forces would establish a desirable distribution of bounty generated by a streamlined efficient capitalist economy. Modern conservatives have also embraced Smith's market determination of economic distribution, a view with which liberals take issue, arguing instead that market imperfections such as monopolies and oligopolies produce undesirable distribution outcomes that need to be corrected by government intervention and regulation. The liberal attachment to individual rights also causes them to argue that rights and human dignity are not just political but include an economic component, since a minimal living standard is necessary for political rights to have meaning. Accordingly, modern liberals have been supporters of transfer payments to low-income individual to create an economic floor or living-standard safety net below which individuals are not allowed to fall. The evolution of both philosophical orientations across two centuries has been great: liberals retain an emphasis on individual rights but shift from a preference for small government incapable of breaching those rights to one endorsing larger government willing to defend and protect them; and conservatives retain an emphasis on maintenance of the existing social structure and system for economic distribution, but shift from supporting primarily governmental enforcement of those goals to market maintenance.

PRESSURES TO INCREASE GOVERNMENT SPENDING

Money is the medium through which the ideology of grand theory meets the pressures of practicality. In this clash of the lofty ideal versus gritty reality, it is the latter that guides the daily processes and practices of government. Ideology is interjected in massive dosages into the system only when there are reform convulsions. At the practical level, the pressures to increase federal spending are not only real, but also substantial.

In describing these pressures, political scientists refer to a powerful relationship called the iron triangle, whose three sides are the congressional subcommittees on appropriations that allocate the spending for a particular federal program, the federal agency that administers the spending for the program, and the constituency or client group that benefits from it. Typically, all three are in favor of increasing spending for the program in question. Caught and buffeted by these forces are both the average member of Congress, most of whose constituents have little interest in the program, and the average citizen who must pay for it.

Why are not members of the subcommittees on appropriations, as well as members of other congressional committees that authorize and oversee the program, better watchdogs for the federal treasury? The answer lies with the internal incentive structure of Congress and the pattern of congressional committee assignments. Members of Congress typically desire reelection and strive for committee assignments overseeing programs that affect their own constituents. The appropriations committees are particularly powerful and attractive, since they oversee the allocation of the federal purse. Once they have achieved committee assignments related to constituent interests, members are motivated to increase spending in order to help constituents and enhance their reelection chances. Additionally, within Congress, controlling large and growing programs is more powerful and internally prestigious than controlling small or shrinking programs.

Bureaucrats have some of the same motives for advocating increases in spending for the programs they administer; large and growing programs are more prestigious and afford more opportunities for upward mobility and personal career advancement than do programs where cuts and retrenchment are the norm. Furthermore, bureaucrats are close to their own program areas and can see legitimate need. Lacking the potential for creating the great wealth that the private sector provides, they are often attracted to government employment with mixed motives, harboring some concern over the public interest or a particular problem area, as well as financial concerns. This proximity to the problem, which the program was constructed to address, and in some instances, public orientation cause the bureaucrat to argue for increases. Additionally, political scientists have noted that agencies, not unlike individuals and governments, develop through stages, and that in later stages, bureaus often become advocates for the industries and groups they were originally created to monitor impartially.

The advantages of increased federal spending to the third side of the iron triangle, the beneficiary constituents or affected interest groups, are obvious. While beneficiaries are most readily identified with transfer-payment programs, almost all federal spending benefits someone. For example, education spending disproportionately benefits teachers and students, while defense spending disproportionately benefits military personnel and defense contractors, to name but a few. Each of these groups has a self-interest in promoting greater federal spending in its particular area.

Interest groups use many tactics to flex their political muscle to keep the stream of federal dollars flowing in their direction. Producer groups often form political action committees (PACs), which become conduits for funneling campaign contributions to members of Congress and candidates for office who promise to support programs favored by the group. Using Federal Election Commission data, Sheler and Black (1984) found that corporate PACs totaled 1,536 in 1983, up from 89 in less than a decade before in 1979. By contrast, there were 378 labor PACs in 1983; 617 trade, health, and membership PACs; and 994 other PACs associated with various public interests and other causes.

Nor are PACs shy about exerting influence. When a vote took place on cuts in dairy-price supports in 1982, 250 of the members who voted against the cuts had collectively received more than $1.7 million from dairy-industry PACs during the preceding five years—an average of $6,837 each. When a House subcommittee in the same congress decided not to place orders with a second supplier for M1-missiles, the chair of the subcommittee, Representative Joseph P. Addabbo, shifted his support to the supplier, Avco Corporation, after receiving a $5,000 PAC contribution from Avco. Prior to a lopsided vote against warranties on used cars, the PAC for the National Automobile Dealers Association contributed more than $750,000 to House members in the preceding election. Additional contributions were made during the debate on the vote, even though it was not an election year.

In addition to PAC contributions, producer groups hire lobbyists to present their viewpoints and cases to key lawmakers. Occasionally, on important votes, producer groups may activate their membership into letter-writing campaigns. Producer groups may also produce expert witnesses to testify before committee and subcommittee hearings on behalf of the group and its programs.

Consumer, labor, and public interest groups employ the same tactics used by producer groups to influence members of Congress, but are more likely to use grass-roots organization and letter-writing campaigns. Despite the fact that they have been outnumbered by corporate groups in recent years, six of the ten largest have been labor PACs, including the United Auto Workers, AFL-CIO, Machinists, Steelworkers, the National Education Association, and the Seafarers. Labor PAC money has the same potency to increase federal spending and achieve desirable legislative outcomes as does corporate PAC money. Before a favorable vote in the House on a domestic content bill backed by the United Auto Workers, which required that American parts and labor be used in cars sold in the United States, the 215 members who voted for the bill had received $1.3 million from the union's PAC in the two preceding elections, more than 18 times the contributions received by the 188 opponents of the bill.

Other factors, including the nature of some policies and the internal norms of Congress, add to the pressure to increase spending. Theodore Lowi, a political scientist, has divided policies into three separate but not always mutually exclusive and distinct categories: distributive, redistributive, and regulatory (Lowi 1969). With redistributive policies in which money is transferred from one group to another and with regulatory policies, which attempt to better match benefits with costs, there are clear winners and losers. The losers provide some force to hold down federal spending. However, distributive policies, such as the so-called "pork-barrel" programs, do not particularly benefit low-income groups. Rather, they distribute money back geographically across all congressional districts. Exemplary of distributive policies are hospital funds, a great deal of military spending in which bases and contracts are distributed across a wide array of congressional districts, water projects, dams, highways, and other types of public works projects. Distributive programs are for desirable social ends and benefit large numbers of constituents in disparate areas and districts, creating an electoral incentive for members of Congress to vote for their support.

Included among the internal norms of Congress that increase spending is legislative "log rolling" in which members vote for increases in spending for programs that their constituents do not particularly value, in exchange for positive votes from other members for programs that do benefit their constituents. This approach to legislative negotiations does a great deal for institutional functioning, but little for holding down federal spending and budget deficits.

Further promoting growth in federal expenditures is the increase in the proportion of the budget that is "uncontrollable," now estimated to be 75 percent of all federal spending. "Uncontrollability" means that decisions about the amount to spend in any particular year have been removed from the budget process and are determined elsewhere, often by economic conditions or other factors beyond immediate congressional control. The separation of the authorization and appropriations functions partially contributes to this. Under current congressional practice, new programs are approved by the authorizing or substantive committees, which set the legislative framework for the program, including any benefit structure and eligibility requirements, while the appropriations committees pass the annual appropriations within those guidelines.

In entitlement programs in particular, which transfer benefits to individuals or groups, this separation removes the actual determination of total levels of spending from the direct control of the appropriations committees. In 1974, Congress reformed its internal budget process and, in an attempt to resume control over entitlement spending, developed a reconciliation phase wherein the budget committees could instruct tax committees to raise more revenues, thus authorizing committees to alter benefit structures and eligibility requirements. Despite these efforts the problem of separation remains.

Entitlement program expenditures are also greatly affected by economic conditions. Several transfer programs designed to assist low-income persons and the needy, such as welfare and unemployment compensation, vascillate inversely with the condition of the economy. When economic conditions worsen welfare and unemployment expenditures increase; when economic conditions improve, welfare and unemployment expenditures decline. This inverse relationship has caused economists to call such spending programs "automatic stabilizers" since they automatically, without overt intervention from Congress, act like a Keynesian rudder, moving in the right direction to provide a countervailing force to economic conditions and keeping the economy on keel. However, until 1981, once benefit structures and eligibility requirements were established, economic conditions, rather than congressional decision making in the appropriations process, largely determined the number of people receiving benefits and, hence, total spending levels.

The stigma in the United States against welfare has caused Congress to impose additional categorical requirements, such as working a specified number of weeks within relevant quarters to receive unemployment, or parenting children, who in some states, still must have no father in the household to receive welfare. This interjects uncertainty and inconsistency into these programs and can increase administrative costs, causing some reformists to move toward solely means-based criteria for receiving government assistance.

The Aid to Families with Dependent Children (AFDC) has been criticized for encouraging recipients to remain on welfare, sometimes over multiple generations, creating a subculture for whom work in the private sector is alien. The categorical nature of this program means that the only way to secure funding is to parent children often born outside of marriage, a factor that perpetuates the welfare culture. Yet crucial to persistence of some recipients on AFDC is the "effective tax rate," or the rate at which they will lose benefits should they find part-time or even full-time employment in the private sector. Effective tax rates for working at low-paying jobs for recipients have been prohibitive in the past, sometimes exceeding 100 percent. These high effective tax rates discourage recipients from attempting part-time or full-time employment in the type of jobs they are most likely to get—low-skill and low-paying jobs. Reform of the entire welfare system, reducing effective tax rates, moving toward means-based qualifications rather than categorical requirements, and integrating the transfer-payment system with the tax system to reduce inequities and inconsistencies when the two meet—all hold the best hope for long-term reductions in welfare spending and diminished reliance on the program both for daily living expenses and as a way of life.

Another source of uncontrollability is contract authority, which provides agencies with the authority to obligate government revenues for payments to contractors in future years. This type of uncontrollability is particularly prevalent in the defense area, in which the Department of Defense purchases huge multibillion-dollar weapons systems, as well as conventional weapons and supplies. Since contracts legally obligate the government in the present to spend money in the future, the decision about spending in subsequent years has been at least partially made. Recent movements toward de facto multiyear budgeting, in which programs expenditures are projected for several years into the future in addition to the budget year, are in part a response to this and other sources of uncontrollability. However, it takes 50 to 100 percent longer to build weapons in the 1980s than it did in the 1950s and 1960s, and the General Accounting Office has estimated that each year added to the production cycle adds 20 to 30 percent to the cost (Pascal 1985).

The nature of contracts, especially defense contracts, compounds the uncontrollability of contract authority. In purchasing a large weapons system, or otherwise procuring a weapon not yet designed but to be developed, competitive bidding, a cost-control procedure highly suitable for standardized manufacturing in which product specification are known and can be identified, is not possible. The Department of Defense, instead, often relies upon sole-source contracts, in which competition in bidding does not occur. When Casper Weinberger became Secretary of Defense in the Reagan administration in 1981, fewer than 10 percent of all Pentagon procurement dollars were allocated through competitive sealed bidding, and one-third of contract dollars were allocated through sole-source contracts. These figures remained unchanged two years later. In 1983, another one-third of dollars were spent through "competitive negotiations," in which bids are limited to a small number of qualified firms. Once a contractor, through the sole-source route or competitive negotiations, has invested in development costs, that contractor usually has moved down the learning curve sufficiently to be able to win subsequent production contracts, since one-fourth of all contract dollars are spent in contract extensions.

Even initial competition does not serve as a cost control for subsequent contracts. Pascal (1985) has noted that, in the initial struggle to win a development contract, defense firms may compete fiercely, but once the award has been made, competition tends to evaporate and incentives for cost control recede, making the production phase the reverse of a free market. Indirectly adding to weapons costs are the personnel practices of the Pentagon, which result in each new weapons program being handled by a succession of uniformed officers who are rotated in and out of their jobs too quickly to build up the long-term knowledge, experience, and expertise for dealing effectively with contractors. One survey of Pentagon procurement officers found that of the 26,000 employed, over two-thirds had not completed mandatory training requirements. Nor do cost-plus contracts, which have been used frequently in the past and agree to cover the contractor's costs plus a percentage of those costs as profit, provide any incentives for cost control. Yet, contractors have resisted attempts to move toward fixed-incentive arrangements.

Borrowing authority provides yet another source of budget uncontrollability. Like contract authority, borrowing authority allows the government to borrow monies now and obligates it to repay the loans at some subsequent prespecified date, with interest. The growth in the national debt and the uncontrollability can remove spending decisions from the current budget process, since Congress, short of national collapse, has no alternative but to repay and service the national debt.

Closely related to borrowing authority has been the explosion of federal credit activity in recent years. While much of the explosion has occurred in off-budget agencies and therefore has not affected the annual budget deficit directly, Ippolito (1984) notes that whether agencies are on-budget or off-budget, the government must still secure funds to cover their lending programs. Most direct loans that require immediate commitment of funds are charged to these off-budget agencies so that their budgetary consequences become apparent only in the event of default when the agencies must actually provide funds to repay lenders holding the guarantees. Nonetheless, with the federal credit activity increasing to $725 billion by 1982, this type of commitment creates a great source of potential uncontrollability.

Nor are the iron triangle or the distributive and uncontrollable nature of a great deal of the federal budget the only forces operating to increase outlays. Wagner's Law, developed in the late nineteenth century, implies that industrial societies, as they develop and become more prosperous, experience increased demand for a greater number of services, especially defense, education, communications, and infrastructure, and these will require an increasing share of GNP (Gould 1983). While cross-sectional empirical correlations testing this hypothesis are not strongly supportive, statistical evidence using a long time frame is more supportive. Wagner's Law implies that government expenditures are income elastic, increasing at a faster rate than GNP as a whole. Changes in demand toward more services and collective goods as national wealth and income rise create additional pressures to increase government spending, sometimes regardless of the ability or willingness to pay.

HOW BAD IS THE FEDERAL DEFICIT?

Not everyone agrees that large federal deficits are a major national problem, but the arguments against continuing and rising deficits are many. Some have argued that as long as the debt used to finance deficits is held mostly by U.S. citizens who are willing to roll it over by purchasing new debt when outstanding issues become due, instead of by foreigners or foreign governments who might not be willing to finance a roll over, the deficit and related debt problems are overstated. However, deficits represent a mortgaging of the future for current programs and benefits, critics contend. The interest costs in the federal budget, which must be borne by all taxpayers, are the costs of trading off future consumption for present consumption.

While the public is aroused by the size of nominal deficits, economists focus on structural and cyclical deficits. The structural deficit is that which would occur aside from cyclical variations in the economy, while the cyclical deficit is that additional deficit which occurs or would occur as employment and the economy vary from the levels used in determining the structural deficit. Sometimes the structural deficit is set at a full-employment level so, if the economy were at full employment rather than the much higher levels experienced in recent years, the government would be running a surplus, given existing spending and revenues, rather than a deficit. Only when the full-employment assumptions would also result in a deficit do adherents to this line of thinking become unduly alarmed.

Nor are federal deficits and debt neutral in their impact on the distribution of wealth, although the nature of the impact is not clear. By selling bonds, rather than financing the deficit through the printing of money, unbacked by debt instruments and loan obligations, the government is creating wealth, which, in turn, is purchased by commercial banks, state and local governments, money market funds, insurance companies, individuals, and foreign governments. In this creation, income and wealth are transferred from the general taxpayer to the holders of federal securities, typically higher-income individuals and large institutional holders in a fashion that is most likely regressive. Yet the monies generated are spent on federal programs that are redistributive, some of which are for transfer payments and are mildly progressive.

Another criticism of mounting deficits is that they cause crowding in the capital markets, so that the government absorbs or borrows as much as one-third of all the funds available for private and public borrowing. This restricts the amount of funds available for private industry to borrow for investment in new plant and equipment, and may slow economic growth. Others point out that a great deal of borrowed funds have been used for corporate mergers and acquisitions rather than investment in new technologies, long-term research and development, or new plant and equipment, so the negative impact on economic growth is overstated.

Related to the argument that federal deficits create crowding in the capital markets is the assertion that they drive interest rates up as a result of the crowding. Yet much of the impact on the capital markets depends on the actions of the Federal Reserve and whether or not it "monetarizes" the debt by pursuing easy money policies that could reduce the crowding impact by as much as 50 percent. Also, when interest rates rise, partially attributable to increases in federal deficits, investment in the United States becomes relatively more attractive to foreign investors who begin to move capital from foreign markets to the United States, expanding the available capital and reducing the crowding effect.

Deficits have been linked to rising inflation, although statistically the relationship is not clear. During the first term of the Reagan administration, in particular, record-breaking deficits were accumulated simultaneously with a drop in inflation to a postwar low by the beginning of the second term. While deficits are one factor in determining inflation rates, clearly other factors during that time period, especially the effective breakdown of OPEC, the glut of oil on the world market and the resulting sharp decline in energy prices, had a salutary effect.

Rising federal deficits have also been linked to rising deficits in the balance of payments and trade. By contributing to high interest rates, which attract capital from abroad, the balance of payments is worsened. High interest rates are also associated with a strong dollar, which in turn hurts exports, worsening the balance of trade. This effect hinges, of course, upon the impact of deficits on interest rates and its relation to the strength of the dollar. As with inflation, many factors, including the quality of American products and U.S. aggressiveness in promoting exporting, also affect the balance of trade.

The budget of the federal government is like neither those of state and local governments nor corporate America. State and local governments and corporations maintain separate capital budgets in which borrowing is customary to finance the acquisition of long-term assets. Requirements to balance the budget typically apply to the operating budget for state and local governments. The federal government, however, has only one unified budget, which includes both capital and operating expenditures.

Eisner compares federal debt to corporate debt and finds that in the 1970s and 1980s, business debt increased much more rapidly than federal debt. In 1952, gross federal debt held by the public constituted 62 percent of GNP while the debt on nonfinancial business was 32 percent. By 1979, federal debt had fallen to 26.5 percent of GNP while business debt had increased to 52 percent of GNP. As a result of the massive deficits in the first Reagan administration, federal debt had increased to 37 percent by 1985, but still lagged behind business debt, which was 55% of GNP.

No one supports massive deficits, but Keynesians contend that at times, deficit spending may be necessary to keep the economy from sliding into recession or depression. Galbraith, however, has observed (1959) that the implementation of Keynesian policy has been a one-sided affair, since the fiscal solutions to combatting recession (increasing government spending and cutting taxes) are politically popular, whereas the solutions to combatting inflation (cutting spending and increasing taxes) are unpopular and may even mean political suicide for politicians, especially in an election year.

Bell and Thurow (1985), in reviewing many of the arguments that the deficit is overstated, find the arguments overstated instead. These authors contend that the fact that U.S. deficits are not much larger than those of its major international competitors is largely irrelevant. Since U.S. industrial competitors save more than do U.S. citizens, those countries can more easily afford to accumulate equivalently sized deficits without an adverse affect on investment. Nor can the United States ''grow its way out'' of a deficit, which would require unrealistically low unemployment rates and substantial improvements in productivity. In short, the federal deficit remains a problem that has not gone away.

THE ROLE OF TAXES

Spending is not the only factor contributing to deficits, which are, by definition, a gap between spending and revenues. Taxes, or rather the lack of tax revenues, also contribute. During the Reagan years, Congress enacted two major revisions in the tax code affecting most individuals. The first was a 25 percent reduction in all brackets for individuals in 1981 under the supply-side philosophy that tax cuts would stimulate productivity and, because of the increase in income and economic activity, would not necessarily result in a loss of revenue. This assumption proved false and required a quick fix, implementing various ''revenue enhancers'' the following year. In addition, the assumption resulted in charges by David Stockman, the administration's ''whiz-kid'' director of the Office of Management and Budget, that Reagan was playing politics with the national purse. The second major change was the simplification of the tax code in 1986, eliminating many loopholes, reducing the number of brackets for individuals from 15 to three, reducing the average rates and shifting over $100 billion of the tax burden from individuals to corporations whose share in revenue contributions had diminished greatly.

It is not without reason, however, that members of Congress often resist raising federal taxes to reduce budget deficits. When the public is asked to rank which tax is least fair, the federal income tax has usually headed the list (38 percent in 1985), followed by the local property tax (24 percent), state sales tax (16 percent), and state income (10 percent). Despite the public dislike of taxes, the U.S. tax bite of 30 percent of GNP ranked nineteenth in 1984 among many industrialized countries as a share of total national output. Heading the list was Sweden, at 51 percent, followed by the Netherlands (47 percent), Norway (47 percent), Belgium (47 percent), Denmark (46 percent), France (44 percent), Austria (41 percent), Ireland (41 percent), and Italy (40 percent). Also exceeding the United States in tax bite were Britain (38 percent), West Germany (37 percent), Finland (37 percent), Canada (35 percent), New Zealand (34 percent), Portugal (33 percent), Greece (32 percent), Australia (31 percent), and Switzerland (31 percent). Japan ranked just below the United States with taxes consuming 27 percent of GNP.

Before the major tax reform of 1986, at least part of the dissatisfaction with the federal income tax resulted from widespread perceptions that the tax was complex, arbitrary, and unfair. The jerry-rigged system has made monitoring difficult and tax cheating prevalent. By 1984, the amount of taxes owed to the Treasury but not paid because of illegal avoidance was estimated at $100 billion, a 226 percent increase over 1973. Popular perceptions that the little and average person pay disproportionately large amounts have contributed to the willingness to cheat, but were grounded in reality. Families right at or below the median income experienced the greatest increase in tax burden during the past generation. Between 1954 and 1984, the tax burden of the median income group increased by 67 percent, while that of families making ten times the median income increased by just 18 percent during the same period. Reagan promoted his revision proposals as populist, despite the reduction in the number of brackets, an essentially antiprogressive measure.

Contributing to its arbitrariness and perceptions of unfairness of the federal income tax was a tendency by Congress to chip away at the tax base, creating special exemptions called "tax expenditures" from taxes that individuals and corporations would otherwise have to pay. Congress raised the number of tax expenditures from 50 in 1967 to 104 by 1982, a year when the total cost to the Treasury of all tax exemptions combined was estimated at $330 billion. In the past, tax expenditures for individuals have included interest on home mortgages, consumer interest, all state and local taxes, capital gains and employer-paid health insurance premiums. The 1986 reforms reduced or eliminated some of these, including the deductibility of consumer interest, state and local sales taxes, and capital gains. Similarly, tax expenditures for corporations, especially rapid depreciation, the investment tax credit and capital gains, were curtailed.

Just like budget subsidies, tax expenditures redistribute the wealth, but are typically favored by wealthy individuals and corporations over budget expenditures for two reasons. These two groups have had a greater incentive to seek tax expenditures because of their higher marginal tax rates. Until the 1986 reforms reducing the maximum personal tax rate from 50 to 33 percent, wealthy individuals benefited far more from income exemptions than did individuals in lower-income brackets. Similarly, the corporate tax rate was 46 percent prior to reforms.

A second reason these groups have often preferred tax expenditures to budget subsidies is the frequency of debate on benefit structures by Congress. While budget subsidies are debated and scrutinized annually, with the potential for reductions being implemented each year, tax expenditures are not regularly debated nor scrutinized with the possibility of changing them. Until the 1974 congressional budget reforms, tax expenditures were not even enumerated regularly. Yet they have constituted a tremendous drain on the federal treasury, with as much as one-third of the federal subsidy budget again being allocated by tax expenditures. Closing tax expenditures but retaining the pre–1986 rate structure would have eliminated the deficit problem. When, however, Congress did move to eliminate many favored tax treatments, it chose to reduce the number of brackets for the personal income tax to three and to hold harmless revenues, a strategy used in part to increase the popular appeal of the reforms, but one that did little to alleviate the deficit.

After World War II, the personal and corporate income taxes combined provided as much as 70 percent of federal revenues, but by the 1970s, this combined share had declined to only slightly more than half of federal revenues. Replacing the corporate income tax as the second most productive revenue source was the social security tax—a payroll tax—which contributed about one-third of all federal revenues by the 1980s. Because of this shift, along with other changes, the federal tax system can no longer be characterized as progressive. Undercutting progressivity not only undermines the ability to pay principle, with those having greater means paying a disproportionate share of the burden, but also undercuts the elasticity of the federal tax system, indirectly compounding the deficit. When taxes are elastic, revenues grow at a rate faster than the tax base, but when they are inelastic, tax revenues grow at a slower rate than the tax base. An inelastic nonprogressive tax structure means that revenue growth will be more sluggish, and without a return to a more progressive system, additional funds to address the problems of federal deficits and debt must be found elsewhere.

Several proposals have been suggested by politicians and academicians to implement new taxes to address budget deficits and national debts. A value-added tax (VAT), now utilized in many European countries, has been suggested most frequently. Under this tax, the value added at each stage of the manufacturing process is taxed, as the partially finished product is sold to subsequent intermediaries in the production chain. The VAT is relatively productive in the countries in which it is used and is largely hidden from the public, which makes it easier to implement. Proponents of the VAT contend that it taxes individuals on what they consume or take out of society, rather than the income from work and savings that they put into it. Because everyone must consume, even those engaged in underground and illegal activities, it provides a mechanism for taxing activities that previously have escaped taxation. Thurow notes that the VAT is also self-enforcing, in that any attempt by a firm to push the VAT tax burden backwards to suppliers or forward to consumers will be resisted by those groups, leaving the government with its rightful revenue.

However, the VAT is the equivalent of a national sales tax, and as such, is regressive. It could also raise the prices of U.S. products, making them less competitive in export markets. Furthermore, it places the heaviest burden on complex manufactured products, including high technology, whose components may change hands several times. It also taxes least services that have little turnover of components but constitute the fastest growing sector of the economy. The VAT may well be an idea whose time has not come.

ATTEMPTS TO REFORM THE PROCESS

David Broder, national columnist for the *Washington Post*, has offered the simplistic, but insightful, advice that the longer Congress struggled with the problem of federal deficits, the more it became clear that the only way to balance the budget was to balance it. While seemingly tautological, Broder meant that there were no shortcuts, no procedural gimmicks, and no painless solutions available to achieve the goal of balanced federal spending and revenue collection.

Yet attempts to reform budget procedure are as persistent if not as frequent as the deficit itself.

Presidential budgeting as we know it today was created by the 1921 Budget and Accounting Act, which centralized executive budgeting in the White House, created the Office of Management and Budget (OMB, then called the Bureau of the Budget) as a presidential budget office, and established the General Accounting Office (GAO) to serve primarily the Congress and provide audits of federal expenditures, and later, program effectiveness. Other reforms in the next 50 years attempted to increase congressional control of the budget, including the Antideficiency Act, which made bureau heads legally responsible for overspending and apportionments and which doled out appropriations in quarterly amounts to prevent overspending early in the year and the absence of funds to meet vital functions late in the year. In 1946, the Council of Economic Advisors was created to provide the president with information on aggregate economic performance and regulatory needs within specific industries.

Other reforms oriented toward limiting spending or making it more effective, or both, have focused on budget formats. Achieving prominence in the 1960s, especially in the Defense Department under Robert McNamara, was the planning, programming, and budgeting system (PPBS), which attempted to move toward a program format, detailed analyses, and multiyear budgeting to streamline expenditures and to spend funds most effectively. Under Nixon, management by objectives (MBO) gained prominence, while under Carter zero based budgeting (ZBB), in which expenditures were justified from ground zero every year, was partially enacted. Each of these reforms attempted to streamline executive budgeting, they have been well intentioned and ultimately have collapsed under their own weight of paperwork and justification, but have left behind a residue of heightened rationality—comparing expenditures as means to objectives and goals—as a legacy.

The guts of controlling spending, however, lies within the Congress. Recognizing that the power of the purse was slipping out of its control when it engaged in hostile debate with Nixon over selected executive impoundments, Congress enacted the 1974 Congressional Budget and Impoundment Control Act to reform both internal congressional budget processes and modify impoundment procedures affecting executive-legislative relations. This act created the Congressional Budget Office (the congressional counterpart to the executive's OMB) and the House and Senate Budget Committees.

Through a series of budget hearings, concurrent resolutions, the development of a congressional budget with aggregate spending and revenue targets and spending targets for major functional areas, a reconciliation procedure and a more realistic timetable, this act attempted to reassert congressional control. In addition, it attempted to invert the budget process from a "bottom-up" decision process, whereby line items and program expenditures drove budget decisions, to a "top-down" process in which macro-economic concerns and national priorities drove decisions. The act did provide Congress with the institutional support and procedures to exert more influence in a more informed way, but as a spending control mechanism, or a mechanism for clearly establishing national priorities and the trade-offs priority setting implies, it failed. Deficits continued to mount. The executive budget, especially in the honeymoon period of Reagan's first term, took precedence over congressional budgeting, and the procedure surrounding the Second Concurrent Budget Resolution collapsed.

Gramm-Rudman-Hollings, passed in 1985, was a somewhat desperate attempt by Congress to reduce the deficit while abdicating responsibility for any pain caused by budget cuts. The act established deficit reduction targets for each of five years, to result in a balanced budget by 1991. Should the budget passed by Congress violate the deficit reduction targets, then the Comptroller General of GAO was to issue automatic spending cuts, allocated equally to defense and nondefense spending, with certain major programs, such as Social Security and some defense contracts, exempt from cutbacks. The constitutionality of the act was immediately challenged on the grounds of violation of separation of powers, since the president appointed the head of the GAO, but could not remove the incumbent. Ruling in favor of the plaintiffs, the Supreme Court forced Congress to create an alternative trigger procedure, and Congress delegated the budget-cutting authority to the director of OMB, increasing presidential power. The first year's budget reduction target was met largely by accounting legerdemain, by shifting expenditures forward into the next fiscal year and by the wholesale sale of government assets. By the second year, Congress was already discussing the modification of the Gramm-Rudman-Hollings budget reduction target.

Other reforms suggested to control government spending have included a presidential item veto and a constitutional amendment to balance the budget. The presidential item veto would parallel the item veto over specific line items in appropriations and capital budgets now held by 43 governors, and has been pushed periodically by Reagan. Congress has accused Reagan of using this proposal to further increase presidential power at congressional expense and to camouflage the fact that all of his proposed executive budgets have included substantial deficits. Furthermore, presidents already have impoundment power to cut back specific spending items though the use of recisions, or permanent executive cuts in spending that must be approved by both houses of Congress within 45 days to become effective. Most likely, the presidential item veto would be used to target specific programs and items unpopular with presidents, and would have little cumulative effect on total aggregate spending or deficits.

A second proposed structural reform to reduce deficits has been to amend the U.S. Constitution to require a balanced budget. Proponents have included Rudolph Penner, the second director of the Congressional Budget Office, and Nobel-Prize-winning public choice economist James Buchanan, while opponents have included political economist Anthony Downs and David Obey, Democratic member of the House of Representatives from Wisconsin (Moore and Penner 1980). Supporters of this proposal contend that political pressures were so great that nothing less than a constitutional prohibition would serve to stem deficits. Interestingly, during the late 1970s, over 30 states, just short of the necessary two-thirds required, passed resolutions to require Congress to call a second constitutional convention to address this issue. While the mechanism of state legislatures mandating Congress to call a constitutional convention to amend the Constitution is provided within it, this procedure has not been used in the history of the country, raising the specter that such a convention would not restrict itself to the deficit problem, but would engage in wholesale revamping of the basic structure of the U.S. government. Also interesting was the then substantial reliance of states and localities upon intergovernmental funds from the federal government, funds most likely to be cut under balanced-budget requirements.

Opponents to a constitutional amendment to balance the budget have noted that it would vitiate the use of taxing and spending as fiscal policy tools to stabilize the economy, throwing the entire burden of stabilization upon monetary policy. Additionally, such a proposal would unduly hamper the effectiveness of the federal government in times of national crises, such as war. Most negatively, it would not alter any of the basic pressures that have contributed to the rapid growth of deficits in recent years, including the influence of special interest groups and PACs in Congress, and the uncontrollability of the budget. After heated debates in the later 1970s and early 1980s, this proposal receded in importance on the national agenda, although it has not totally faded away.

LONG-TERM SOLUTIONS TO THE DEFICIT PROBLEM

There are no easy nor painless solutions to the deficit and debt problems, but there are solutions. Anthony Downs, however, has cautioned that there is no perfect society, and solutions consist of substituting one set of problems, hopefully less extensive and less troublesome, for another, Perhaps most fundamental is reducing the pressure of special interest groups upon Congress, without reducing the accountability of members of Congress to citizens, or citizen access to members.

As long as Congress is "for sale" to the most affluent PACs, the pressures to increase spending from the bottom up will prove irresistible. To break this dependence of members of Congress upon the financial largess of special interest groups seeking real deficit-creating benefits requires public financing of political campaigns for members of Congress. Contributions of PACs to congressional campaigns need to be limited, just as the 1974 campaign reform act limited individual contributions to presidential candidates receiving public monies. Members not dependent upon special interest for reelection could more impartially judge national priorities and make the trade-offs that priority setting requires.

Nor would this diminish the accountability of members to citizens, for each member must still appeal to a majority of voting constituents to be reelected. With monies for campaigns publicly provided and limited, the tendency toward perpetual campaigning and ever-mounting campaign costs would be held in check. While adding an expenditure category to an already bulging budget, the long-term payoffs of public financing of congressional campaigns are tremendous. When proposals for continuing agricultural supports, tax expenditures, new weapon systems, and expansion of entitlement programs are being debated in Congress, members would not have their immediate reelection potential jeopardized by voting for cuts in the national interest.

This proposal would not render special interest groups totally ineffective for, like any group, they would still be able to influence congressional outcomes by rallying votes for candidates who support their particular programs and positions. Hence, in order to be completely effective, campaign laws would have to be strengthened to prevent PACs from spending large amounts to influence election outcomes supposedly without the candidate's knowledge, but in sufficient volume to continue the dependence of congressional candidates upon special interests.

One solution for minimizing the spending of special interest groups on electoral outcomes that is not coordinated with the candidate's campaign, but still creates a financial dependency of the candidate upon the interest group, is to limit total election spending by individual PACs. Such legislation could limit total campaign spending by PACs for both direct and indirect support of candidates but would not limit the ability of PACs to publicize and push specific issue positions—a debate healthy to the development of national priorities and dissemination of information on public policy issues.

Many constitutional issues surrounding this proposal need to be resolved. However, partial public financing of presidential elections already exists and, while not without problems, as Anthony Downs (Moore and Penner 1980) has noted any solution is preferred if it works better than the system that preceded it. Some will contend that the cost of this proposal is too great. If each congressional race costs, on the average, $2 million for all candidates involved and each Senate race averages $5 million, then the total costs of 435 House races in any election year will be $870 million, while the total cost of 33 Senate races will be $165 million.

Total election costs per election year would approach approximately $1.04 billion, presumably an astounding sum. At costs projected in 1987 for the ill-fated B–1 bomber, which were in excess of $250 million a copy (with many costly improvements yet to be installed to make the plane effective), the entire cost of financing congressional campaigns would about equal the cost of four B–1 planes. With a national budget now in excess of a $1 trillion annually, or over $2 trillion on a biannual basis, the cost of financing congressional campaigns ($1 billion) would be less than 1/2,000 of the $2 trillion plus in spending those members will oversee. Posed that way, public campaign costs seem less daunting, as a means to elect representatives able to eschew the deficit-inducing allegiance and budgeting that financial reliance on PACs brings.

Other less drastic proposals might be implemented immediately. One is more stringent training of procurement officers, especially in defense where purchases of large weapons systems involve billions of dollars. In fact, many experts believe that a completely separate and independent agency is needed for defense procurement, similar to that found in other countries with large defense budgets. Congress is already moving toward multiyear budgeting, by requiring five-year projections on the costs of any proposed new programs and, in many instances, projections for future years for existing expenditures, but this trend might be accelerated. Additionally, the reconciliation process might be strengthened by increasing the ability of the budget committees in each house to instruct the revenue committees to find new revenues to diminish projected deficits or authorizing committees to change program structure to reduce spending for the same purpose.

Finally, given public resistance to raising current taxes, the government must explore new revenue sources. Since services and information transfers are a growing part of the now service-and-information-oriented U.S. economy, taxing that base is an obvious candidate. Unlike basic commodities, services are more typically consumed by middle- and high-income groups, so that taxing them would be less regressive than general sales taxes. The federal government already has a history of implementing selected sales taxes through the use of excise taxes imposed on luxury goods.

Even more radical, however, is the proposal that the federal government explore ways to make money. Under our current conception of government, its role is to perform many of the functions not profitable or not otherwise being filled by private industry. We have limited government to taxing as the predominant source of revenue. Yet increasingly we are demanding that government act with the efficiency of a business that must produce profits or go bankrupt. If we cannot allow the government to deficit spend indefinitely, could we not allow it the same privilege of making money today from productive enterprises to finance future activities and cover future costs? In short, we are imposing the responsibilities of private-sector behavior upon government without the same privileges—making it assume risks without the potential for gain—while limiting it to taxing an increasingly reluctant and resistant public as its main revenue source. We should not be surprised that this is a tough act, performed by politicians who must please the public or forego future curtain calls.

An alternative to taxing is to allow government to make money—a proposal most likely to be resisted by private industry fearing unfair competition from the government and encroachment of government enterprises into highly profitable areas that private investors would prefer to keep for themselves. Yet there are many areas in which government could make money without jeopardizing existing private industry. One innovative individual has suggested that the federal government sell advertising space on all its postal trucks, military bases, and other properties clearly visible to the public. The federal government owns huge amounts of property, which could be used productively to raise revenues in this way, without increasing taxes.

Yet another suggestion is that the government charge a license fee for drugs and products authorized by the Food and Drug Administration (FDA); these are often highly profitable products for the large pharmaceutical companies. The fees would be based on total product sales for approved products for a fixed number of years, just as private companies who buy product rights must pay a fee for every item sold within a specified period. Since the FDA has often been accused of acting too slowly and cautiously, keeping potential life-saving drugs off the market too long, these monies could be plowed back to evaluate potential life-saving drugs more quickly to provide for more rapid marketability, as well as to decrease deficits and the debt.

Another suggestion, even more controversial, but not unlike the actions of now over 20 states, is that the federal government adopt a national lottery. At the state level, lotteries have been well regulated, preventing organized crime from taking control. They have been small but stable sources of revenue, netting from 2 to 4 percent of total state funds. Should a national lottery be similarly productive, however, the trillion-dollar-plus size of the federal budget means that it could produce in excess of $40 billion annually, enough to make any interest group salivate and pressured congressional hearts palpitate.

Critics contend that lotteries are regressive, since lottery ticket expenditures constitute a larger proportion of the income of low-income individuals than of high-income individuals. At least one study shows, however, that the participation rate of middle-income individuals in state lotteries approaches that of low-income individuals. Furthermore, the lottery is voluntary, unlike the proposed VAT and the current flattening of the income tax rates, which are also regressive.

Another suggestion is for the federal government to retain control of the space shuttle, instead of selling it off to private industry the minute it becomes profitable, after years of start-up costs and billions of dollars in initial investment, all paid by the taxpayer. No sane private investor would pour billions of dollars into a project, and then sell it the minute the project begins to turn a profit, so that someone else reaps the benefit of all the initial costs. Yet selling the space shuttle is asking the federal government to do exactly that—an option that is bad business and inconsistent with demands to balance the budget. Furthermore, the government pioneering in the development of space, just as city governments develop infrastructures of water and sewers to facilitate urban and suburban development, could sell rights to travel, research, and production in space. Space is a commodity going to the pioneer who gets there first, something the federal government could use to turn a profit and reduce deficits and debt without increasing taxes.

Often the federal government disposes of military surplus at bargain prices or dumps it into the ocean to keep private markets from being inundated and private suppliers from complaining. This extravagance would be more understandable, from a business viewpoint, if we were running huge surpluses instead of deficits. Clearly military surplus as well as other government surplus can and should be sold at prevailing market rates to raise revenues to reduce the deficit, something far more likely to occur if members of Congress, because of public campaign financing, do not have to rely on special interests for funds.

The military flies many sorties to maintain flying time for pilots. While politicians may catch rides on military transports, how about selling vacant space to private citizens when it is available? Military buffs, fascinated with and anxious to learn about the military, would prefer this means of transport when available.

Many federal office buildings with auditoriums, classrooms and other training facilities stand idle between 5 P.M. and 8 A.M. the next day. Guards are already paid to secure the integrity of offices, so why not rent out the idle space to civic and corporate groups when possible?

Nor has the federal government achieved maximum revenue potential from naming its great array of property. Private individuals now have the opportunity to make donations to colleges and other institutions, in turn for having their names imposed on some building. Such is the power of ego for recognition. The federal government, with its vast array of property, could capitalize upon the same motivation. Private individuals willing to make modest contributions toward debt reduction might have a small conference room or other such hall named for them. Larger contributions might purchase the right to have a whole building named for the contributing individual. A huge contribution might be worthy of having an entire military base named for the contributor. In a land that values money and the ability to "make it" in the private sector, can anything be more patriotic than so honoring those who have made it and are willing to donate a small portion toward debt reduction? Currently we frivolously and nonproductively name buildings after living politicians who spend money rather than contribute it.

Perhaps the largest service currently produced by the federal government is the public good, defense, a great deal of which protects Japan and West Germany, whose economies are outperforming the U.S. economy in recent years. Exploration should begin on methods of charging these and other countries for the police services provided by the United States. In times of plenty, the Untied States could more readily afford to give away police and defense protection. In more idealist and naive times, the United States might think that it could and should influence the internal development of other countries, something we have been willing to impose on others but would be horrified to have imposed on us. Now that times are tough, and Korea and Vietnam have punctured naive idealism, we could explore charging for this huge commodity that the United States produces so well. Selling defense services would keep defense contractors, unions representing defense workers and military operations happy, since production and income streams to those sectors would not be disrupted. Liberals would be happy that the revenues rather than further cuts in social spending could finance defense development and growth. Citizens concerned about protecting America would be pleased that the Untied States could use the revenues to fund a technologically superior military that is better maintained and might be employed in times of national emergency. This is a more efficient way to protect the United States than fighting nonwinnable civil guerilla wars abroad at the taxpayers' expense.

The U.S. military currently runs excellent language schools for soldiers being transferred to duties abroad. Given the inability of many U.S. citizens to speak anything but English, and the need for U.S. exporters to acquire greater language facilities, the government could capitalize on this training ability be expanding facilities to include private individuals wanting crash courses. Not only would this raise a small amount of revenue, but it would also facilitate exporting to address the balance of trade.

The U.S. intelligence agencies currently collect a great deal of information on agricultural, industrial, and economic forecasts for many countries. This could be sold to potential exporters at a profit. Agencies dealing with international trade (the existing International Trade Administration or the proposed Department of International Trade) could collect and sell credit ratings and other relevant information on foreign buyers.

Finally, many foreign nationals come to the United States to take advantage of U.S. education, especially higher education. The federal government could develop educational programs to sell abroad in technical, computer, engineering, business, and health-related areas. These programs—whose structure is yet to be determined but may involve classes via satellite in the buying country along with periodic visits by professors—could be sold to raise money. The money could be used to upgrade education in the Untied States and to reduce deficits and debt. Not only would the Untied States benefit, but also conflict might be reduced as the classes help other nations to raise their living standards. Proponents of capitalism would like the inclusion of business courses to teach students in developing countries about the advantages of markets, financial instruments, and other procedures for making capitalism work.

These are but a few ideas—some more realistic than others—which might raise revenues without raising taxes. A creative and vibrant nation, like the Untied States once was and could become again, could come up with many more. Making money is what America is all about, and as a nation we need to make about $2 trillion to reduce our grandchildren's loan.

4

EDUCATION FOR TOMORROW

SIGNS OF TROUBLE

Ominous signs abound that American schools, once the paragon of broad-based mass education, are no longer excellent. In fact, critics charge that they are no longer even good, citing the following statistics, among others ("The Brain Battle" 1987, pp. 58–64):

- Japanese high school graduates completing the twelfth grade have the equivalent of three to four more years of school than do U.S. high school graduates. Half know as much as the average U.S. college graduate.

- Soviet students typically devote five years to physics and algebra, four years to biology, and two years to calculus. In the United States, most teenagers take neither physics nor chemistry and only 6 percent study calculus.

- When 22 experts in comparative education were asked to rank elementary and secondary education systems in six countries, they ranked those of the United States next to last in mathematics and science, ahead of only Britain and behind top-ranking Japan and second-ranking Soviet Union, France, and West Germany. In no area did the United States rank first, although it was second, after West Germany, in social studies.

- In use of the country's own language, the United States astoundingly and abysmally ranked last, surpassed, in order, by top-ranking France, the Soviet Union, West Germany, Japan, and Britain. In use of foreign languages, skills useful if not necessary for exporting and global competitiveness, the United States ranked fourth behind West Germany, the Soviet Union, and France, and ahead of Japan and Britain.

- While nine out of ten Japanese youths earn high school diplomas, nearly one-fourth of American youths drop out of high school, resulting in about one million untrained teenagers entering the job market and often the unemployment lines every year. Of those who stay in high school, experts note that many are motivated to do so only to take driver's education and get a driver's license.

- In a 1982 testing of thousands of twelfth graders in 15 different countries administered by the International Association for Evaluation of Education Achievement, the United States finished fourteenth, just ahead of Thailand and just behind Hungary. Hong Kong ranked first, barely ahead of Japan.

- In a United Nations survey of knowledge of foreign cultures given to students in nine countries, U.S. students scored the lowest. Another test of American 12-year-olds showed that 20 percent could not even locate their own country on a map.

- According to Xerox Chairman David Kearns, U.S. industry spends $25 billion a year training poorly educated workers. Harry Gray, former chairman of United Technologies, believes that "A battle for the technological future of the world is being waged—and the U.S. is losing."

- A 1987 report published by the National Assessment of Educational Progress found that 700,000 functionally illiterate U.S. high school students graduate every year, and another 700,000 drop out.

In an era in which future economic success is tied more closely than ever before to a high-quality, highly educated, and highly competitive labor force, many experts are calling for a reexamination of U.S. educational institutions and a possible overhaul from the ground up.

EDUCATION AND THE BABY BOOM

The United States' educational institutions in recent decades have acted like accordians—pushed and pulled by the baby boom. Marching forward in huge numbers, this generation has been called by various names, including the war babies, Sputnik generation, Pepsi generation, Vietnam generation, and me generation. Regardless of the name used to describe it, this generation more than any other has strongly affected the institutions through which it passed, especially the schools.

In 1951 and 1952, the first of the postwar babies entered kindergarten, exploding enrollments in the schools. These students, born in 1946 and 47, were the beginning of a cohort 38 percent larger than the one immediately ahead of it. For the next 12 years, each class graduating from high school was replaced by a kindergarten class on average 1.5 million students larger and, on occasion, up to 2.5 million larger. Only when the 1946 cohort began graduating from high school did the size of the class of entering kindergarteners begin to shrink. When that happened in 1964, one in four Americans was enrolled in public schools. In 1970, the absolute number of students began to decline, after having peaked at 51.3 million.

Each year demographers would predict that the birth rate would slow and the baby boom would end. Each year, until 1964, it did not. The schools became very overcrowded. Although 50,000 new classrooms were built in 1952, they were not enough. California opened a new school each week during the 1950s, but nationally there was still a shortage of 345,000 classrooms, despite 78,000 makeshift classrooms in churches and vacant stores. Three out of five classrooms were considered overcrowded and a student teacher ratio of 45 to one was not uncommon. Students shared desks and books. Teachers were in short supply and in great demand.

Despite expansion to meet the need, the educational system was in overload during the baby boom. Since substantial federal aid to education did not begin until the mid–1960s with the 1965 Elementary and Secondary Education Act, additional needs were predominantly met and financed locally. Then, in the mid–1960s, the reverse retraction in elementary and secondary education began.

However, the first baby boomers were receiving their high school diplomas and college enrollment expanded from 20 percent of those graduating in the 1950s to 30 percent of those graduating in the 1960s. Not only did the baby boom have greater numbers, but also its members attended college at a higher rate, doubling the total enrollment in all higher institutions of education between 1963 and 1974 from 4.7 million to 9.6 million. The annual growth rate of colleges rose from 2 to 9 percent, and five new professors were hired for every older professor who died or retired in order to meet the demand.

The deluge of numbers greatly increased competition for the more prestigious universities and colleges. Standardized testing and large anonymous introductory classes with hundreds of students became the norm in most universities. Protests over crowding and living conditions eventually became focused on the Vietnam War and civil rights, as the age of student protest began. No other group had so many college graduates, creating an education gap between the baby boom and their parents. An astounding 85 percent of the baby boom graduated from college, although only 38 percent of their parents did. As the last of the baby boom began to graduate in the 1970s, higher education confronted the same overcapacity that had been confronted earlier by the public schools.

Having expanded to meet the baby boomers' needs, the college and university system was now too large. Some small and marginal colleges closed. Faculty salaries fell relative to those of other occupations, and the numbers of new faculty hired declined as the earlier expansion in higher education ended. The bloom was off the educational rose. In a retrenching educational system, teaching at all levels became less prestigious, less well paid relatively, and less desirable. The accordion effect of the gargantuan baby boom generation transformed the focus of college curricula to concern over relevance, placed additional stress upon schools at all levels, and made it more difficult for educational institutions to achieve their goals.

RACE AND EDUCATION

For most of the nation's history, public schools, along with other major public institutions, were racially segregated. Plessy v. Ferguson in 1896 embraced the principle of ''separate but equal'' accommodations for blacks and whites. This principle was extended by southern states to include educational facilities as well as public accommodations, transportation, parks, and recreational facilities. By

1950, the 14 states requiring legal segregation provided 14 medical colleges, 16 law schools, 15 engineering schools and 5 dentistry schools for whites; only 5 black law schools and no black medical, dental, or engineering schools were available (Burns et al. 1987, p. 111).

After filing law suits since the 1930s protesting the separate-but-equal doctrine, blacks won a victory in 1954 in Brown v. Board of Education. The U.S. Supreme Court reversed the Plessy doctrine and ordered school boards to proceed with "all deliberate speed to desegregate public schools at the earliest date." In 1969, the Supreme Court ruled that continued operation of racially segregated schools was no longer constitutionally acceptable, and school districts must move immediately to eliminate dual systems based on race. The court endorsed busing to eliminate the effects of earlier *de jure* segregation, segregation by law, but refused to order cross-district busing between predominantly white suburbs and predominantly black center cities to reduce or erase de facto segregation resulting from housing patterns within metropolitan areas.

In the mid–1980s, most racial minorities were still behind white students in making progress through the educational pipeline. Despite gains in the 1970s and 1980s, minority students lagged behind their white counterparts in reading and writing skills. By the eleventh grade, 68 percent of whites could read at or above average, compared with 52 percent of Hispanics and 31 percent of blacks. While 83 percent of white students graduated from high school, only 72 percent of blacks and 55 percent of Chicanos, Puerto Ricans, and American Indians did so. Thirty-eight percent of whites entered college, compared with 29 percent of blacks, 22 percent of Chicanos, 25 percent of Puerto Ricans, and 17 percent of American Indians.

College graduation numbers declined for all racial groups, but more for non-whites than for whites. Twenty-three percent of whites graduated from college. Only 12 percent of blacks, 7 percent of Chicanos and Puerto Ricans, and 6 percent of American Indians did so. Fourteen percent of whites entered graduate or professional school, and 8 percent completed their graduate education. Eight percent of blacks entered postcollege education, and 4 percent completed their graduate studies. The equivalent numbers are even smaller for Hispanics, averaging 4 percent entering graduate education and 2 percent completing it.

These numbers portend dismally for America's long-term ability to compete in global markets. With birth rates of blacks and Hispanics exceeding those of whites, racial minorities constitute growing proportions of the population and future labor force. As these proportions grow, quality black and brown education must become a priority to restore competitiveness. Yet recent federal reports show enrollment of minorities, excluding Asian-Americans, in colleges to be stagnating.

' In 1976, 1,691,000 minority students in two- and four-year colleges constituted 15.4 percent of all students. By 1984, 2,063,000 minority students on campus constituted 17 percent of all students, but the figures varied widely by race. Black enrollment peaked in 1976 when blacks constituted 9.4 percent of the college population. By 1984, this figure had dropped to 8.8 percent. During the same time frame, Hispanic enrollment dropped from 4.3 percent of the total to 3.5 percent. American Indian enrollment, less than 1 percent of the total, also decreased slightly. Only Asian-American enrollment increased, from 1.8 percent of the total in 1976 to 3.1 percent in 1984.

One current issue complicating public school administration and teaching is the question of bilingual education. In the 1960s, migration to the United States began to increase, especially from of Puerto Rico and Cuba, and subsequently from Mexico and Central America. Many Indo-Chinese refugees also entered the United States following the Vietnam War. Concentrations of minorities varied by geographic location. New York City experienced large influxes of Puerto Ricans. Miami had large numbers of Cuban refugees, and San Francisco received immigrants from mainland China and Vietnam. Much of the Southwest was the relocation choice of immigrants from Mexico and Latin America. Increasing numbers of children could not speak or had only a limited understanding of English, so that by the mid–1980s, 10 percent of California's students were either non-English or limited-English speaking.

Several court cases, including Lau v. Nichols, established the right of these students to receive effective instruction and equal access to educational services. Federal funds for bilingual education were provided. Several states also established financial assistance programs to help local districts fund bilingual programs. Quickly, dispute arose over whether bilingual education should assist in explaining and sustaining the students' cultural heritage, or merely enable the student to learn English as quickly as possible.

More recently some, including many immigrant parents, have questioned the wisdom of conducting non-English classes and have pushed for a reevaluation of English-only classes. Under the Reagan administration, the federal Office of Bilingual Education, which had previously pushed dual-language instruction, began studying English-immersion techniques. Schools in Dade County, Florida, began a three-year pilot program in 1984 to assess whether students who speak little or no English learn subjects better using their native language or English only. Yet many Hispanics and members of other ethnic groups are opposed to wholesale immersion techniques, which they blame for high dropout rates when children are unable to learn by immersion methods. Educators have not reached a consensus on which approach is the most effective for non-English-speaking students. Many are convinced that in the absence of a consensus, the best solution is the use of a variety of methods. Properly employed in the long run, bilingualism could be used to increase the foreign language capacity of U.S. citizens, thus helping to redress one of our major shortcomings in competing on a world-scale foreign language proficiency. On the other hand, if the English language is not mastered by minority groups, their intregration and adapation to the main streams of American society can be profoundly affected.

RELIGION AND EDUCATION

The linkage between religion and education is constitutionally defined, yet underlying religious sentiment influences any attempt to upgrade U.S. schools. The U.S. Constitution provides two Bill of Rights guarantees in the First Amendment to limit the influence of religion on American secular life, including education. Congress is prohibited from "making any law respecting an establishment of religion, or prohibiting the free exercise thereof." Yet the judicially defined relationship between religion and schools in the United States approaches an intricate dance searching for guidelines to implement these freedoms. While ruling in Lemon v. Kurtzman, the Supreme Court developed a three-part test to judge when the establishment clause had been violated: laws must have a secular legislative purpose; their primary effect must neither enhance nor inhibit religion; and government must avoid excessive entanglement with religion.

Schools may not introduce devotional exercises into their curricula, nor may public school authorities sponsor or encourage prayer. In 1985 in Wallace v. Jaffree, the Supreme Court struck down an Alabama law authorizing teachers to hold one-minute moments of silence for meditation or voluntary prayer, stating that the law plainly had a religious purpose. Nor may a state prohibit teaching evolution or discussing Darwin's theory of evolution. Religion and religious literature may be studied as part of a secular program of education, but in a startling 1987 decision issued by Alabama Federal District Judge W. Brevard Hand, the lower court ruled that secular humanism may be defined as a religion and therefore could be taught in the schools. Following an earlier decision in Tennessee that children of religious conservatives may be excused from reading textbooks they find offensive, segments of the judiciary seemed willing to question previous rules for separating religious teachings from school curricula.

Equally significant as court rulings defining the content of public school curricula are decisions that influence financing of public and parochial schools. Church property, often used for religious-sponsored schools serving as alternatives to public schools, is tax exempt. Yet until recently, parent-paid tuition for private and parochial schools was not regarded as tax deductible. In 1983 in Mueller v. Allen, the U.S. Supreme Court in a close decision upheld a Minnesota law allowing all taxpayers to deduct from their state income taxes, up to a specified ceiling, monies paid for tuition, textbooks, transportation, and other school costs for children attending both public and private schools. Since public schools charge no tuition, the primary beneficiaries were parents sending their children to private schools. The Supreme Court reasoned that the primary intent of the law—to promote a better educated population—was secular, not religious.

When ruling on the permissibility of public funds for parochial and private schools, the Supreme Court has drawn a fine distinction between expenditures that benefit the student and therefore are allowable, and those that benefit the school and therefore are not allowable. Hence, tax funds have been used for textbooks, standardized tests, lunches, transportation to and from schools, diagnostic services for speech and hearing problems, and other types of remedial services in church-operated elementary and secondary schools. The Supreme Court has not allowed tax funds to be used for teachers' salaries, equipment, counseling for students, teacher-prepared texts, facilities repairs, or transportion of students to and from field trips in religious schools.

In the past, issues of religion, race, and school funding have been intertwined. Confronted with forced desegregation in Brown v. Board of Education, many white parents who did not want their children to attend racially integrated schools transferred their children to private schools. Especially in the South, these "segregation academies" were often sponsored by churches. Diverting public funds to private religious schools with a primary intent of maintaining racial segregation would undermine the intent of Brown and subvert public tax dollars to funding continued racial separation in education.

While segregation has diminished in the South, housing patterns in major metropolitan areas, especially in the North, continue to leave public schools in center cities predominantly black. Middle-class whites move to predominantly white suburbs with "private public schools," protected by court prohibitions against cross-district busing. Whites living in center cities often opt for parochial and other private schools. Center-city public schools remain disproportionately minority in student enrollment.

Despite the fact that court rulings have upheld the principle of separation of church and state, in general, and have applied it to the public school specifically, in a 1984 Gallup poll, 68 percent of public school parents said that a top goal of schools should be to develop moral standards—traditionally a function of religion. This percentage of parents who felt that the schools should develop standards of right and wrong was second only to 74 percent who felt that the most important goal of schools was to teach students to read and write properly.

As a greater number of parents and teachers have challenged the notion that learning can be accomplished without discipline and values, educators across the country have been struggling with methods of introducing ethics into the curriculum without offending any group. A Baltimore, Maryland, task force addressing this issue drew upon the Constitution and Bill of Rights to develop a common core of 24 values, ranging from compassion to truth, that should be taught in the schools.

In more than 15,000 elementary classrooms in 1985, values were taught with materials from the American Institute for Character Education in San Antonio, Texas. The materials included stories about children faced with value decisions and the consequences of various outcomes. While some positive results have occurred from the renewed emphasis on value (e.g., significant reductions in vandalism in some schools adopting a values-clarification program), educators warn that school enrichment in this area is no substitute for the teaching of values at home. The entire question remains a controversial one in American education (Mathews 1985).

FINANCING PUBLIC EDUCATION

Education has become big business in America. Constituting only 3 percent of the GNP in the 1930, it rose to 8 percent by the mid–1970s. By the 1980s, the proportion of GNP devoted to education had declined to 7 percent—still a large share of national resources. Almost 61 million of a total population of 232 million in 1982, or one in four people, had education as their primary activity (Aronson and Hilley 1986). This included 57.2 million students and 3.6 million teachers and administrators.

The education policy process is very political, yet uneasiness marks the attitudes of Americans toward the linkage between education and politics. With politics viewed as seedy and sometimes corrupt, separate school boards were constructed to create a wall between politics and education. School boards typically have their own taxing authority to diminish the influence of other politicians. They are often elected in nonpartisan elections and are presumed to represent the entire city or jurisdiction. Voting frequently occurs at a time different from other municipal elections to further reduce the connection between politics and education. Especially with the issues of taxes and financing, politics and education policy become intertwined.

Despite some federal involvement, financing public education remains primarily a state and local function and, with over 15,000 school districts, highly decentralized. Some states, such as Texas, Nebraska, and California, have more than 1,000 local administrative units for the public schools. By contrast, southern states typically organize educational units to coincide with county boundaries rather than municipalities, and therefore have fewer, geographically larger school districts.

School districts differ in their power, although most have power to set tax rates for school financing independently of their cities or counties. Despite increased reliance on state funding, schools remain heavily dependent upon the local property tax, a factor that links school funds to the value of real estate in the local jurisdiction. Throughout most of this century, patterns of school finance and distribution have resulted in unequal tax burdens and expenditures. In 1984, for example, New York spent $4,364 per public school pupil, while Alabama spent only $1,978.

Poorer districts, despite heavier school tax burdens, have often experienced lower per pupil revenues. However, although wealthier states, on average, tend to spend more per pupil than poor states, differences in underlying fiscal capacities do not totally explain the variation in per pupil spending. Price, socioeconomic status, and preferences of citizens also have been shown to influence educational spending. Overall, though, the fact remains that poorer states and localities find raising education revenues more difficult with schools in those districts less well funded.

The constitutionality of existing systems for financing education was challenged in suits filed in 27 different cases between 1960 and 1982. Despite this questioning of the use of the locally based property tax to fund schools, the U.S. Supreme Court ruled in the 1973 case of Rodriquez v. San Antonio that unequal state systems were not unconstitutional as a violation of the equal protection clause of the Fourteenth Amendment. However, some state courts, including the California Supreme Court in Serrano v. Priest, did rule that such systems were in violation of state constitutions.

Consequently, the decade of the 1970s saw many states adopt education improvement and reform acts, which were designed to diminish inequities from property-tax-based funding of schools at the local level. By 1982, the state share of funding for all educational institutions was 38 percent, exceeding the local share of 25 percent. Federal expenditures constituted a much smaller 10 percent and private contributions about 26 percent of total expenditures. For public schools, the state share is even larger, reaching 48 percent in 1984. Local spending on elementary and secondary public schools contributed less than half of total expenditures, constituting 45 percent with federal spending composing almost 7 percent.

Improvements in equity varied greatly by state, and in the 1970s, school finance was complicated by a wave of tax and expenditure curbs imposing fiscal limits on state and local jurisdictions. Coinciding with declining enrollments after the passage of the baby boom, many districts found themselves facing constant budgets or cuts. The great diversity in state financing patterns is illustrated by the extreme examples of Hawaii, which has a highly centralized system and uses state and federal funds exclusively, and New Hampshire, which has neither a state income nor sales tax and where localities finance 88 percent of educational expenditures.

States use three types of school finance systems, the oldest and most prevalent being the foundation plan. States employing foundation plans establish a dollar level of per pupil expenditure that is guaranteed to all districts taxing a rate greater than or equal to some state-specified minimum rate. Districts wishing to spend above the minimum level may do so, although this places poor districts at a disadvantage. Some foundation plans have been criticized for setting the minimum funding level too low.

A second system of school finance is a district power-equalizing plan. Under such plans, states finance matching grants to ensure that poor districts may spend as much for education as if they had tax bases equivalent to those of wealthier districts. State-matching rates are tied directly to the fiscal capacity of school districts. Equivalent percentage tax rates will raise the same amount of revenue in both poor and wealthier districts, since the state supplements poor districts.

Some states, including Maine, Minnesota, Missouri, Montana, Texas, and Utah, have adopted a hybrid of the foundation and district power-equalizing plans. In these mixed systems, matching funds to locally raised revenues is applied by the state up to the foundation level of spending, but not beyond.

FEDERAL INVOLVEMENT IN EDUCATION

The federal government has played a long-standing but relatively minor role in education. In the 1787 Northwest Ordinance, Congress allocated land grants for public schools in new territories. The 1862 Morrill Land Grant Act provided land for establishing land grant colleges specializing in agriculture and mechanical arts. A federal Office of Education was established as early as 1867. In 1917 the Smith-Hughes Act funded grants to promote public school vocational education in agriculture, home economics, trades, and industries. Grants and commodity donations were provided to both public and private schools through the 1946 National School Lunch and Milk programs. In 1950, the Federal Impacted Aid program provided fiscal relief to school districts with high concentrations of federal employees to partially compensate for the removal of federal property from local school district property tax rolls.

Widespread concern over Sputnik when the Soviets beat Americans into space prompted the 1958 National Defense Education Act, which provided funds to improve instruction in science, mathematics, and foreign languages; to strengthen guidance counseling and testing; and to improve statistical services. In order to improve teacher training, the act also established a system of loans to undergraduates, fellowships to graduates, and funds for colleges.

The first large-scale federal aid to education, however, did not materialize until 1965 with the passage of the Elementary and Secondary Education Act (ESEA), which provided federal funds to local education agencies serving areas with a high concentration of children from low-income families. Monies were also provided for both public and private schools to acquire school library resources, textbooks, and other educational materials.

A separate cabinet-level Department of Education with nine regional offices was created in 1979 and continued throughout the Reagan years despite his intentions to abolish it. Under the urging of the Reagan administration, Congress replaced ESEA and several other educational programs in 1981 with the Education Consolidation and Improvement Act, a block grant with priorities to be determined locally. The Reagan administration de-emphasized national involvement in education and proposed budget cuts in federal funding.

Recently, the influence of the federal government on education policy has disproportionately exceeded its actual financial contribution to that function. Despite various federal legislative acts, the federal share of school financing has never risen beyond 10 percent of the total cost of education. Federal contributions constitute only 5 percent of primary education and 15 percent of higher education revenues. Typically, the federal government does not operate educational institutions but must work through state and local education agencies to have its policies implemented.

In the past, federal policies have been directed toward specific national needs, including manpower training, enhancement of economic productivity, and ensuring equality of educational opportunity. The federal government has also been the primary supporter nationally of scientific research and the primary provider of student financial support. Several federal programs were established in the 1970s to help students finance college costs. Among them were Pell grants, originally created as Basic Educational Opportunity grants, which were received by about 1.8 million students annually; guaranteed student loans received by 2.8 million undergraduates and 2.4 million graduate and professional students; direct student loans; supplemental educational opportunity grants; and college work-study funds received by about one million students annually.

Several programs have been criticized for abuse, especially the guaranteed student loan program, for which the default rate is 12 percent. The Reagan administration cited such problems when proposing to reduce student aid as well as overall federal support of education. Given the need to develop a competitive and well-educated labor force, especially in the areas of science and technology, Reagan's approach was very short sighted. The levels of federal involvement it proposed were insufficient to propel the nation forward into global competitiveness. An active and aggressive federal education policy is essential to restoring American economic health and developing a qualified and literate labor force capable of meeting the demands of tomorrow's technology.

A NATION AT RISK

In 1983, the National Commission on Excellence in Education reported to the president and the American people that the nation was "at risk" from an inferior and deteriorated education system ("A Nation at Risk" 1983). The commission found cause for optimism in the public's commitment to improving education and redressing the problems in the public schools. However, those problems were and are considerable. The following are some of the more significant findings.

Secondary school curricula have become "homogonized, diluted, and diffused" to the point that purpose has been lost. With cafeteria-style offerings in most high schools, students have shunned more rigorous college courses and vocational courses in favor of less rigorous "general track" courses. The proportion of students taking these general courses increased from 12 percent in 1964 to 42 percent in 1979, with 25 percent of the credits earned by general-track high school students concentrated in physical and health education, work experience outside the school, remedial English and mathematics, and personal service and development courses such as adulthood and marriage. While more rigorous courses were widely available in most high schools, only 31 percent of recent high school graduates completed intermediate algebra, 13 percent French I, 16 percent geography, and 6 percent calculus.

The commission also found glaring deficiencies in the expectations of student performance held by students themselves, as well as others in the secondary school system. The amount of homework for high school students had decreased to where two-thirds reported doing less than one hour a night, yet with grade inflation, grades had risen even as average student achievement had declined. In many other industrialized nations, mathematics, biology, chemistry, physics, and geography courses begin in the sixth grade and are compulsory for all students. About three times as many class hours are devoted to these subjects in those countries as are in the United States, even by the most science-oriented U.S. students.

By comparison with other nations, state standards in the United States for high school graduation are extraordinarily lax. In 1980, even though eight states required high schools to offer foreign languages, no state had mandatory foreign language graduation requirements. One year of mathematics was sufficient for a high school diploma in 35 states; one year of science was enough in 36. In 13 states, 50 percent or more of graduation credits could be electives. Minimum competency tests, required in 37 states, set standards too low, and often the "minimum" became the "maximum" expected with the perverse impact of lowering educational standards for all. Competency tests for high school teachers have also begun to spread across the country. The aim here is not only to rid the schools of incompetent instructors, but also to upgrade the professional status of teachers.

High schools were not solely to blame for the sorry state of American secondary education. The National Commission on Excellence in Education found fault with U.S. colleges and universities as well. One-fifth of all four-year U.S. public colleges must accept every high school graduate within the state regardless of high school courses completed or grades. This allows high school students to pursue nonrigorous high school curricula or to perform poorly and still attend college. Of more selective colleges and universities, 23 percent reported a decline in the 1970s in their general level of selectivity, and 29 percent reported reducing the number of specific high school courses required for admissions, frequently dropping foreign language requirements. Currently only one-fifth of U.S. colleges have foreign language requirements for admission.

During the past 15 years, many textbooks and other materials for secondary education have been "written down" by publishers to ever-lower reading levels in response to market demands and to accommodate declining literacy. The commission contended that too few experienced teachers and scholars are involved in writing textbooks, which are often produced by professional writers removed from the direct educational process. Many assigned books are too easy and do not challenge students, leaving them bored and restless. A study by the Education Products Information Exchange revealed that a majority of students were able to master 80 percent of the material in some of the texts before even opening the books. Between the late 1960s and early 1980s, expenditures for textbooks and other instructional materials declined by 50 percent. Despite a recommended level of spending on texts of between 5 and 10 percent of the operating costs of schools, the budgets for basic texts and related materials have been dropping for the past two decades, falling to only 0.7 percent.

That most precious of resources—time—is squandered and used inefficiently in American public schools. The commission found that compared with other nations, American students spend much less time on school work, with the typical school day in the United States lasting six hours and the typical school year 180 days. By contrast, in England and other industrialized nations, eight-hour school days and 220-day school years are common.

Nor is time spent in the classroom and on homework used efficiently. Some U.S. schools provide students with only 17 hours of academic instruction during the week, considerably below the already low average of 22 hours per week. One California study of individual classrooms revealed that because of poor management of classroom time, some elementary students received only one-fifth of the reading comprehension instruction other students received. The commission further criticized schools for failing to help students develop the study skills needed to use time well or the motivation to spend more time on school work. Teaching study skills in most schools is haphazard and unplanned, leaving high school graduates entering college without disciplined and systematic study habits.

Underlying the deterioration of elementary and secondary schools has been a significant deterioration in the quality of U.S. teachers. The commission found that too many teachers were being drawn from the bottom quarter of graduating high school and college students, and that not enough academically capable students were being attracted to teaching. Low teacher salaries with little room for advancement exacerbate this trend. In 1983, the average teacher's salary after 12 years of teaching was only $17,000 annually. Many teachers have found it necessary to supplement their income with part-time and summer employment. Educational curricula in many U.S. colleges, required for preparation in teaching, are inadequate and often heavily weighted with courses in "educational methods" at the expense of courses in the subject matter to be taught. A survey of 1,350 institutions training teachers found that 41 percent of the time spent by college students majoring in elementary education was in education courses rather than in specific subject courses. Teachers also have little individual influence in such professional decisions as textbook selection and curricula development.

Despite an overabundance of teachers in some areas, severe shortages, particularly of mathematics and science teachers, exist. In 1981, 45 states experienced shortages of teachers in math, 33 states in earth sciences, and all states in physics. The commission found that half of the newly employed mathematics, science, and English teachers were not qualified to teach those subjects, and that fewer than one-third of U.S. high schools offered physics taught by qualified teachers.

Additionally, overall teaching shortages are predicted in the future as children of the baby boom enter public schools, especially if teaching conditions and salaries do not improve. The traditional source of teacher supply—women and some minority groups—now have expanded opportunities in higher-paying fields, further contributing to the future teacher shortage. The U.S. Department of Education has estimated that about 1.3 million people will have to be drawn into teaching between 1987 and 1993 to adequately staff the nation's elementary and secondary schools. Anticipated shortages are particularly great in certain states, including California, Texas, and Florida.

The National Assessment of Educational Progress (NAEP), a program financed by the Department of Education and administered by the Educational Testing Service in Princeton, New Jersey, has also criticized the preparation today's students are receiving to meet tomorrow's challenges. A report issued by the NAEP found that many youths, especially those from minority groups, lacked the reasoning and literacy skills necessary for job success. In the future, jobs will be restructured, on the average, every seven years, and only the literate will be able to perform them. Yet U.S. high schools graduate 700,000 functionally illiterate young people annually, and another 700,000 drop out each year. Despite the fact that the 1980 dropout rate of 28.1 percent had declined by 1986, the national rate was still 25.9 percent with one out of every four high school freshmen absent on graduation day. In some of the nation's largest metropolitan areas, the dropout rate often exceeds 40 percent ("The Brain Battle" 1987).

Businesses have been forced to teach the basic skills that workers should have received in high school. A survey of 200 businesses conducted by the Center for Public Resources, a nonprofit think tank, found that most companies reported significant deficiencies in reading, writing, science, mathematics, reasoning, speaking, and listening skills among personnel in most of the job categories held by high school graduates. Examples of the inadequacy of high school graduates abounded.

At considerable cost, 75 percent of the businesses surveyed conducted some type of basic-skills competency program within the firm for already hired personnel. A Carnegie Foundation for the Advancement of Teaching report verified that training by business, including remedial and basic skills, has become a major part of American education with more than 8 million adults enrolled in corporate-sponsored courses at a cost of more that $40 billion annually. Ironically, improvements in the unemployment rate increase the need for remedial corporate training as people with greater deficiencies are hired ("As Businesses Turn Offices into Classrooms" 1985).

HIGHER EDUCATION

Higher education in the United States consists of approximately 2,000 colleges and universities, with an enrollment of over 7.5 million full-time students and an additional 3.2 million part-time students. Three-fourths of college enrollment is in public institutions, including community colleges serving a local or regional population. State Boards of Higher Education or Boards of Regents are typically responsible for public colleges and universities within a state.

Lester Thurow (1985) has noted that Americans, while considerably behind their economic competitors in other nations upon graduation from high school, have taken solace in the fact that part of the ground is recouped in college.

However, some of the problems afflicting U.S. elementary and secondary schools are spilling over into its universities and colleges.

Just as the passage of the baby boom caused painful contractual constrictions in the public schools, subsequent declines in college enrollments have caused adjustments in higher education, mostly negative in terms of restoring U.S. competitiveness in global markets. The number of Americans in the normal college age range of 18 to 22 years will fall by 24 to 28 percent between 1984 and 1996. Declining enrollments imply a reduction in the overall number of faculty. Under conditions of retrenchment, the best and the brightest, and those with the most marketable skills, leave first.

American higher education is characterized by a tenure system. Tenure is granted by the department of a particular institution. All faculty members must eventually get tenure in their departments—the American Association of University Professor rules to which most colleges and universities adhere specifies within seven years—or leave. Originally devised to protect freedom of speech within universities, tenure has become the great lifetime security blanket for university and college professors, protecting the competent and productive, as well as the incompetent and unproductive. Once securing tenure, a professor cannot be fired except for gross malfeasance of job performance or heinous violation of prevailing moral standards. In public institutions as well as in many private ones, annual cost-of-living salary increases and unionization have almost totally severed the tie between monetary rewards and productivity, further eroding faculty accountability for job performance.

Newsweek reports that at some colleges, faculties are so underworked that they joke about the "leisure of the theory class" ("Fuming Over College Costs" 1987). The standard nine-month academic calendar translates into only 30 weeks of teaching a year. Robert Iosue, president of York College of Pennsylvania has noted a considerable decline in the teaching load of college faculty over the past few decades. Whereas 30 years ago, faculty routinely taught 15 hours a semester, today, nine credits is often the norm. These teaching loads are justified if accompanied by substantial research activity. However, the Carnegie Foundation found that only 40 percent of all faculty have written or edited a book and 32 percent have never published an article in a journal.

In periods of retrenchment, more senior, tenured faculty are the last to be let go. As the number of positions decline through attrition where retiring faculty are not replaced, and as untenured positions are abolished, the ranks of professors become older and often further removed from current research. While in the 1960s, turnover in American colleges and universities approached 8 percent of employed faculty, by 1972 turnover dropped to 1.4 percent. By the 1980s, turnover among academic institutions granting life-time tenure had dropped to below 1 percent.

Since tenure is granted by individual academic departments rather than the institution as a whole, it also diminishes incentives for faculty retooling and retraining to meet market demands for new skills. Fields with declining enrollment and relevance are overtenured. New, especially technologically oriented fields with booming enrollments, such as computer science in recent years, are understaffed with few tenured faculty. Unlike corporations, which can order employees to shift jobs as corporate needs change, colleges and universities do not have the flexibility to order tenured faculty to change their teaching focus and areas of specialization as majors wax and wane in popularity. Only when a department is disbanding or when personnel cuts are required, can tenured faculty be terminated.

Suggestions to alter the tenure system are met with bitter resistance by professors and their organizations, including the American Association of University Professors (AAUP). Professors counter that tenure is an "up-or-out" system, not unlike the military, failing to note that the up-or-out nature of military promotion persists throughout the working life of the career military officer, but not beyond the tenure decision for the professor.

Some educational experts have suggested renewable long-term contracts for university professors to replace the permanency of tenure. Productive professors would be rewarded with progressively longer contracts, while nonproductive professors would not. After several shorter contracts with opportunities to perform, nonproductive professors could be dismissed by institutions and replaced by younger unproven or more productive professors. Critics of this system argue that most older, more expensive professors would always be dismissed, regardless of productivity, and replaced by less costly younger professors, as institutions moved to cut personnel costs. Supporters argue that it would enhance accountability and provide an incentive for professors to produce, a process that is currently missing from American higher education.

Evaluating faculty performance is difficult, contributing to the subjectivity involved in tenure, promotion, and salary decisions in academe, which historically have worked against women and minorities. In using peer review and secret voting for tenure and promotion, personnel decisions sometimes resemble legislative decisions more than bureaucratic ones based on merit. Traditional criteria for university faculty evaluation are research, teaching, and service.

Critics of the "publish-or-perish" emphasis argue that only research matters, creating pressure that has sometimes led to fraudulent presentation of falsified research results, especially in medicine and medically related fields where continued funding from government agencies may depend upon positive results. Despite the peer review process for publication of scientific studies, little rigorous oversight of research conducted in academic settings exists. One recent example of fraudulent work was that of Dr. Stephen E. Breuning, one of the nation's most influential researchers in the field of mental retardation treatment. According to Daniel Greenberg, editor and publisher of *Science and Government Report*, a verdict of "serious scientific misconduct" was rendered against Breuning by a panel of distinguished specialists who concluded that Breuning "did not carry out the described research" and simply invented the results. Federal issues in 1987 barred Breuning from receiving further research grants for ten years and referred the case to the Department of Justice for possible prosecution. Greenberg has also reported on numerous other such cases in the field of hard sciences ("Trouble in the Groves of Academe" 1987). Other critics of the peer review process for evaluating the quality of research claim that it is biased toward the status quo and existing paradigms, making it difficult to publish truly innovative ideas challenging basic premises in a field, and that by emphasizing positive results, it does not reward the tedious but necessary scientific activity of study replication.

Evaluating teaching proves even more nettlesome than evaluating research. Currently most colleges and universities rely upon standardized written evaluations filled out by students at the end of a course. Critics contend that such evaluations turn into popularity contests rather than serve as an accurate measure of what students learned, and that students may be unduly influenced by the course grade they anticipate. Nor do such evaluations readily distinguish between the challenges of teaching large lecture sections versus smaller seminars.

Some observers of higher education feel that, partially due to evaluation difficulties but also other forces, teaching has become devaluated, especially in major public and private universities. Faculty are often consumed by their own research, writing, and consulting agendas, recognizing that rewards are based upon publications and not excellence in teaching. Undergraduates are forced into large lecture classes, sometimes containing hundreds of students in order to reduce faculty teaching loads. Graduate students, rather than full-time faculty, end up teaching many introductory classes.

As tenure grows more difficult to get, the number of academic "gypsies," teachers who roam from one part-time or temporary job to another, is increasing. In 1984, federal figures revealed that gypsy faculty, including graduate students who teach part-time, filled 35 percent of college teaching jobs, up from 22 percent in 1970. According to the *Wall Street Journal* (" 'Gypsy' Faculty Stir Debate" 1986), gypsies earned an average of $1,500 a course. Schools hire them to ease shortages in some areas and to exploit the oversupply of teachers in others, such as liberal arts. Gypsies are cost efficient for institutions who can hire up to four part-timers for what a single tenured professor would cost. Critics of this approach argue that temporaries and part-timers are often overburdened and resentful of low salaries, and that quality instruction is more uncertain and often inferior.

In large part, due to the retrenchment of higher education, faculty salaries have experienced a real decline in purchasing power of over 40 percent from the early 1970s to the present. Faculty salaries rose 73 percent in the 1970s, considerably behind the 112 percent inflation rate. While nonproductive faculty may still be overpaid, despite this significant decline, productive faculty may be underpaid. Additionally, the relative decline vis-à-vis other professions has increased the difficulty of attracting faculty in scientific and technical fields where Ph.D. holders can earn substantially more in industry and work with state-of-the-art equipment.

By contrast, many college laboratories and technical facilities are supplied with obsolescent equipment 15 to 20 years old, which frequently has been donated by industry after its industrial usefulness has passed in exchange for tax deductions. In some instances, the age of the equipment exceeds the age of the students using it. The 1986 Packard-Bromley Report on the Health of Universities estimated that the federal government should spend about $10 billion in the short run upgrading university facilities to retain scientific competitiveness, since $10.6 billion of the total $118 billion spent on research and over half of the nation's basic research is conducted in universities.

Academics and other technology experts contend that backward equipment and facilities are hindering research by discouraging leading researchers from remaining in academia. About 8.5 percent of funded engineering faculty positions were unfilled in 1986, and shortages in computer science and math were growing. Equally crucial is the fact that universities and colleges train the nation's future engineers and scientists, handicapped by outdated and outmoded equipment.

University administrators argue that the equipment shortage is the result of a long period of federal underfunding that began in the 1960s as expenditures on the Vietnam War increased and monies after Sputnik dried up. Between 1958 and 1964, federal funding for university research grew at an average of 22 percent annually in constant dollars. After 1964, federal funding flattened until the 1970s, and of those funds received, higher percentages were allocated to salaries and materials. The proportion of federal funding devoted to instrumentation fell from 12 to 6 percent. Facility funding, measured in constant 1972 dollars, dropped from $212 million in 1966 to under $20 million in 1981. Federal grants often deleted the equipment portion of research monies, expecting universities to provide for that. Yet universities failed to compensate for declining federal equipment dollars, spending unearmarked dollars for research personnel (Solomon 1987).

Along with the decline in enrollments, relative faculty salaries, equipment, and facilities, critics note that American universities have also declined in recent years in overall research competitiveness. A great deal of nondefense civilian research and development, which is more directly tied to exporting than defense research and development, is conducted within universities. Donald Kennedy, president of Stanford University, notes that currently U.S. expenditure on civilian research and development is about 1.8 percent of GNP, whereas equivalent figures for Japan and West Germany, major U.S. competitors, are 2.5 and 2.6 percent ("Does College Cost Too Much?" 1987).

Despite the shortage of monies available for certain types of research, tuition costs have been increasing more rapidly than in other sectors of the economy. College tuitions rose 10.6 percent between 1980 and 1986, exceeding increases during the same time period in medical care (8.5 percent), houses (6.1 percent), all goods and services (4.8 percent), food (3.9 percent), new cars (3.8 percent), and energy (0.4 percent). The total cost of a four-year degree at a quality private university can now rival the cost of a small home.

From the academic year 1970–71 to 1986–87, tuition at Harvard rose 338 percent to $11,390. Stanford rose 367 percent to $11,208, while Tulane and Vanderbilt rose 378 percent and 365 percent. Lower-cost public universities experienced equivalent percentage increases. The University of Michigan rose 360 percent and the University of Texas 380 percent for in-state students. About 60 percent of the recent increases in tuition is the result of rising personnel costs. There has been an attempt to recoup some of the faculty salary losses during the 1970s. Colleges also cite replacement of antiquated facilities and the high cost of periodicals and books for libraries. Another factor is uncontrollable on-going expenses such as insurance and utilities.

As tuition costs have increased, so has the financial burden of a college education, increasing from 9 percent of total family income for an average family of four in 1960 to 19 percent in 1987. Simultaneously, the Reagan administration has been hostile toward higher education and has reduced student financial aid, especially for middle-class students. Reagan's Secretary of Education, William Bennett, has charged that greed and inefficiency are to blame for increased tuition costs. At the three-hundred-fiftieth birthday of Harvard, Bennett called U.S. colleges "rich," with Washington lobbyists "very good at getting their funds from a Congress seemingly enraptured by the pieties, pontifications and poor-mouthings of American higher education" ("Does College Cost Too Much?" (1987).

Elsewhere, Bennett has described college students as "sun-worshipping, car-driving stereo buffs" (Feistritzer 1985). Yet with the passage of the baby boom and the increase in part-time and older students, Bennett's mental picture of college students is surprisingly out-of-date. In 1985, only 57 percent of college enrollment came from the 18- to 24-year-old age group, down from 68 percent in 1963 to 1964. Likely future declines make this traditional-age college group a minority. The number of older students working at full- or part-time jobs has increased greatly. Part-time students now account for almost half (44 percent) of total student enrollment in higher education. Two-year college enrollments have increased 116 percent since 1970, compared with a 17 percent increase at four-year institutions.

The attitudes evidenced by Bennett and other top administrators of the Reagan administration did little to solve the complex problems currently confronting American higher education or to develop solutions to restore competitiveness. Yet both tax and budget changes pushed through by the administration undercut higher education. The Tax Reform Act of 1986 made charitable gifts to colleges and universities less attractive to upper-income donors, taxed custodial educational accounts for children at the parents' tax rate, and placed a cap on tax-exempt borrowing by colleges. Total federal student aid was cut from $7.9 billion in the 1985 fiscal year to $6.3 billion in the 1986 fiscal year. Students from families earning more than $25,000 a year were ruled ineligible for Pell grants, college work-study funds, and national direct student loans. Those from families earning more than $32,500 became ineligible for guaranteed student loans. Support for graduate programs was abolished.

STRATEGIES FOR IMPROVING AMERICAN EDUCATION

Proposals to improve American education are as varied as the problems currently plaguing the system. The National Commission on Excellence in Education has recommended an increased emphasis on English, mathematics, science, social studies, computer science, and foreign languages. Specifically, high school English should equip students to comprehend, interpret, evaluate, and use what they read; write well-organized and effective papers; listen to and discuss ideas intelligently; and relate literature to daily living. High school mathematics should include algebra, geometry, applied math, and estimation, approximation, and measurement skills.

Science in high school must be revised to not only convey basic physical and biological concepts, laws, and processes, but also to impart methods of scientific inquiry and reasoning. Social studies should equip students to understand the functioning of political and economic systems, the differences between repressive and free societies, and the implications of social structure and culture. Through the introduction of computers and computer science in school curricula, students should understand the capacity of computers as information, computation, storage, and communication devices, be able to use computers in the study of other subjects and develop some understanding of electronics and related technologies. To recover from a severe disadvantage internationally in fluency with foreign languages, the commission has recommended that foreign language study be introduced into elementary schools, since proficiency in a nonnative language usually takes from four to six years of study.

In addition to more rigorous curricula and graduation requirements, the commission has recommended that schools, colleges, and universities adopt more rigorous and measurable standards and higher expectations for student performance. The administration of standardized nationwide tests of achievement at major transition points from one level of schooling to another would certify student credentials, identify the need for remedial work, and determine for whom accelerated or advanced work is appropriate.

College and university professors should assist public school teachers in preparing more rigorous materials for secondary schools. States should adopt more rigorous instructional materials and, when possible, insist that publishers provide data on the effectiveness of their texts. Funds should be available for special students with smaller markets, such as disadvantaged, learning disabled, and gifted students. New materials should reflect current applications of technologies and the most recent research and scholarship in respective fields.

Other commission recommendations deal with increasing the amount and effectiveness of student time spent on learning, including the assignment of more homework, the introduction of study skills in elementary school, the adoption of seven-hour school days and 200- to 220-day school years, and more time devoted to learning within the classroom. If necessary, additional time should be devoted to disadvantaged and gifted students. Teacher energy devoted to discipline should be diminished by the consistent application of fair standards of conduct, and by placing disruptive students in alternative classrooms and programs. Enforcement of attendance policy should be coupled with incentives and sanctions to reduce absenteeism and tardiness. Additionally, teacher administration should be reduced when possible to increase the time available for instruction and teaching preparation. The commission attacked social promotion by recommending that graduation be based on achievement and academic progress rather than age.

The quality of teachers needs to be greatly improved, partially by requiring persons preparing for teaching to meet high educational standards in an academic field and to demonstrate an aptitude for teaching. Teacher salaries must be raised to attract professionally competent, performance-oriented individuals. A comprehensive teacher evaluation system, including peer review for salary, tenure, promotion, and retention, should be developed to reward superior teachers, encourage average ones to improve, and eliminate ineffective ones. Teacher competency tests should be required for entry into the teaching profession, along with periodic certification renewals to ensure that teachers are keeping abreast of their fields.

Teachers should be employed for 11 months, to ensure time for curriculum and professional development, to allow for adequate teacher compensation, and to accommodate an expanded school year of 200 to 220 school days. Extra resources should be devoted to training, recruiting, and retaining mathematics and science teachers. Loan programs, grants, and other incentives should be developed to attract outstanding students into teaching. Master teachers, in addition to administrators, should help create teacher-training programs and supervise probationary teachers.

At the college level, colleges and universities should place much more emphasis and attention on tenure decisions and consider ways to increase productivity, while protecting academic freedom. Experimenting with short- and long-term contracts may be one way to do this. More effective methods for evaluating teaching should be developed so that teachers are judged by student gains in knowledge and skills as well as popularity. To combat declining enrollments and to facilitate job transitions, colleges and universities should adopt a philosophy of life-long learning, expanding the current trend of educating older students to new fields. Alternative collective incentive systems that teach and reward teamwork should be considered when appropriate.

Funding for education should be increased at all levels, most especially at the federal level. In particular, the federal government should support curriculum improvement to a far greater extent than it does at present. Student aid for postsecondary education should be expanded and available for nontraditional as well as traditional students. Extra funds should be devoted to upgrading the educational skills and achievements of minority students who are currently behind. The president should give a report to the nation annually on the progress of the country toward the goal of education excellence.

The objective of the nation in the twenty-first century should be to provide all of its citizens with as much training and education as they are capable of receiving. The loss of brain power through unfulfilled talent is a waste of resources that this nation can no longer afford if it is to compete successfully. A new and universal GI Bill for Education is highly desirable. Although the costs may necessitate its gradual implementation, the goal of equal educational opportunity for all who are capable and meet acceptable performance criteria is a standard against which progress should be measured. Enhanced public educational opportunities should be coupled with the idea of public service.

This could be meshed with a mandatory Youth Service Corps that all student youths between 18 and 20 would join. Those inclined could join the military. Those not interested could do domestic service, including a National Sanitation Corps, which would maintain a litter-free environment. This would make students more mature before entering college, provide a rationale for student aid, and solve some pressing domestic problems while rebuilding the intrastructure. It could also help with the dropout problems. Students who dropped out of high school would have to enter the Youth Corps immediately and serve extra years until they too reached the age of 20. Hopefully this would provide youth employment and encourage youths to stay in school. Those who did drop out would be forfeiting educational benefits, but would at least be working and doing something constructive. They could hopefully acquire some job skills and/or qualify for technical or vocational training.

Quality in education costs, but an uneducated, unqualified labor force costs more.

5

THE NATION'S HEALTH

THE UNHEALTHY HEALTH CARE SYSTEM

A healthy vibrant labor force is essential to global competitiveness. Sick and absent workers reduce productivity and increase mounting health care costs. Over the past 20 years, health care in the United States has grown into a multibillion-dollar industry with dramatic increases in the number of physicians and other health care workers. Modern hospitals have expanded in size and technological complexity. Despite these advances, health care remains essentially a nonexportable service. It is not easily transferred nor sold to other countries and has little direct positive impact on the balance of trade. While health care expenditures are necessary to maintain a strong and viable labor force, inefficiencies in health care represent opportunity costs that undermine America's competitiveness.

In recent decades, the United States has achieved preeminence in medical research and technology, if not in service delivery. A supportive infrastructure, including the funding of medical research by both the government and corporate laboratories, has contributed to this preeminence. Government-sponsored research in the chemical, biological, and engineering fields has directly and indirectly facilitated the growth of medical knowledge and technology. Comparatively high levels of funding, prosperous economic growth during much of the post-World War II period, and the American fascination with gadgets have added to its technological supremacy in medicine.

Yet, according to one Harris poll ("Americans' Satisfaction" 1985), Americans have grown less satisfied with their health care. In 1985, only 36 percent of those questioned said that they were "very satisfied" with the health care services they had received in the past few years, a decline from 52 percent in 1980. Respondents who were only "somewhat satisfied" increased from 33 to 46 percent while those "somewhat dissatisfied" rose from 13 to 16 percent.

In recent years, there have been three major criticisms of the health care system that have become evident: rising costs, lack of adequate access to health care by substantial portions of the population, and quality of care (Hoadley 1987). Despite an expansion of health insurance coverage, many people still do not have benefits for significant periods. Third-party payments of health care services have fueled spiraling health care costs. A decline in the approval and respect for physicians has been accompanied by an increase in the number of malpractice suits. In short, some examining the medical system itself claim that it is ill.

RISING HEALTH CARE COSTS

In recent decades, the proportion of total GNP devoted to health care costs has risen at an alarming rate. In 1950, national health expenditures totaled $12.7 billion, or 4.4 percent of GNP. By 1980, that proportion had risen to 10.6 percent of GNP, with the largest increase occurring in the late 1960s after the inception of Medicare and Medicaid.

The proportion of health care dollars derived from federal sources declined slightly between 1981 and 1984, from 42.6 percent to 41.4 percent, but this share is 15 percentage points higher than it was prior to 1965 when both Medicare and Medicaid were enacted. Medicare, operating similarly to the overall Social Security system, provides federally sponsored health insurance to persons aged 65 or older and covers people with some specific disabilities, such as end-state renal disease. Medicaid is a cooperative federal-state program that pays for hospital, physician, and additional health services for eligible indigent recipients.

Nor have the costs abated in the 1980s. By 1987, the United States spent $425 billion annually on health care (Easterbrook 1987). As a nation, the United States spends more on health care than it does on national defense. For individuals, health care expenditures exceed amounts spent on automobiles and gasoline combined.

Several factors have contributed to the increase of U.S. health care costs. The first is a general rise in inflation during recent decades. This has contributed to a price increase in most services, including health care. Yet health care costs have increased at rates faster than can be explained by either inflation or population growth. Figures available in 1987 showed a 7.8 percent increase in health care costs, compared with a 1.1 percent increase in the Consumer Price Index (CPI) (Hoadley 1987).

Medical Technology and the Shift to Chronic Diseases

A second factor is the prevailing attitudes favoring increased usage of sophisticated and costly medical technology among significant parties involved in the medical system, including patients, hospitals, and physicians. Additionally, some reimbursement structures have encouraged the purchase and use of new and more technologically advanced equipment. Once in place, new technology generates its own incentive for use through extended services and additional patients, for the greater the number using the equipment, the lower the per capita fixed costs.

A third factor contributing to rising health care costs is the changing nature of diseases confronting Americans. Until the advent of acquired immune deficiency syndrome (AIDS) in the 1970s, the nature of disease and morbidity had been gradually changing from a predominance of infectious diseases prevalent at the beginning of the twentieth century, largely involving short-run treatments, to chronic incurable diseases not readily caused by a virus. Chronic diseases include heart and kidney disease and cancer. By 1986, approximately six million patients a year were hospitalized for heart disease, and more than 2.5 million annually were treated for cancer. Almost 21 million each year underwent some type of surgery (Trafford and Dworkin 1986). Strokes, which require a long rehabilitation process for patients who partially recover and constant care for those who do not, afflict 400,000 people a year, killing 160,000 ("Living with Strokes" 1985).

The origin of these diseases appears to be very complex, and cures are not available. Compared with curing infectious diseases in the pre-AIDS era, medical treatment of chronic diseases has involved controlling their spread and impact, and the further deterioration of the patient. Often, persons suffering from chronic diseases undergo treatment for the remainder of their lives. Both the long duration and high capital intensiveness of treatment of these diseases have contributed to escalating medical costs.

Present technologies are known as "halfway" for their inability to bring about a cure and their focus upon disease control and abatement. None is cheap. Kidney dialysis, heart bypass surgery, and chemotherapy and radiation therapy for cancer are but a few examples. Though incredibly expensive, they continue to be employed as they represent the state-of-the-art treatment for many chronic diseases.

Yet recent studies have questioned the effectiveness of several halfway technologies to treat chronic diseases. A 1985 study conducted by the Yale School of Medicine found that about a third of all suspected heart attack victims face virtually no risk of dangerous complications, and that keeping them out of intensive care units could cut national health care costs by over $600 million annually. Furthermore, ordinary electrocardiograms can be used to predict which people with heart pains can be treated safely in less sophisticated and less costly hospital units.

Organ transplants are also performed with increasing frequency in modern medicine and often with dubious results. Among the more successful, judging by one-year success rates (with the patient still surviving) are heart transplants. Of 172 performed in 1983, at an average cost of $100,000, 80 percent of the patients were still alive after a year. For the 6,116 kidney transplants, costing on the average $30,000, the success rate varied between 60 and 85 percent. One hundred and sixty-three liver transplants that same year cost on average $135,000 each and had a 65 percent success rate. Pancreas transplants (218 in number) had a 35 to 40 percent success rate and cost an average of $30,000 each. Nor is the end of the market for organ transplants in sight. Some experts estimate that from 50,000 to 75,000 people could "benefit" from heart transplants. At $150,000 per operation in the future, the total bill for heart transplants alone would approach $71.5 billion (Friedrich 1984).

Hospital expenditures have also increased at an alarming rate during the past three decades. This has prompted a number of states to adopt certificate of need (CON) legislation requiring that capital expenditures in excess of $100,000 receive a certificate of need from the state. The goal of CON legislation is to lower health care costs by preventing needless duplication of facilities. In 1974, Congress extended CON requirements to all facilities receiving federal health funds. Hospitals have consistently fought the legislation and have engaged in several nearly successful attempts to have it repealed.

Health Care Demand and Payment Schemes

The peculiar nature of health care demand contributes to rising health care costs. Health economists note that demand for health care services is inelastic compared with demand for other goods and services, implying that the quantity of service demanded is relatively insensitive to the price of the services. Restoring health or maintaining life becomes such a priority when illness or accidents occur that price becomes secondary, if not incidental, in service utilization.

Decisions to purchase health care services occur in a two-stage process. First, the consumer decides whether or not to enter the health care system. Second, once having self-selected into the system, consumers make subsequent decisions based on physicians' recommendations. Primarily the second stage contributes to health care demand inelasticity. After an initial visit to a physician, most patients allow the physician to determine the need for prescription drugs, future office visits, specialists' services, laboratory tests, surgery, and hospitalization.

Physician control over patient use of health care services is enhanced by relative consumer ignorance of the effect of medical care on health. In essence, physicians make the health care purchasing decisions for most patients. Yet physicians are not disinterested parties, since they are simultaneously suppliers of many of the services they encourage patients to buy.

In the United States most doctors are reimbursed on a fee-for-service-rendered basis, the equivalent to a piecework basis in a factory system. The more service rendered, the greater the income of the physician. Fee-for-service-rendered reimbursement schemes further enhance physician interest in promoting the use of health care services, since their personal income is directly and positively related to the amount and type of services they perform. In American medicine, the person who makes purchasing decisions is the supplier, who directly financially benefits from deciding that services are needed.

Increased availability of health insurance, as well as the third-party nature of insurance coverage, have contributed to escalating health care costs. Under third-party payment systems, most of the cost of service delivery, especially hospitalization costs, are passed along to a third party—either a private insurer or the government—after the patient has paid out-of-pocket costs or deductibles. Under this system, no one except the remote third-party payer has a direct interest in holding down costs.

The inelasticity of health care demand, plus the incentives created by fee-for-service-rendered reimbursement schemes have meant that traditional supply and demand controls of competitive markets do not apply to health services. Yet the strategy of the Reagan administration in dealing with health care costs was to restore competition into health service delivery. A physician-instituted traditional ban on advertising health services and prices has further eroded market functioning in the supply of medical services, since consumers are often unable to obtain cost information for competitive pricing.

Attempts to raise "copayments" or "deductibles" paid by the consumer before payments are made by the third party raise real questions about, and often conflict with, the goal of extending access to health care. High copayments fall most heavily upon low-income consumers. Furthermore, data-based studies have found conflicting evidence about the impact of increased cost sharing between the consumer and the third-party payer on service utilization, often differing by a factor as much as three or greater in the degree of increase in health services utilization when an average uninsured person becomes fully insured (Kronenfeld and Whicker 1984, p. 114).

Medical Malpractice and Defensive Medicine

Further fueling health care cost increases is the rising number of malpractice suits against physicians brought by unhappy patients. The basis for physician fear of malpractice, however, is real since jury awards to defendants have been increased even faster than the number of suits. In 1987, the average medical-malpractice jury award was $1,179,095, up from $166,165 in 1974. The largest award at that time exceeded $29 million.

In recent years, the courts pushed the scope of malpractice suits against physicians even further by legitimating the concept of "wrongful birth"—parental claims of prenatal negligence by doctors as a valid type of malpractice action. By 1985, the highest courts in California, Washington, and New Jersey all upheld suits brought on behalf of a child under a related concept of "wrongful life," in which the physicians charged should have realized that, due to hereditary and other fetal risks early in pregnancy, the child never should have been born. Many states are considering following the lead of Minnesota, South Dakota, and Utah, which have prohibited one or both of these types of suits, but currently court rulings in the various states constitute a patchwork of what is permissible and what is not (Otten 1985).

Although most cases are settled out of court, and of those that do go to trial, juries rule in favor of the doctor three-fourths of the time, malpractice insurance premiums for physicians have begun to reach the stratospheric level of their previous incomes. By 1987, annual premiums exceeded $100,000 for some specialists in large cites. Since physician malpractice insurance costs get added to patients' bills, which are paid by health insurers and ultimately the health consumer, they contribute to overall health care costs as well as to immediate physician expenses.

In response to rising malpractice premiums, doctors in some fields, especially high-risk specialties, have stopped practicing medicine. A 1985 survey conducted by the American College of Obstetrics and Gynecology showed that 12.3 percent of its members stopped delivering babies because of high malpractice premiums (Otten 1985). Nearly half of all the family practitioners in one state, North Carolina, stopped their obstetric practice. Doctors who continue to practice have begun to use defensive medicine by ordering more tests and laboratory work, increasing the nation's health bill. The American Medical Association estimated in 1987 that such defensive medicine costs an additional $15 billion per year.

The increased willingness of medical consumers to sue their physicians, an action almost unheard of in earlier times, reflects both the increased number of lawyers and litigiousness of the population and also indicates a building anger over the unwillingness of physicians to regulate malpractice and shoddy medical care within their own ranks. Little discipline of physicians occurs apart from lawsuits. Ralph Nadar's Public Citizen Group reported that only 563 doctors out of almost 400,000 practicing received any punishment in 1983 from state review boards. Nadar's solution was to charge each practicing physician a $500 annual license fee, creating a pool of $200 million, which could be used to review and discipline doctors in an effort to improve the quality of medical care and reduce malpractice costs ("The Malpractice Mess" 1986).

ACCESS TO HEALTH CARE SERVICES

Health services delivery in the United States is pluralistic, characterized by a variety of subsystems, each specializing in location and type of clientele. Three other systems deliver services in addition to the private practice fee-for-service-rendered system for middle- and upper-class citizens. The poor inner-city minority consumers use local government health systems, especially county hospitals. Active-duty military personnel and their dependents use the military system, while U.S. veterans use the Veterans' Administration (VA) health care system.

According to a 1985 Census Bureau study, three-fourths of all Americans were protected by private insurance, with the Northeast having both the highest percentage of coverage and the longest hospital stays ("Most Americans" 1985).

Adding the people covered by government programs, including Medicare, Medicaid, and military insurance to those covered by private insurance increased the scope of coverage to 85 percent of the population. Since job-related insurance is the major type of insurance protecting most Americans, and since whites have the lowest unemployment rate, more whites than blacks or Hispanics have private health insurance. The share of people protected by insurance increases with age.

The South had the lowest rate of total insurance coverage, at 81 percent, leaving almost 20 percent of the population of that region without access to health coverage. The Midwest ranked second in total coverage at 88 percent, not far behind the 90 percent coverage in the Northeast, while the West ranked third, with 82 percent coverage.

The Census Bureau also found differences in total health coverage by racial group. Eighty-six percent of whites had some type of health insurance, but only 78 percent of blacks and 71 percent of Hispanics did so. At 86 percent, women had slightly higher rates of coverage than men (84 percent). Among different age groups, the elderly had the highest amount of coverage, with over 99 percent of Americans aged 65 and over covered by some form of insurance ("Most Americans" 1985).

The expansion in numbers of individuals covered has camouflaged recent cutbacks in coverage available to individuals, especially for employee-related coverage. As costs of providing coverage have mounted, many employers have moved to reduce health benefits. In a 1985 Harris survey, 30 percent reported insurance payment increases, 5 percent reported a reduction in benefits, and 14 percent reported both.

During the Reagan administration, funding for Medicaid was also cut back. Under Medicaid, the federal government reimburses states an average of 55 percent of their costs for medical care for the poor, chiefly for those receiving Aid to Families with Dependent Children (AFDC), and Supplemental Security Income for the aged, blind, and disabled. Recipients of these two latter programs automatically qualify for Medicaid. By 1975, the number of people eligible for Medicaid was 22 million.

At Reagan's request, Congress reduced the number of people eligible for AFDC in 1981, and consequently reduced Medicaid, by more than one million. The Congressional Budget Office estimated a cut of $3.9 billion in federal Medicaid payments to states between 1982 and 1985, with 3, 4, and 4.5 percent cuts in each of those years. Twenty-five states began to require copayments for eyeglasses, drugs, and dental services. Twenty-one states started limiting the number of days in the hospital for which Medicaid would pay, and 14 states reduced the number of people eligible for Medicaid. Thirteen states reduced or eliminated some services (Rich 1985).

Despite expansion of health insurance coverage in recent decades, especially prior to the Reagan administration, some segments of the population still fall between the cracks, including those working for employers who do not provide benefits, and those who are poor but fail to meet specific Medicaid eligibility criteria and are unable to obtain other forms of insurance. A 1985 Florida report found that only one-third of the Floridians below the poverty line were covered by Medicaid. In Florida, a family of four that year was considered ineligible for welfare and Medicaid if its income was more than $284 per month. A Robert Wood Johnson Foundation study in 1983 reported that 28 million Americans were considered "truly medically disadvantaged" because they were too poor to afford medical care or because they didn't have health insurance.

The poor have differed from the nonpoor not only in the amount of health care available, but also in the source of that care. Low-income persons are more likely to be without a source of regular care than middle- and high-income persons, and often the only form of medical care regularly available to indigents without health care coverage has been use of emergency room services at county hospitals.

This method for service delivery to the poor, even for services that could be handled at a physician's office, has placed a large financial burden on county and public hospitals, particularly in large cities where high numbers of the poor live. Racial differences in access to regular health care have also been considerable: 13 percent of whites compared with 20 percent of blacks and 19 percent of Hispanics. The absence of regular access to health care is particularly disturbing in light of the higher birth rates of blacks and Hispanics and, consequently, of adequate prenatal care for a growing part of the population.

Other questions surround the commitment to maintain health care systems designed for special groups, specifically, the system of Veterans' Administration hospitals. Squeezed by federal deficits, national budgets were closely examined in the 1980s with many cuts in proposed increases as well as actual cuts in social services. Some feared the nation's largest medical system—the VA network of 172 hospitals, 228 outpatient clinics and 115 nursing homes, caring for 3 million veterans at a cost of $10 billion a year by 1986—was in jeopardy. Four-hour waits in Florida VA facilities were common, and that year, the number of inpatients was reduced by 62,000. Staff shortages were considerable, contributing to episodes where patients were accidentally injured, killed, or committed suicide while in VA medical facilities. Data from 1984 showed 80,273 "incidents" that year, 1,124 of which were serious enough to report to headquarters, including 134 suicides. Increasingly overworked staff relied upon volunteers to perform various jobs within VA facilities.

In anticipation of the projected aging of the population as well as its clientele, the VA shifted funds in the mid–1980s from care for younger veterans to providing long-term care for elderly ones. Forty-two million dollars of VA grants were spent by states as part of the effort to provide the 175 percent additional nursing-home space needed by 2010. Expecting a jump to 760,000 veterans at home, the administration planned to add more home services. Costs of home-based services averaged less than $20 per day, compared with $250 for inpatient care. But just to stay abreast of the projected increase nationwide, the VA was expected to need 54,000 additional beds beyond the 80,000 it already maintained to meet demand. Experts expected the VA medical operating budget to triple to more than $25 billion and to require an equal amount in new construction. In April of 1986, Reagan signed a "means test" to limit free medical care for veterans over aged 65. While veterans with service-connected conditions would continue to receive lifelong free care, other veterans would not qualify unless they earned less than $15,000 per year (Powell 1986).

QUALITY OF HEALTH CARE

Medical Training and Personnel

Quality education for physicians and other health care professionals is a critical component of maintaining the overall quality of health care. Unlike 1910, when Flexner published a searing and now classic critique of U.S. medical education, charging that medical schools were often nothing but pure business ventures, the average individual today seeking the services of a physician can be assured that he or she will be dealing with a well-trained professional (Raffel 1984, p. 536). In 1981, there were 136 fully accredited medical schools in the United States, with 78 being part of publicly owned universities. Additionally, there were 20 primary specialty boards, each with different requirements for the training and testing of physicians wishing to become board certified in a specialty.

In the United States, becoming a physician takes longer than in most other countries. Typically, prospective doctors earn four-year B.A. or B.S. degrees before embarking on another four years of medical school. About 7 percent of entering medical students do not have an undergraduate degree, but rather are part of specially designed programs that telescope premedical and medical training into six years. Those studying a specialty continue for an additional one to three years even beyond medical school.

Medical school selection processes have been criticized for overemphasizing high undergraduate grade point averages and high test scores on MCATs, the standardized medical college entrance exam, at the expense of encouraging creativity and communications skills later needed to deal with patients. Other criticisms of medical training are that it fails to emphasize knowledge of drugs, diet, nutrition, and research skills to an appropriate degree. Racial and sexual discrimination by medical colleges also persisted until recently. Now about 30 percent of entering medical students are women, and formal barriers to both women and blacks are gone.

Medical education is expensive, so that without some type of subsidy, only students from wealthy families can afford it. In the past, subsidies have been available from federal and state governments, in the form of research grants, scholarships, and loans. The average medical student today leaves medical school over $30,000 in debt, although some individual debt burdens exceed $60,000.

Expenses are also high for the medical colleges themselves. The average U.S. medical school had an operating budget of $33 million in 1980–81. This did not include any of the costs of medical education borne by an associated hospital and funded from outside sources. While critics have charged that the American Medical Association restricts the number of schools and thereby the supply of physicians, Raffel (1984) found no evidence to support this assertion, contending that the cost of starting and running a medical school is the primary control. The federal government was interested in and provided funds for developing new medical schools in the 1960s and 1970s, but greatly reduced such funding in the 1980s.

Graduate medical education includes supervised training in an approved clinical setting following medical school graduation as a prerequisite for obtaining a state-issued license to practice medicine. In 36 states, an internship that typically lasts one year is a basic requirement for licensing. Residencies, a second type of postmedical school supervised training, last from three to five years, depending upon the medical specialty being supervised.

Medical residencies are known for long and grueling hours, leaving young residents chronically fatigued, overworked, and bitter over exploitation by the hospitals that provide the residencies they must have to obtain licensure. These attitudes, in turn, often engender a subsequent callousness among residents toward a system that brutalized them, raising questions of the long-term as well as short-term impact on health care quality.

Recent testimony before a New York grand jury contended that the long and grueling hours of interns and residents trained in hospitals in that state have resulted in patients' deaths. One resident testified of beginning duty at 6 A.M. on Friday, and not being relieved until 5 P.M. on Monday. The state proposed new hospital regulations that limit such hours, a rational move given the considerable power even physician trainees have in hospital emergency rooms. Often, hospital emergency rooms are staffed by interns and residents on weekends, the time period when major accident and trauma cases are most likely to occur. Those limits in the interest of protection of the consumer would be similar to regulations already in place in the trucking and airline industry that limit the number of continuous hours truckers and pilots are permitted to spend on duty.

Laws on licensure of physicians vary from state to state, creating a complicated maze in which physicians accused of misconduct can hide. Without national licensing standards and procedures, physicians stripped of practicing privileges or threatened with such action in one state can move to another state and set up practice there. The reluctance of physicians as a group to censure their own members further enables incompetent physicians to continue practicing. A 1984 study by the General Accounting Office observed that doctors who lose their medical licenses in one state and move to another to practice also continue to receive federal Medicare and Medicaid payments for treating the elderly and the poor ("Doctors Who Lose Licenses" 1984).

William L. Wood, executive director of the New York State Office of Professional Discipline noted a "crying need" for states to share more information on disciplinary actions taken against doctors, dentists, and other professionals. Although 20 states have formed a clearinghouse to share such information, many doctors are only asked for voluntary information about misconduct when they apply for licenses in other states ("Doctors Who Lose Licenses" 1984).

Compounding physician discontent with working conditions is a doctor glut in recent years, which has been driving earning increases down. Concomitantly, physicians have experienced a decrease in autonomy, prestige, and authority. The number of physicians grew more than 40 percent between 1975 and 1985, despite a tightening market in health care. For example, the number of surgical procedures in hospitals decreased slightly between 1979 and 1985, but the number of surgeons increased by 19 percent. Physicians have begun to compete with each other for patients, and the surfeit of doctors has given leverage to government and industry to implement new reimbursement and service delivery systems.

Once among the highest paid professional group, physicians have now dropped below top earners in investment banking, finance, high-level corporate management, and certain other select lucrative fields (Work and Walsh 1987). Despite all the changes, the income levels remain considerable. The professional journal, *Medical Economics*, calculated the median practice income of doctors in 1985 both before and after professional expenses (Trafford and Dworkin 1986). Median net income varied considerably by specialty, ranging from $193,000 for neurosurgeons to $72,000 for general practitioners. Besides neurosurgeons, other high-paying specialities were orthopedic surgeons ($169,000), plastic surgeons ($155,000), thoracic surgeons ($152,000), and radiologists ($150,000). The median income for anesthesiologists was $134,170; $121,000 for obstetrician-gynecologists; $121,000 for general surgeons; $90,000 for internists; $80,000 for psychiatrists; and $79,000 for pediatricians.

The decrease in relative lucrativeness, the diminution of prestige and autonomy, and the fear of AIDS have caused a 26 percent drop in medical school applications between 1975 and 1986, with 1987 applications expected to drop another 10 percent. The ratio of applicants to places has gone from three to one in the mid–1970s to less than two to one today, and students who apply have lower grade point averages. According to Dr. August Swanson of the Association of American Medical Colleges, the applicant pool may be approaching the minimum threshhold for acceptable quality. Those more sanguine about this change argue that the diminished competition may help attract a different breed of student not just interested in profits, and that more room will be made in the profession for women and minorities (Work and Walsh 1987).

Enrollment in nursing programs has also diminished in recent years, dropping 24 percent since 1983. Nurses may be differentiated by skill level and amount of training into three groups: registered nurses (RNs) may hold two-year associate degrees, three-year diplomas, or four-year baccalaureate degrees; licensed practical nurses (LPNs) are trained for nine to 15 months and operate under the supervision of an RN; and nurse's aides deal with more menial aspects of patient hygiene, although some institutions require a high school degree for this category. Current efforts are underway to abolish two- and three-year programs for RNs, standardizing requirements to the four-year college degree.

Compared with physicians, who until recently have been disproportionately male, nurses have lower status and have been disproportionately female. Nursing is poorly paid in comparison with other occupations demanding similar levels of education and involving similar responsibilities. Furthermore, the income gap between nurses and physicians has worsened dramatically since World War II. In 1945, nurses' incomes averaged one-third of physicians' income, but by 1980, doctors earned over five times more than nurses (Mechanic and Aiken 1982).

Nor do nurses' salaries compare favorably with those of other female-dominated professions. In 1980, nurses' salaries were about equal to those for secretaries, even though the educational requirements are considerably greater for nurses. Nor does the typical salary structure reward career nurses, since a nurse beginning her first job will earn only slightly less than a nurse with years of clinical experience (Donovan 1980).

Over two-thirds of all nurses in the labor force work in hospitals, where traditional work schedules and working conditions have been undesirable. Nurses work on rotating shifts, weekends, evenings, late nights, and holidays. The average number of patients each nurse is expected to attend has been increasing in many hospitals to control costs. More recently hospitals have begun innovative scheduling to try to attract more nurses, including paying a full week's salary for working two weekend shifts of 12 hours each.

Hospital nurses often confront a monopsonistic (one employer) or oligopsonistic (only a few employers) marketplace, since over 70 percent of the hospitals in the United States are located in one-hospital communities. Lack of competition for nurses' services, as well as the absence of any strong labor organization or union further drives down nurses's wages. In recent years, higher-paying career options previously closed to women have opened up, including engineering and medicine. In 1987, for the first time ever, there were more women in four-year college programs intending to become physicians than nurses.

Disagreement exists among experts over whether there is an absolute shortage of nurses, or just a shortage of nurses willing to work under the conditions and for the wages they are typically offered. However, nationwide, vacancies in hospital nursing jobs have more than doubled, from 6.5 percent in 1985 to 13.6 percent in 1986. Even though the total number of nurses has increased slightly each year, many are avoiding hospital jobs to work in health administration, home- and ambulatory-care facilities, doctors' offices, and clinics. Desperate, many hospitals have attempted to recruit nurses from countries abroad, such as Ireland, Canada, England, and the Philippines, but report that foreign-trained nurses are not used to providing the all-around care that American nurses are expected to give.

Less attention has been directed to the supply of allied health professionals, such as laboratory technicians, medical records professionals, occupational and physical therapists, and medical technologists. These people are trained in various settings, including proprietary schools, hospitals, junior and technical colleges, and allied health schools that are part of university medical centers.

One problem for many individuals in these specialized jobs is lack of career advancement. Furthermore, the highly specialized and technical nature of many of these jobs, coupled with licensing and regulatory restrictions, reduce mobility from one allied health field to another. Within each allied health field, there are only a few administrative positions to which health professionals can advance without acquiring different training in order to change their job designation. Despite such limits, these jobs impact significantly upon the overall quality of medical care, especially within hospitals.

Midlevel health professionals include nurse practitioners (NPs) and physician's assistants (PAs), jobs created under federal encouragement with federal training funds to alleviate the projected shortage of physicians. Medics trained in and leaving the military serve as a ready pool of labor for PAs, who are predominantly male, while NPs are predominantly female. Given the current glut of physicians, the future of these professions is in doubt.

Quality Control

Quality control is difficult to measure in the health care system, more so than in standard manufacturing processes where quality control consists predominantly of sampling outputs and testing the selected products for defects. A traditional way to define health is the absence of disease or illness, yet this definition focuses almost exclusively upon physical health with little attention to mental health and none to social health.

Yet mental health particularly affects job performance and productivity of employees. Experts estimate that serious depression costs American society more than $16 billion and 20,000 lives through suicide annually, much of which could be reduced with preventive treatment. Three to 4 million adults, 2 to 3 percent of the adult population, suffer from depression at any time. The cost of their illness includes $2.1 billion for direct care and $14.2 billion in lost productivity, according to Richard Frank of the Johns Hopkins School of Public Health. Treatment for depression accounts for about 11 percent of the total cost of treating mental illness, which approaches $200 billion annually.

Despite the large incidence of depression and the assumption by psychiatrists that depression is the most common form of mental problems in the United States, a six-year study conducted by the National Institute of Mental Health (NIMH) revealed that anxiety disorders, including phobia, panic disorder, and obsessive-compulsive behavior are more widespread (Leo 1984). One American in five, about 29 million total, suffer from some form of mental problem. Only one-fifth of that total sought any type of professional help, reflecting the social stigma still attached to mental problems, as well as a lack of access to mental health professionals. Of those who did seek help, most turned to general physicians who are not trained to deal with mental illness or problems, rather than to mental health specialists (Leo 1984).

Close behind the 8.3 percent of the U.S. adult population afflicted by anxiety disorders (13.1 million, 23 percent of whom received treatment) was 6.4 percent of the population suffering from alcohol and drug abuse (10.0 million, of whom 18 percent receive treatment). Third in incidence, those suffering from depression, was 6.0 percent of the adult population (9.4 million, of whom 32 percent received professional help). Rates of disorder, especially for alcohol and drug abuse, were much higher for those younger than 45 than for those over 45. Education reduced mental problems, for college graduates had far fewer mental illnesses than did noncollege graduates. Only 1 percent (1.5 million adults) suffered from schizophrenia. Despite the severity of this illness, only half of those received help.

Many mental health experts believe that the nation's primary system for caring for those with chronic and severe mental problems is in chaos. Partially in response to dehumanized conditions in some larger state mental hospitals, the nation has embarked on a course for the past two decades of "deinstitutionalization" of the mentally ill. Since 1955, the residential population at state and county mental health hospitals has dropped by nearly 450,000. In 1986, 900,000 people were still institutionalized for mental problems, including 150,000 in mental hospitals. However 1.5 million people with mental problems resided in the community. Of those, 110,000 were in short-term treatment at hospitals, 290,000 were in halfway houses and other group quarters, and 1.1 million lived in private homes, either by themselves or with family.

On the positive side, the level of care for those who remain in long-term confinement has improved, and up to 65 percent of discharged mental patients have adapted successfully to outside life. For the rest, deinstitutionalization has failed, partially because the government has not provided the kind of community-based support services needed to sustain them on the outside, since most mental health dollars are spent on institutions that now contain a fraction of their former residents (Morganthau 1986; Maloney 1985). Unable to live normal lives, estimates now place a third of the nation's homeless as mentally ill. The number of homeless estimated for 1986 varied widely from 350,000 to 3 million, placing the figures for the mentally ill homeless at 117,000 to 1 million.

Complicating service delivery for the mentally ill are legal reforms that have made involuntary institutionalization for all but the most severe of cases impossible. There is now a recognition that deinstitutionalization may have gone too far, but neither its reversal nor the development of an adequate alternative community-based system has occurred. Budget cuts and the conversion to block grants in 1981 reversed 1980 legislation that earmarked more funds for housing, training, and other support services for community-based mental patients. In 1985, federal expenditures for community-based mental health totaled only $243 million, a reduction from 306 million federal dollars spent in 1981.

Quality control will become more important in the VA system as the number of veterans aged 65 and older is expected to triple from 3 million in 1980 to 9 million by the year 2,000. This aging of the veteran population will precede the crescendo of aging for the population at large by about ten years. A key issue confronting the system is maintaining quality while simultaneously controlling costs. By 1984, operating 172 medical centers and 99 nursing homes, the VA's operating budget had approached $8.2 billion a year.

The VA has been criticized by a presidential commission for construction costs of its nursing homes, which greatly exceed those of private nursing homes. The administrator for Veterans Affairs, Harry Walters, countered that VA facilities are required by law to be built to more rigorous specifications than most private facilities, including being earthquake resistant (Spolar 1985). Other upfront construction costs are for designs or items that will later minimize maintenance. The agency hopes to increase administrative efficiency by implementing modern computer systems.

Quality of care provided in the military health care system has been particularly criticized in recent years (Spolar 1985). Audits of Navy, Army, and Air Force hospitals have revealed numerous deficiencies, including the cursory review of 13,704 physicians approved for practice, unrestrained access by many physicians to military pharmacies, and the practice of some physicians to work at private jobs on military time at sites more than 200 miles from their military bases. As a result of poor care as well as the general increase in litigiousness, malpractice suits against the military health system cost taxpayers 41 percent more in 1984 than two years earlier, for a total of $41 million.

In a 1984 audit report ordered by Secretary of Defense Caspar Weinberger after the government lost a $2.1 million negligence suit, the military's largest malpractice loss to that date, numerous problems with quality of care were uncovered (Spolar 1985). Air Force hospitals in 1982 delivered 29,000 babies, but the mothers experienced twice the national average rate of severe cuts and tears. Army doctors were authorized to practice without proper verification of their training or experience. Of the 366 Army doctors' files reviewed, 362, or 99 percent, did not provide information on training or competence. None of the Air Force hospitals surveyed complied with the Air Force credentials requirements. Nor did Navy recruiters obtain data on or verify first-time military doctors. Of the 243,000 admissions to Air Force hospitals that year, admissions data showed patterns of probable poor performance. In response to this report, the military planned an upgrade in monitoring of physician credentials and a crackdown on other problems.

Nor is the private health care system blameless. Experts argue that an enormous medical problem currently plaguing the United States is the lack of a coherent system to deal with serious injuries (Clark; February 16, 1987). This gap in quality care exists despite the fact that injuries cause 142,000 deaths each year, and trauma is the leading cause of death for Americans under the age of 34 years. Half the victims of major trauma never reach the hospital alive, but of those who do, another 25,000 die needlessly. Despite the fact that trauma costs the United States $100 billion a year in death and disability, the study of trauma receives only one to two cents of every federal research dollar.

Nearly 50,000 die each year in automobile accidents, and another 30,000 of gunshot wounds. More than 13,000 jump or fall to their deaths, and accidents maim or disable another 80,000. According to Dr. Kenneth L. Mattox, chief of surgery and trauma care at Ben Taub General Hospital in Houston, Texas, there is a "golden hour" after injury during which, with proper treatment, the victim's life could be saved—but often isn't. The American College of Surgeons has argued for a regional system of trauma centers so that accident victims are no more than 20 minutes away from proper trauma care. Since a great deal of trauma occurs at night, each center would be staffed 24 hours a day with a trained surgeon, anesthesiologist, radiologist, nurses, and technicians, and would have CAT-scanning devices and other equipment available. While experts estimate that 350 trauma centers are needed, only 150 are currently available, and of those, only 50 are prepared to offer top quality trauma care.

A major flaw in the private insurance employer-provided health care system with potential long-run impacts on the quality of health care is the absence of legislation requiring employers to fund promised health care benefits for retirees (English 1985). American companies face huge and growing financial obligations, mostly unfunded liabilities, for the health care costs for their retirees. In 1985, the total unfunded liability for this type of benefit was estimated at $125 billion and was increasing at $5 billion per year, according to Department of Labor statistics. Private experts have estimated the total as high as $2 trillion.

Since most companies pay for current medical expenditures out of current revenues and collections, few have set aside funds to pay the future costs of retirees' health care. The liability has grown as more employees retire at earlier ages and as Medicare coverage has been altered to shift more financial responsibility to beneficiaries. Court rulings have also limited the ability of employers to alter health benefits for those already retired. Yet unlike legal protection for pension benefits, no federal law requires employers to cover future health care benefits for retirees.

The accounting firm of Coopers & Lybrand and the benefits-consulting firm of Hewitt Associates found that only nine out of 4,000, less than 1 percent, were voluntarily funding their liabilities (English 1985). Tax law changes effective in 1986 further reduced incentives for companies to fund health care liabilities, by capping the amount of contributions that are deductible, and by making the earnings on the set-aside contributions taxable.

To cut future drains, many companies are dropping health care benefits for future retirees. The Employee Benefit Research Institute found that the percentage of employees who were promised employer-sponsored health plans for their retirement fell from 60 percent in 1980 to 57 percent in 1984. Experts are demanding tax breaks from Congress to alleviate some of the disadvantages of funding liabilities for future retirees' health care plans, and suggest that, eventually, a system of vesting of retirees' health care benefits much like the current system of vesting in pension benefits could emerge.

Ultimately, quality care clashes with costs and raises the specter of rationing or limiting some types of services. According to William Schwartz, coauthor with Henry Aaron of the Brookings Institution of *The Painful Prescription: Rationing Hospital Care* (1984), the increasingly expensive care of the terminally ill, plus the extraordinarily high costs associated with organ transplants and other procedures that are becoming more common may force the United States to move into the rationing of medical care. In 1984, then Governor Richard Lamm of Colorado provoked national controversy by declaring that elderly people who are terminally ill, not only have a right, but also a duty to die. Today, 80 percent of Americans die in hospitals or nursing homes while receiving expensive treatment. Yet legal problems involved in allowing the elderly to die have created dilemmas for hospitals and physicians, even when the wishes of patients or their families are clear.

Nor does Medicare, despite significant improvements in coverage for the elderly, cover all the expenses associated with extensive hospital stays. Among costs borne by beneficiaries in 1984 were an initial deductible of $356, an additional $89 per day for the sixty-first through the ninetieth day of a single hospital stay, and drawing on 60 lifetime "reserve days" for any stay exceeding 90 days and paying $178 for each reserve day used. Other beneficiary-borne costs include private-duty nursing and nursing home care. After three days of hospitalization, part A of Medicare helps beneficiaries pay for up to 100 days in a skilled nursing facility, but not in a nursing home. Part B, which covers doctors' services plus outpatient and physical therapy care included a $75 once-a-year deductible in 1984, and only paid 80 percent of approved charges.

The gaps force many of the elderly who are able to afford it to obtain additional private coverage to fill in the gap. In 1984, one-third of health care costs for the elderly were paid with private monies, while two-thirds were paid with federal, state, and local monies. Forty-nine percent of health care spending for those aged 65 and older came from Medicare, while 33 percent came from private funds and insurance. An additional 13 percent came from Medicaid and 6 percent from other public funds.

To improve this situation, the Reagan administration proposed legislation providing additional protection against excessive hospital costs. Unfortunately, it did not cover Alzheimer's disease, which afflicts 3 million Americans, nor Parkinson's disease, which afflicts 1.5 million. It also did not cover long-term home care, prescription drugs, hearing aids, dental, eye or foot care, nor routine physical exams. Representative Claude Pepper of Florida, "Mr. Senior Citizen of Congress," introduced a bill addressing the costs of catastrophic health insurance. It provided for comprehensive catastrophic health care coverage for Medicare beneficiaries while promising to reduce the total health bill of the average older American. As of this writing (1987–88) the bill has only been introduced but not passed.

Besides rationing and scope of coverage for the elderly, several ethical issues in health care promise to impinge upon the quality of care in the future (Dedek 1975). Among these are the extent and scope of surgery performed, questions of who shall receive organ transplants, and the degree of human experimentation and testing in medical research. Other ethical questions affecting quality of overall care deal with contraception and sterilization, transsexualism, genetic manipulation, abortion, euthanasia, and psychosurgery for behavior control.

Prevention versus Acute and Long-Term Care

Health care may be conceptualized as a continuum that ranges from the prevention of illness for healthy people to the maintenance and restoration of health for those with acute illness, to the preservation at the highest possible level for those with long-term and terminal illnesses. Generally, the U.S. health system has placed the greatest emphasis upon the last two, with much less emphasis upon prevention.

The success of prevention policies is even more difficult to measure than that of acute medical care. Yet some positive trends have occurred. Heart disease mortality has been decreasing since 1950, with especially dramatic decreases after 1970. Death rates from strokes have similarly decreased. The picture for cancer is less clear. Total cancer mortality started to decline among people younger than 45 in the 1970s, but the rate for lung and other respiratory cancers has continued to rise. Breast cancer is still the most common cause of cancer death among women, and lung cancer is increasing, despite a decrease in smoking among both adult males and females. Discouragingly, during the same time frame between 1969 and 1980, the rate of smoking for teenage girls increased, in contrast to a decline in that of teenage boys.

Americans have become more concerned about the amount and type of food they eat, but what they actually eat has not changed much. Despite talk about lighter and healthier meals, most Americans still consume a diet high in fat and low in complex carbohydrates, thereby increasing their risk of heart disease and cancer. While the notion that U.S. consumers are avoiding red meat is widely held, red meat consumption dropped only 6 percent between 1970 and 1985 and still remains a large part of the average diet, with per capita consumption higher than that of 20 years ago.

Many Americans continue to be overweight, despite studies that show that obese people have three times the normal incidence of high blood pressure and diabetes, an increased risk of heart disease, a shorter life span, and an unusually high risk of developing respiratory disorders, arthritis, and certain types of cancer. When obesity is defined as 20 percent over ideal weight, more than 34 million Americans, about one in five, fall into this category. Of these, 11 million are severely obese, exceeding their ideal weight by more than 40 percent. More employer- and community-based programs are called for to encourage long-term changes in diet.

Particularly distressing are recent reports that American youths—the work force of the future—are flabby and out of shape. Not a new problem, poor youth fitness so alarmed President Eisenhower when U.S. youths of all ages lagged behind their European counterparts on tests of strength and flexibility that he created the President's Council on Youth Fitness. The cause was renewed under President Kennedy, but 25 years later in 1985, American young people continue their poor performance on fitness tests. In one test of 8,800 youths, ten-year-old boys could only average 2.7 chin-ups and took more than ten minutes to run a mile. Forty-seven percent of tenth grade boys and more than half of all junior high and high school girls performed poorly in the 600-yard run. Third and fourth graders in a low-income San Francisco, California, neighborhood could not even complete ten minutes of moderate exercise.

The consequences of an unfit youth go far beyond the immediate ability to perform on a test. Deteriorated physical conditioning is associated with poor mental performance. Studies from other countries have demonstrated that not only does the physical conditioning of youngsters increase when they exercise vigorously, but their academic performance improves as well. Unfit young people are also developing major health problems, including many of the illnesses that afflict their unfit parents. When Charles Kuntzleman of Spring Arbor College examined the fitness and health of 360 elementary school children in Jackson County, Michigan, he found that 98 percent showed at least one major risk factor for heart disease. Twenty-eight percent had high blood pressure, 42 percent had abnormally high levels of cholesterol in their blood, and more than half had a combination of three or more risk factors (Carey 1985).

Part of the blame for unfit youth rests with a dearth of adequate physical education programs in the schools. Some schools that do emphasize athletics often specialize in competitive varsity sports, which affect only a small percent of the total student body. According to the National Children and Youth Fitness Study, only 36 percent of American students have daily gym classes, and many of those classes emphasize team sports like dodgeball and baseball, which do not ensure overall fitness and conditioning. Other factors contributing to the lack of fitness are an increase in the proportion of fast foods in diets, and the considerable amount of time spent viewing television (an average of seven hours a day for U.S. teenagers (Carey 1985)). Substantial changes are necessary in each of these factors to get American youth into shape.

One area related to health and quality of life in which preventive measures could have a substantial impact, is teenage pregnancy. Each year, 1 million U.S. teenagers become pregnant, a rate of one teenage girl out of every ten—the highest rate of any developed country. Nearly 40 percent of white girls and 63 percent of black girls become pregnant by the age of 20. The problems facing children of teenage parents are considerable. Only one in five girls under the age of 15 receives any prenatal care during the first three months of pregnancy. Teenagers are 92 percent more likely to have anemia and 23 percent more likely to have complications related to prematurity than mothers between the ages of

20 to 24. Teenagers have twice the normal risk of delivering a low-birth-weight child (under 5.5 pounds). Low-birth-weight babies are in danger of serious mental, physical, and developmental problems that may require costly treatment, possibly lasting throughout life. Many children of teen mothers are victims of child abuse. Many children of teen mothers often repeat the cycle and become teen mothers themselves.

Teen pregnancy imposes hardships on the mother as well as the child. Teen mothers are many times more likely than other women with young children to live below the poverty level. One study found that only half of those who give birth before age 18 finish high school, compared with 96 percent who postpone childbearing. Teen mothers earn less money and are more likely to be on welfare. Seventy-one percent of female AFDC recipients under age 30 had their first child as a teenager.

While teenage birth rates were actually higher in 1957 than today, most births then occurred within marriage. The 1950s were an era of early marriage and social stigma attached to illegitimate births, often prompting shotgun marriages if pregnancy occurred from premarital sex. In 1950, fewer than 15 percent of teenage births were illegitimate, but by 1983 more than half were, and in some regions the figure rises to 75 percent. Unwed motherhood has become a normal state of affairs. Despite the pervasiveness and social costs of teen pregnancy and a 1984 Harris poll, which showed that 84 percent of Americans regard teen pregnancy as a serious national problem, controversy continues over the appropriate solution.

Martha R. Burt of the Urban Institute argues that marriage for pregnant teenagers is actually detrimental in the long run (Levine 1987). Married teens are more likely to drop out of school. Marriage decreases the ability of both boys and girls to support themselves and increases the probability of having more children more quickly. Conservatives and liberals often clash over how much and how far to push the preventive measures of sex education in the schools and the use of contraceptives. Although fear of AIDS has added a new urgency to the need to use condoms, the controversy remains. The quality of health, and indeed, of life, for whole segments of the population await its resolution.

By the late 1980s, AIDS had reached epidemic proportions in the United States. By August 1987, the census of deaths from AIDS reached 22,000 by conservative government count, and by 1991, it is expected to reach 179,000 with 270,000 cumulative cases of AIDS. While 90 percent of the known casualties are male homosexuals or drug users, the disease is spreading to the heterosexual population with frightening rapidity. Although some promising clues to controlling the AIDS virus have been uncovered, as yet no reliable or tested cure has been found. On October 11, 1987, over 200,000 gays and supporters of homosexual rights marched in Washington, D.C., beseeching the federal government to spend more money on AIDS research and treatment and to end discrimination against homosexuals. The problem promises to become a major public health issue by the end of the decade when AIDS deaths threaten to reach 60,000 Americans a year, and 5 million people will be infected with the AIDS virus.

The Impact of New Payment Reimbursement Schemes

Traditionally, hospitals have employed retrospective payment systems and "cost shifting" to cover nonpaying patients. Under retrospective payment schemes, payment levels were set with the third-party payer after a service was delivered. The retrospective nature of payments, in fact, allowed cost shifting, whereby health care providers charged more to patients with private resources to cover other losses. A 1982 study found that typical hospital bills to commercial insurers were "marked up" 27 percent, while the markup to Blue Cross was 17 percent. Medicare broke even and Medicaid was marked down 10 percent (Easterbrook 1987).

In the early 1980s, the federal government shifted to an alternative prospective payment scheme called "diagnostic-related groups" (DRGs). Entering patients are diagnosed as belonging to one of hundreds of treatment groups, and the hospital receives a fixed fee reflecting the average cost of curing that condition. If the patient is worse than average and requires additional services, the hospital must pay the needed amount beyond the DRG funds. However, if the patient is better than average, the hospital keeps and profits from any leftover payments. If the patient is severely ill, an "outlier" payment becomes effective, recognizing the unusual nature and extraordinary expenses attached to the case.

The rate of increase in federal health care expenditures began to slow almost as soon as DRGs were enacted. From 1983 to 1984, Medicare expenditures grew by only 8.6 percent, the smallest increase in the history of the program. The following year, the rate fell further to 5.5 percent. Dr. Charles Sanders, former director of Massachusetts General Hospital, among other experts, has argued that the reduction in cost growth rates was achieved by radically changing the relationship between hospitals and patients, hospitals and doctors, and doctors and patients. Patients' hospital stays became shorter, and doctors began using fewer tests and more alternative facilities to hospitals. For Medicare patients, the average length of a hospital stay dropped from ten days in 1981 to less than eight in 1985.

Most experts also agree that patients should not spend any more time in a hospital than is absolutely necessary, for quality of health care as well as cost control. During hospitalization, patients typically are immobilized and have increased risk of acquiring infections they did not have upon admittance. For example, in 1983, nearly 2 million patients came down with new illnesses while in U.S. hospitals, and 96,000 died as a result. The expected stay for many ailments, consequently, has declined.

Partially as a result of earlier hospital discharges placing greater demands upon the posthospital network of nursing facilities and home health services, that system appears to be overloaded. In the first 18 months after prospective payment was enacted, hospital discharges to nursing homes increased 40 percent, despite a shortage of nursing home beds in many states. The biggest problem, especially for the elderly when they leave the hospital, is that they often find themselves not sick enough to stay but not well enough to go home, trapped in a no-care zone. Patients whose Medicare home-health-services benefits have run out but who are not poor enough to qualify for Medicaid must pay for the services themselves, or rely upon their children.

To deal with issues of quality of care exacerbated by prospective payment systems, the federal government has established a network of peer-review organizations to monitor health care, but Richard Kusserow, inspector general of the Department of Health and Human Services (DHHS), has found deficiencies in the system (Trafford and Dworkin 1986). Of 4,724 reported suspicious cases, patient records were lost in 43 percent. Since the new payment system began, DHHS has issued only eight sanctions to doctors and hospitals due to poor quality. In 1986, however, the government released a controversial list of 269 hospitals with abnormally high or low death rates.

RECENT CHANGES IN THE HEALTH CARE SYSTEM

Diminution in hospital stays has been accompanied by an increased emphasis upon outpatient services. These are provided to patients at hospitals without admitting them for overnight stays. Ambulatory services are provided at locations other than hospitals. Simple operations, such as those for hernias or cataracts, are increasingly conducted on an outpatient basis. Ambulatory surgical centers, usually owned by doctors, have also grown in number in recent years. Because ambulatory centers do not fall under certificate of need regulations, they have had more flexibility in meeting market trends, and now offer surgery for cataract removals, cosmetic surgery, hernia repair, gynecological procedures, "sports medicine" (sometimes called "Yuppie orthopedics"), and fat removal. Ambulatory centers often resemble hospitals in every respect except that patients do not spend the night. Ambulatory centers, especially those that provide routine care as well as surgery, have been nicknamed "doc-in-the-boxes," and have been criticized by some for "stealing" patients from hospitals. With the expansion of the number of physicians and hospitals, the medical industry in many areas is facing oversupply, with not enough patients to go around. In 1986, the United States had 553,000 licensed physicians, or 22 doctors per 10,000, a third more than in 1976 when the ratio was 17 doctors per 10,000. Unless trends change, there will be 26 doctors per 10,000 by the year 2,000, with most of the surplus concentrated in medical specialties and in big cities. An influx of foreign medical school graduates, although slowing down in recent years from a high of 45 percent of new medical licenses in 1973 to 17 percent in 1981, has exacerbated the surplus. Others criticize that in the current deregulated environment, the growth in ambulatory centers will lower the overall quality of care, although little evidence exists yet to support this charge.

Another innovative service delivery system has emerged during the past two decades called health maintenance organizations (HMOs), whose growth was partially stimulated by the Health Maintenance Organization Act of 1973. During the development of block grants for health in the Reagan administration, the federal government moved from supporting HMO expansion to a neutral stance. The HMOs consist of prepaid health care service, where annual fees are assessed per subscriber, regardless of services delivered. Health maintenance organizations were designed to contain the total cost of medical care by creating different financial incentives than those underlying the fee-for-service-rendered payment system. Under the latter, physicians benefit from increased numbers and costs of services provided. Under the HMO system, physicians are often paid a salary, rather than on a piecework basis, offering little incentive to provide unwarranted services for income maintenance. The HMOs benefit financially when patients remain healthy or are quickly restored to health, since these subscribers experience lower than average service delivery costs. Health maintenance organizations lose financially when patients become very ill and require extensive and costly services. Both HMOs and DRGs essentially employ the same prospective payment principle. While critics argue that HMOs do not provide adequate incentives to provide quality care, supporters contend that the incentive structure for HMOs places greater emphasis on prevention and health maintenance than traditional delivery and payment systems. As alternative delivery systems that lower physicians incomes, the HMOs have been bitterly opposed by the American Medical Association. One of the largest and oldest HMOs in the United States is the Kaiser plan.

With health care consuming so much of GNP—more than twice that of defense—it has attracted the interests of profit-oriented enterprises. Once considered the terrain of those with altruistic and humanistic impulses, increasingly in the United States, health care is provided on a for-profit basis. A large increase has occurred in the number of Wall Street-listed corporations providing primary services and health care, creating what Stanley Wohl (1984) calls "the medical industrial complex." Wohl divides the listed corporations in this complex into six categories:

—those owning or managing health care facilities, such as hospitals, nursing homes, surgical centers, community psychiatric facilities, sports medicine centers, and rehabilitation centers (examples include Hospital Corporation of America, National Medical Enterprises, and Beverly Enterprises);

—those that have purchased, bought out, or otherwise acquired large medical partnerships (e.g., ARA Services, which now owns Spectrum Medical Care; and Humana, which now owns Emergency Medical Services);

—those such as pharmaceutical and medical supply companies whose primary business is supplying goods and services to the health care field (e.g., Eli Lilly, Johnson & Johnson, and Baxter Travenol);

—corporations whose primary business is elsewhere, but over the past 20 years have established subsidiaries in the health care field (e.g., Du Pont and Dow Chemical, which began pharmaceutical divisions; and Monsanto Company, which formed a health care division to purchase biotechnology companies);

—companies that supply goods and services to a variety of markets, but whose products account for large expenditures by the health care system (e.g., IBM, Hewlett-Packard, General Electric, and EMI, which sell high-technology equipment to hospitals and clinics; and banking and insurance companies, which finance medical purchases and services);

—companies emerging in recent years to capture very specific fields in health care (e.g., Cetus and American Surgery Centers).

Despite the rapid growth of the medical industrial complex in recent years, as well as the expansion of specific companies that comprise it, some experts question whether or not the proportion of GNP devoted to health care can continue to rise. With constant or declining health care dollars and increased competition for patients, some shakeup in this industrial complex is anticipated.

HEALTH CARE ISSUES FOR COMPETITIVENESS

Most developed nations in the world have decided that prepayment of health costs and entitlement to health services for the entire population is the best way to provide universal service while containing costs. The nationalized health care system in Great Britain, for example, costs only 5.5 percent of GNP, compared with 10.6 percent GNP spent on health care in the United States (Wohl 1984).

The decentralized political system in the United States undermines national planning and leaves often conflicting and incomplete policies developed through responses to crises. Nowhere is the crisis development of policy more evident than in health care, where the federal role has expanded incrementally over the twentieth century, first responding to control of traditional infectious diseases, then encouraging physician training and hospital development, then extending health care coverage to previously excluded groups. Most recently national health care legislation has focused upon cost containment. At no time has the nation established as a goal the provision of high-quality health care to all its citizens, and designed the most efficient system for providing and delivering those services. The current hodgepodge of institutions and vested interests in the health care industry mitigates the development of such a goal and rational planning to achieve it. Yet without a healthy vibrant labor force, the United States cannot compete effectively in global markets. With an inefficient health care system consuming a disproportionate share of the GNP, resources that could be used to restore international competitiveness are diverted elsewhere.

Future crises loom on the immediate horizon. One is concern over the development of catastrophic insurance to help individuals with terminal illnesses and diseases requiring expensive halfway technologies cope with the costs. Most proposals continue the current ills of the existing system: the absence of incentives to hold down costs embodied in third-party payments, and reversions to retro-spective payment systems that drive up costs. Another issue is legislation pro-posed by Senator Edward Kennedy to require all employers to provide health care coverage—an attempt to cost shift health care expenses to employers and to extend coverage to the 37 million Americans not covered by health insurance. This proposal still falls short of universal coverage and allows many individuals to still fall through the health care system cracks.

Both of these issues, however, are dwarfed by the upcoming national furor over who will pay for the high costs of caring for AIDS victims. With current projections of 1.5 million people infected, and often unknown carriers, and estimates of the number of future victims rising almost daily, the high cost of dying in America has become even more apparent. The achievement of high-quality universal health care at an acceptable cost does not have to be an elusive dream. It will increasingly become a necessity to compete abroad and will require cooperation at home at a level Americans have rarely, if ever, seen before.

6

INCOME DISTRIBUTION AND WELFARE

INCOME INEQUALITY AND INTERNATIONAL COMPETITIVENESS

Since the 1970s, income and wealth in the United States have been changing in such a way that the rich are getting richer while the numbers of poor are increasing and the middle class has been having an increasingly difficult time holding its own (Thurow 1987). That this is disturbing in its own right is obvious to anyone who is concerned about equity and opportunity for all citizens. That it has the potential of a significant negative impact on international competitiveness is somewhat less obvious. Yet the equation is not hard to discern: an increase in poverty equals reduced educational and economic opportunities for much of the labor force. In turn, reduced opportunities result in a more poorly trained labor force unwilling, because of the inadequate but still significant welfare system, to compete for subsistence level wages and unable to compete for high-tech jobs.

Citizens permanently excluded from the good life can hardly be motivated to sacrifice for international competitiveness to ensure that other Americans have it. Additionally the welfare system is expensive and counterintuitive. Paying potential workers not to work hardly promotes long-term productivity. Underlying the change in income and poverty statistics is a sad tale of waste of precious human resources, touching not only many heartstrings, but also the nation's bottom line.

Some contend that restoring competitiveness will exacerbate inequality, at least temporarily, since the adoption of high technology does not necessarily imply the adoption of high or more equitable wages. In recent times, the number of high-paying blue-collar jobs disappearing as plants close or move abroad has not been offset by an increase in high-paying jobs in new sectors of the economy. High tech often means low pay for production workers who manufacture or assemble electronic components, as well as for many service workers.

How much has the inequality in income increased in recent years? The U.S. Bureau of Statistics reports that the share of total income going to the top 20 percent of all families in 1985 was 43.5 percent, the highest level since 1947 when those statistics were first compiled. By contrast, in the intervening years, the share of income going to the top fifth of the population had fallen to 40.5 percent at one point. The bottom three-fifths of the population in 1985 also received the smallest share of total income ever: 32.4 percent. The grim reality of these statistics is that the top fifth received 11 percent more income than the bottom three-fifths combined (Thurow 1987).

Federal Reserve Board (FED) data include items not included in the Census Bureau's definition of income and show even greater income inequality. FED statistics show the bottom three-fifths receiving only 28 percent of total income in 1982, a decline from 32 percent in 1969, while the top 10 percent increased its share during the same period from 29 to 33 percent. Nor is the income distribution racially neutral. Racial minorities continue to lag behind whites in earnings and to have higher incidences of poverty. In 1983, for example, 34 percent of all blacks lived below the official poverty line, contrasted with 11.5 percent of whites.

Wealth is even more unequally distributed than income. While the top 2 percent of the population receives 14 percent of total income, members of this group own 28 percent of total net worth. The top 10 percent owns a whopping 57 percent of net worth, compared with their 33 percent share of total income. The bottom half of the population owns only 4.5 percent of net worth. While about half of top-wealth holders earned their accumulations through their own efforts, the other half inherited theirs through no effort of their own. Nor is the distribution of wealth color blind, since 98 percent of top wealth holders are white (Thurow 1987).

Despite the fact that well-heeled America continues to exclude minorities, middle-income white males have also been hard hit by recent shifts. When middle-income male jobs are defined as those paying 75 to 125 percent of median male earnings (from $13,334 to $22,224 in 1985), the number of those jobs declined from 1976 through 1985 from 23.4 to 20.3 percent of the male work force. Despite a total growth in total male employment in that period of 7.4 million jobs, 400,000 middle-income male jobs disappeared, with only small offsetting gains in upper-income jobs. Most of the job growth occurred in lower-paying jobs.

Thurow traces the following sequence by which these disturbing shifts have occurred to determine exactly where greater inequality has entered the system. A decline in output growth—a drop from 3.8 percent in the decade of 1960–69 to 2 percent for the period from 1979–85—begins the pressure toward greater inequality. Smaller output growth heightens the competition at home for smaller shares of additional output. With declining productivity, unemployment has risen from 4.8 percent in the 1960s to 8.1 percent in the 1980s, further exacerbating the difference between the well-off and those struggling to survive.

Ironically, this pressure has narrowed the still substantial gap between the average pay of men and women. The reason is not that women are experiencing faster gains, since their rate of increase in earnings is actually smaller than in the past, but rather because men have experienced substantial reductions in income. Male incomes remain substantially above female incomes, with a median for full-time workers for males of $24,999, compared with $16,252 for women. With considerable gains in the proportion of elderly living in poverty, women, especially single heads-of-households, and the children of single-parent families have become the "new poor."

With the decline in competitiveness continuing in the late 1980s, the U.S. Census Bureau reported that the average pay of women who work full time was up to 70 percent of men's wages in 1986, compared with only 62 percent in 1979, a statistic that had remained constant since 1973 (Thurow 1987). Gains were attributed to the greater number of women college graduates filling higher-income professional and managerial jobs traditionally held by men. Part of the remaining wage gap was attributed to the fact that men were still twice as likely to enter high-paying fields, such as accounting and engineering. Furthermore, women more frequently interrupt employment for childbearing and child rearing, undercutting seniority and availability for promotion. The remaining portion of the wage differential between the sexes is a function of sex discrimination against women ("More Gains . . . " 1987).

Solutions to continuing discrepancies between male and female earnings are not politically easy. They include stricter prohibitions against employment discrimination on the basis of gender, including the passage of an Equal Rights Amendment to provide constitutional guarantees of equality. Comparable worth programs in which equal pay is grated for comparable work performed by men and women remain controversial, but also are a strong option for reducing discrimination against "pink-collar" fields in which women are concentrated, such as teaching, nursing, and secretarial work, where wages are low in large part because women predominate (Whicker and Kronenfeld 1986). As the number of single-parent, female-headed households increases (44 percent of all black families and 14 percent of all white families in 1985), failure to address gender-based income disparities means that more children are raised in poverty, with reduced opportunities for educational and economic success.

Thurow traces the recent slowdown in growth to a threefold reduction in productivity, from 2.7 percent between 1960 and 1970 to 0.9 percent between 1979 and 1984. Nor were Germany and Japan, the major competitors of the United States where the growth in productivity is three to five times the U.S. rates, similarly affected. Slow rates of increase in productivity are, ironically, connected to high employment. If each worker is comparatively less productive, it takes more workers to produce the same output. Hence, despite the poor productivity performance of the United States since 1970, and indeed, because of it, the United States has created 28.4 million jobs. Yet European employment, where productivity has been high, is at about the same level as in the 1970s.

Even though employment gains are associated with low rates of increase in productivity, income gains are associated with high rates of productivity increase. When productivity gains were higher in the United States, between 1960 and 1969, compensation to labor rose 2.7 percent per year. When U.S. productivity gains were scant, between 1979 and 1985, increases in per hour labor compensation fell to 0.4 percent per years, despite rapid job creation.

That most of the new jobs created during periods of sluggish productivity growth are low paying is illustrated by the fact that of the 10.7 million new earners in the United States between 1979 and 1985, almost half (48.6 percent) were paid less than $10,000 in 1985 dollars. Another 30.5 percent earned between $10,000 and $25,000 (less than the proportion of the labor force—37.6 percent—in this income category in 1979 before the influx of new jobs). Fewer of the new jobs (20.9 percent) were paid more than $25,000 compared with the proportion of old jobs in that category in 1979 (23.2 percent) (Thurow 1987, p. 32).

Another source of inequality is the unequal distribution of wealth, which is less evenly distributed than income. Since wealth is capital and earns income independently of labor, individuals who own wealth get richer faster than individuals who do not, even given equal efforts in the labor force. Omitting homes and real estate, the distribution picture that emerges for net financial assets (stocks, bonds, or pension funds) is one of extreme inequality. The top 2 percent of all families own 54 percent of all net financial assets. The top 10 percent own 86 percent of net financial assets, while the bottom 55 percent have zero or negative financial assets (meaning they are in debt). As overall income rises, the inequality in wealth contributes further to the inequality in income, and since income can be used to purchase assets, also to wealth.

How important is the slowdown in productivity to the recent exacerbation in income inequality? Thurow argues that this slowdown outweighs cutbacks and demographic changes (increases in unskilled and inexperienced baby boomers in the labor force) in the amount of pressure applied to spiraling inequity. He contends the two major forces that have caused the rising inequality in earnings distributions are intense international pressures coupled with high unemployment, and the rising proportion of female workers in the labor force. A trade deficit of $170 billion has had the impact of squeezing four million workers out of higher-paid manufacturing jobs and into lower-paying other jobs.

Not only is the United States more heavily dependent upon international trade, and competition in world markets stiffer than before, but also the United States must now compete with its technological equals, rather than from the position of technological superiority that it previously enjoyed. When technology is essentially equal across major players, then the country with the lowest production costs wins the international markets game, an area in which the United States, with shrinking productivity gains, has fallen behind.

Not only are major U.S. competitors not plagued with the same sharp declines in productivity gains as the United States, they also do not have the amount of income inequality that is present in the United States. Inequality in Japan and

Germany is about half of what it is in the United States. Most of the improvements in equality in those countries are brought about by redistributive actions on the part of government. For example, before taxes and transfer payments, the percent of the population in the United States and Germany with less than half of the median income is about the same: 28 percent in Germany and 27 percent in the United States. After taxes and transfers, however, 6 percent of the West Germany population, compared with 17 percent of the U.S. population, has less than half the median income.

PUBLIC OPINION AND REDISTRIBUTIVE POLICIES

Thurow contends that the heart of the income distribution problem lies in increasing international competitiveness. Yet if surges in inequality become too great, before adjustments from heightened competitiveness are realized, then political unrest and instability may result. Traditionally, the United States has moved to address inequities potentially fueling such unrest before system-threatening instability or even revolution occurred. In the twentieth century, the New Deal response to the trauma and misery of the Great Depression, a period in which radicalism and communism were gaining in appeal, reflects one such solution. The Great Society programs, geared to reinstate groups economically marginal and politically disenfranchised into the mainstream, reflect a second.

Despite these periods, the government's role in redistribution remains controversial. Public finance theorist Richard Musgrave has identified three basic functions of government: allocation (the purchase of collective or public goods); stabilization of the economy (countering the business cycle to lower unemployment and inflation and to promote stable long-term growth); and redistribution (shifting resources and income from one income group to another). Of these three functions, redistribution remains the function with the least popular consensus underpinning it.

Public opinion data show that the poor feel that government should take a more active role in reducing income differences than do the affluent ("Opinion Roundup" 1987). Forty-two percent of respondents in a national opinion poll who earned less than $15,000 agreed that government should do something to reduce the income differences between the rich and the poor, while only 33 percent of those earning between $15,000 and $39,999, and 14 percent of those earning $40,000 and over agreed with the statement. While only 13 percent of those below $15,000 felt the government should not concern itself with income differences, 16 percent in the middle-income category and 34 percent in the top-income category agreed with this laissez-faire position.

The differences between the income groups were only slightly less marked when queried about the role of the government in improving the living standards of all poor Americans. Thirty-nine percent in the lowest group, 29 percent in the middle-income group, and 21 percent in the top-income group agreed with a statement that the government should pursue that type of improvement. A higher proportion in each income group, but still a majority in only the lowest group, agreed that the government had a responsibility to help people in paying for doctors' and hospitals' bills. Fifty-four percent in the low-income group felt that the government should provide assistance in financing medical care for the poor, compared with 49 percent in the middle-income group and 40 percent in the high-income group.

Despite the decreasing desire for government redistribution of income the higher the income class, even the lowest income class does not support those policies by a majority. Those data reflect the strong cultural bias in the United States for individualism and capitalism, and pervasive support for the work ethic. In few other countries in the world today is individualism so valued and entrenched. Belief in individualism has translated into a concomitant belief that the individual is responsible for his or her own economic well-being, and that work and individual effort are the primary routes to economic success.

Nor have economists been willing to specify desirable limits on inequality, nor link income inequality to productivity and GNP growth empirically in any systematic way. Measures of inequality are not as highly developed, fine-tuned, and frequently used as measures of other economic concepts, such as total national product, balance of trade, price inflation, and unemployment. Nor has a systematic index to assess the redistributive impacts of all government policies been developed.

Neoclassical economists find inequality a troublesome if not irrelevant concept, since classical economic theory and its updated neoclassical version are essentially theories of production, not distribution. The goal of both theories is to lay out the conditions under which supply and demand reach an equilibrium, and output is maximized (Thurow 1983). Neoclassical theory says little about distribution, except that factors of production receive rewards in proportion to their contribution to output production. More profitable activities and firms receive greater rewards, either by addressing unsatiated demand or by lowering production costs, or both. Their disproportionate gains serve as a guide to steer new competitors into areas in which demand exceeds supply, thereby eventually restoring equilibrium. The potential of high profits also encourages competitors to adopt new technologies and become more cost competitive.

Despite this scholarly inattention of neoclassical theory to questions of distribution, the slow development of widely used measures of inequality, and the lack of consensus of the desired level and nature of government redistribution, redistributive concerns underlie every collective action, often driving the politics, if not the public debate surrounding public choice. Public debate on any particular proposed government policy typically focuses upon the allocation and stabilization impacts. Yet the politics of the action revolve around the redistributive impact—who gains and who loses, and by how much?

Supply-side proposals illustrate this duality of debate versus political reality, as well as the fact that redistributive policies may be regressive, penalizing the poor and rewarding the rich in their impact. They can also be progressive when resources are transferred from the rich to the poor. Supply-side policies were pushed mostly by a right-of-center Reagan administration and by administration supporters. The central supply-side idea was to cut taxes in the face of inflation rather than pursue the traditional Keynesian solution of raising taxes to lower aggregate demand. Since prices are a ratio of demand (total money in the economy at the aggregate level) to supply (total goods in the economy), the ratio may be altered by changing either the demand numerator or the supply denominator. Price inflation means that the ratio is rising, which implies that the demand in the numerator is growing faster than the supply in the denominator.

Keynesian solutions to inflation have focused upon the numerator, attempting to lower aggregate demand by reducing the amount of money in the economy, a solution that required lowering government expenditures and raising taxes. Supply-side theorists broke from Keynesian solutions by arguing that stabilization goals would best be served by lowering taxes in the face of inflation, a policy directly contrary to traditional wisdom.

Supply-siders developed an elaborate rationale to justify a huge tax cut, a policy coincidentally with a major redistributive impact especially benefiting the Reagan constituency. Here is the rationale: lowered personal taxes will increase personal savings, which, in turn, will be employed in productive investments and used to purchase new plant and equipment. The new plant and equipment will incorporate new technologies that will raise productivity. As productivity increases, the amount of goods in the economy—the denominator of the ratio of demand and supply that makes up prices—will increase. Hence, inflation could be lowered by increasing the productivity and the amount of goods rather than by relying strictly upon lowering aggregate demand.

Scant empirical evidence existed to bolster the supply-side view and several links in the preceding theoretical chain proved weak. When personal taxes were cut, Americans spent the money, rather than dramatically increasing their savings rate, which at 4 percent of disposable income, is the lowest savings rate in the industrialized world. Of those funds that were saved, some were not used in domestic investments, but rather were used to pursue more lucrative opportunities abroad. Of the investment that was retained within the country, a great deal went to fuel the corporate merger mania, rather than toward the purchase of new plants and equipment. With American productivity increases during the early 1980s sinking to one-third their former level during the 1960s, supply-side attempts to increase productivity were abysmal failures.

Other notions connected to supply-side theory, for example, the famous Laffer Curve, were also not based on empirical evidence and mostly provided further rationale for the redistributive tax cut that rewarded the Reagan constituency. Laffer posited a curvilinear relationship between the amount of taxes collected and tax rates, arguing that if tax rates rose above a certain point, people would begin to substitute leisure for work, thereby lowering total tax revenues. According to Laffer, there were two tax rates, one high and one low, which yielded identical tax revenues (Lekachman 1982). On the basis of no evidence, Laffer concluded that the United States, despite the existence of tax rates among the lowest of industrialized countries, was taxing at the high level. He extrapolated that taxes could be reduced by one-third without reducing the total tax revenues collected. Presumably, people not then working because of high marginal tax rates would begin to work, and those already working limited amounts would work more. The increased tax revenues gained from additions in the total number of people working and in the total hours worked would offset the loss of tax revenues from significantly reduced rates. Hence, tax revenues would not be reduced and the deficit would not grow from the major tax cut.

Again, many of the theoretical links in the logic chain proved weak. Employment tends not to be sensitive to tax rates except at extremely high marginal rates, rates not yet approached in the United States where the maximum rate had, at that time, been lowered to 50 percent on earned income and half of that on capital gains. Nor were there hard data that the relationship between tax rates and tax revenue was curvilinear, or that the United States was on the high side of the curve if it were curvilinear.

Experience proved that Laffer and his fellow supply-siders were not just slightly wrong. Their estimates were wrong by huge amounts. With tax rates on personal income cut by one-fourth and taxes on business cut considerably as well, budget deficits ballooned. Inflation did fall, but not because of the increase in productivity predicted by supply-side theory, since the rate of productivity increases fell during this period. Rather, an oil glut fragmented a fractious OPEC, producing a sharp decline in energy prices, which, in turn, reduced inflationary pressure throughout the economy.

The appeal of supply-side economics was its redistributive impact. Not only were monies redistributed from the government sector to the private economy by the tax cut, but across-the-board percentage cuts particularly benefit the affluent who experience a larger absolute decrease in taxes than do the poor. The political rhetoric of the day focused upon the stabilization impacts of supply-side theory, which were mostly conjecture at the time, rather than its redistributive benefits for Reagan constituencies.

THE ROLE OF TAXES IN REDISTRIBUTION

The redistributive impacts of supply-side economics also emphasize the power of the tax code as well as the budget to affect the distribution of income within the country. While the predominant redistributive effect of supply-side policy was derived from across-the-board percentage cuts, more typically exceptions to the tax code—tax expenditures—are employed. The term "tax expenditure" came into vogue in the past two decades as a less biased expression for the transfer of benefits through the tax code. Furthermore, the newer terminology emphasized the granting of government largess upon tax expenditure beneficiaries. Benefits received through tax expenditures are deemed no less desirable or beneficial than benefits bestowed by "budget expenditures," which transfer income from the general taxpayers to recipients.

A tax expenditure is a legal reduction in effective tax rates for certain classes of taxpayers, resulting in lower taxes due than from nominal tax burdens. Tax expenditures create effective tax rates lower than nominal tax rates for beneficiaries. Often they also create discrepancies between the lower effective tax rate of beneficiaries and the higher effective tax rate of non-beneficiary individuals or corporations with similar incomes who are not eligible for the tax expenditure.

Critics of the newer terminology, as well as the concept of tax expenditure, contest the notion that the government is bestowing a benefit by "allowing" recipients to keep private income earned through market activities. Supporters, however, counter that this simplistic opposition ignores collective decisions to purchase public goods and services, and to allocate the burden of paying for those goods and services across different classes of taxpayers. Supporters of the concept of tax expenditures often oppose their reality, and sometimes charge that recipients of tax expenditures use political clout to avoid paying their "fair share" of the tax burden.

As noted in Chapter 3, the use of tax expenditures is not class neutral. More affluent income classes and corporations are frequent recipients of government benefits granted through the tax code, whereas poorer income classes more commonly receive government benefits through transfer payments allocated by direct budget expenditures. Several reasons underlie this class preference in method of receiving government benefits.

First, low-income groups that do not pay tax do not benefit from tax expenditures. The poorest income groups fall below the income level which is a minimum for paying income tax, may own no property and hence are not directly billed for property tax (although they may bear some of the burden of property tax through higher rent payments), and may purchase few large-ticket items subject to sales tax. For people below the poverty line, a reduction in taxes—especially income taxes they do not owe—is hardly a benefit.

Second, high-income groups often have higher marginal tax rates, and therefore benefit more from income exclusions than do moderate- or low-income groups. Reduction in nominally progressive taxes, such as the federal income tax before the recent reduction in tax brackets and many state income taxes that are very mildly progressive, benefit high-income classes more than lower-income classes. Under progressive tax systems, high-income groups theoretically pay higher marginal tax rates (and average tax rates) than do lower-income groups. Hence, income exclusions, exemptions, and deductions of the same dollar amount are worth more to higher-income groups who would lose more of the deducted amount through higher marginal tax rates than they are worth to lower-income groups in lower marginal tax brackets.

Third, politically sophisticated groups prefer tax expenditures because they are less visible than direct budget expenditures and therefore are less subject to opposition. The visibility of direct budget expenditures may cause them to become a target of groups opposed to distributing monies to any set of recipients. Welfare and social service expenditures are very visible, with recipients clearly identified along with the dollar amount individual beneficiaries receive, and total expenditures made for those purposes.

By contrast, tax expenditures are much less visible to the public. Often identifying who and how many beneficiaries are receiving a particular tax expenditure is difficult. Calculating the actual total dollar amount of benefits received may be equally or more difficult, and may involve making some assumptions about the economic behavior of recipient groups. Higher-income groups and corporations are considerably more sophisticated politically than are low-income, less educated groups, and realize that lack of public visibility is a plus in ensuring a steady benefit flow.

Fourth, tax codes and the benefits they bestow through tax expenditures continue indefinitely once enacted, since debate over existing tax expenditures and tax reform occur infrequently and irregularly, if at all. By contrast, budget appropriations are debated annually nationally and in most states. Even states with biennial budget processes often have smaller stopgap supplemental appropriations bills in the off-budget years. Hence, every year, recipients of direct expenditures must defend their budget base and justify continuation of government benefits.

However, neither the nation nor the states annually scrutinize their entire tax code in the same fashion. Tax codes and the distribution of tax expenditures they bestow are scrutinized irregularly, with long periods of years existing between waves of reform. During these intermittent years, no one in either the legislative or the executive branch typically questions the continuation of tax expenditures present in the tax code. As more sophisticated political players, higher-income groups and corporations realize that receiving tax expenditures, which must be defended only infrequently and irregularly, is greatly preferred to receiving direct budget expenditures, which must be defended frequently and regularly against competing groups.

Fifth, tax expenditures, as methods of achieving public purposes and goals, are not held to the same rigorous standards of performance as are direct budget expenditures. Direct budget expenditures not only are more visible, but also are often subject to performance evaluation studies by the General Accounting Office and the Office of Management and Budget at the federal level, or by state legislative audit councils, executive budget agencies, and evaluation staffs within the agencies themselves. Inadequate and unclear performance standards enable interest groups benefiting from tax expenditures to prevent their discontinuance.

Finally, tax expenditures reduce overall funding for government and hence coincide with the preference of political and social elites for lower taxes and smaller government. At the federal level prior to the tax reforms of 1986, tax expenditures approached an amount equaling one-third the size of the direct federal budget. While many specific tax expenditures were abolished or limited as a result of the reform, the pressures that created the abolished tax expenditures have not died. Without vigilance and a change in the method by which congressional campaigns are financed, tax expenditures pushed by various special interests will gradually creep back into the tax code, until it is as riddled as it was before 1986.

The decided preference of high-income groups and corporations for tax expenditures over direct budget expenditures does not mean that low-income groups never are the beneficiaries of tax expenditures. Some tax expenditures, such as property tax circuit breakers, homestead exemptions, and sales tax exemptions on necessities at the state level, or personal exemptions and energy tax credits at the federal level, were designed to benefit lower-income groups. Other tax expenditures, such as home mortgage exemptions on federal and state income taxes, benefit middle-income home owners as well as high-income groups. Overall, however, tax expenditures in the past have eroded the progressivity of the federal income tax, mitigated the ability of the tax structure to redistribute from the rich to the poor, and contributed to income inequality.

In addition to tax expenditures, tax systems redistribute income through their rates. Before the 1986 tax reforms, nominal rates were progressive, but exclusions and exceptions had eroded effective rates to such a point that the federal system was proportional in impact throughout most middle-income levels. The system remained mildly progressive at the lowest income levels and regressive at high-income levels. The 1986 reforms eliminated many tax expenditures and reduced the number of income brackets from 14 to three. The top rate fell from 50 percent to 33 percent. Reform advocates pushed the proposal as "fair," not on the basis of improvements in vertical equity of nominal rates, which was clearly eroded, but on the basis of increases in horizontal equity. (According to vertical equity, high-income groups should pay proportionately more; horizontal equity implies that people in the same income class should pay equal amounts.) Proponents also contended that actual vertical equity would increase, due to the imposition of a more strict minimum tax and abolition of many tax expenditures favored by the affluent. Yet presumably four-fifths of all taxpayers would owe smaller tax bills after the reform. Clearly, the redistributive impact of the 1986 tax reforms is muddy at best. Politically, the population proved willing to trade off nominal vertical equity for greater horizontal equity.

The other major federal tax—the social security tax—is regressive in impact. The tax is levied on payroll, a fixed percentage of wages applied to all workers below an income cap. Proportional up to the cap, the effect of the cap is to make the tax regressive. Reforms to keep the system solvent have raised the percentages paid by both employee and employer, until by 1987, the combined share approached 15 percent of wages.

Unlike the federal personal income and social security taxes, which are direct taxes levied on individuals, the corporate income tax is indirect. Assessing the redistributive impacts of indirect taxes is difficult. Conclusions made in such analyses often depend upon the assumptions made about the degree of shifting of tax burden that occurs. If markets are competitive or demand is elastic (sensitive to price changes), passing corporate income taxes forward to consumers is more difficult, and they are more likely to be borne by the stockholders. Under these conditions, corporate taxes are less regressive. However, if markets are not competitive or demand is relatively inelastic, corporate taxes can be passed forward to general consumers and have the impact of sales taxes, which are clearly regressive.

Assessing the redistributive impacts of some state and local taxes is equally troublesome, with conclusions about those impacts highly dependent upon the assumptions made. In particular, local property taxes and state corporate income taxes are difficult to assess.

Economists have developed several techniques to measure the redistributive impacts of taxes. One is to measure the tax policy when it is enacted and then again after it has been implemented, using a Lorenz Curve technique to express the inequality in the distribution of two variables, called a Gini coefficient. If the distribution of income becomes more equal, the tax is viewed as progressive. If the distribution of income becomes less equal, the tax is seen as regressive.

The Gini coefficient technique is unsatisfactory for assessing redistributive effects of proposed tax changes for several reasons. First, since it relies on measurement of before-and-after income distributions, it can only be employed after the policy has been implemented and therefore is of little value when the proposed change and various alternatives to it are being debated. Second, accurate measures of income distributions are difficult to obtain, especially when the adjusted gross income reported on tax returns omits various types of nonwage income. Third, this measure confounds the budget impacts from the tax change with the tax change itself. If taxes are increased, then the monies are spent for programs that also affect the income distribution, and the two effects are difficult to sort out since both occur simultaneously. Other measures of tax incidence (who pays) are similarly plagued by one or more of these problems.

Lester Thurow (1980) in his now classic book, *The Zero-Sum Society*, has noted that the United States has avoided making redistributive decisions overtly and hence makes them inadvertently. The redistributive decisions that politicians and policymakers cannot make personally are made impersonally through budget deficits and inflation. Yet since political debate often focuses on the allocation and stabilization impacts of any proposal, redistributive impacts are not clear, especially to average citizens.

To facilitate public debate over the redistributive impacts of policy proposals, Congress could mandate that a redistribution impact statement be attached to any new program or policy submitted to either house, not unlike the current requirements for five-year cost projections for new program starts, and environmental impact statements for policies that have an impact upon the environment. If hard choices need to be made, and if they need to be made overtly rather than inadvertently, then both politicians and the public need to be better informed of the redistributive consequences of all new proposals. New attention needs to be directed to the development of adequate and readily comprehensible indices of these redistributive impacts. A redistributive index is particularly needed for proposed changes in the tax structure, where beneficiaries are more difficult to identify than with direct budget expenditures and final impacts are less clear.

Since major redistribution occurs through the tax code, it should be reevaluated regularly, rather than infrequently and irregularly. While a five-year reevaluation is desirable, a ten-year reassessment is acceptable and would constitute a considerable improvement over the status quo. The Senate Finance and House Ways and Means Committee could begin the process shortly after each census, when new income data are available, and complete it within the same session. Sunset legislation should be used to introduce all tax expenditures. Hence, tax expenditures introduced during the decade would expire at the reassessment period and would only continue if reenacted and approved by both houses of Congress and signed into law by the president. Under this reform, the explicit allocation, stabilization, and redistribution goals of each tax expenditure must be attached to it, to facilitate rigorous evaluation of its effectiveness at the ten-year reassessment. Shorter life spans for tax expenditures more temporary in nature could also be used.

These proposals would place redistribution directed through the tax code on a more equal footing with redistribution through the budget process and appropriations process, requiring the same evaluation standards for each. In short, there is not tax process now by which Congress regularly reassesses the effectiveness of the tax system to meet any goal, redistributive or otherwise. It needs to create one.

SOCIAL AND WELFARE SPENDING

Besides tax subsidies, there are several types of direct budget expenditures that transfer income from the general taxpayer to a particular group. Lump-sum transfers are used only occasionally, as in cases of disaster aid. "In-kind" subsidies involving transfer of particular goods or services, such as housing subsidies, food stamps, and Medicaid, are used more frequently. Cash payments, such as Social Security, Supplemental Security Income for the indigent elderly not eligible for Social Security, unemployment insurance, workmen's compensation, veterans' pensions, and Aid to Families with Dependent Children (AFDC), constitute the most common method of transfer.

Growing rapidly as an additional method of transfer are credit subsidies. While direct credit subsidies tie up government funds through low-interest loans, credit guarantees to private lenders also constitute a benefit to the lendee. Credit guarantees are particularly popular with politicians concerned about budget deficits, since they do not have an immediate impact on the current budget and, if the lendee does not default to the lender, do not have a budget impact at all.

The development of welfare and income-transfer programs in the United States has been spasmodic, unsystematic, and uncoordinated. Because of the strong bias toward individualism and capitalism, politicians developed programs in response to crises and interest-group pressure, rather than with any conception of what an adequate distribution of income is, how it might be achieved, and the appropriate role of the government in attaining it. Because individuals, especially in previous decades, often felt responsible for their own economic poverty, shame was attached to accepting welfare. This chaotic development has led to a severely flawed transfer-payment system. Here are some major criticisms of it:

Transfer payments and welfare in the United States are not based strictly on need, but are also categorical in nature. To be eligible, individuals must not only be needy—and what is defined as needy varies from program to program—but they must also fit into some predesignated category. This reflects the "widows and orphans" syndrome needed to justify transfer payments in a system in which individualism is prized and poverty is assumed to be the fault of the individual. Under this individualism-based logic, poverty alone is insufficient cause to warrant government support. Rather, individuals, such as widows and orphans, impoverished by forces beyond their control, must be deserving of government aid as well.

Several consequences of this categorical approach are very negative. First, impoverished individuals needing government transfers who do not initially fit into a "deserving" category have a strong incentive to try to fit in to become eligible for public assistance. The most obvious example of this occurs with Aid to Families with Dependent Children, which is only available to females with children. In states without the unemployed-father option, the females may not be living with an unemployed male, even the father of her offspring. Low-income women with few or no job options can only receive government assistance if they become pregnant and, at least in some states, raise illegitimate children. Since the first implementation of the program, whole welfare cultures have developed, in which generation after generation knows no other existence but to live on and for AFDC payments.

When morality is stripped aside, the federal government is providing direct incentives to low-income women to produce illegitimate children. The more children they produce, the higher their payments; hence, greater financial incentives exist to produce more babies in an impoverished environment. While politicians rave about the immorality and undesirability of this cycle, the system they have designed, or rather failed to design, encourages the exact cycle of poverty they presumably abhor.

How might this perverse situation be addressed? Deleting the categorical requirements to receive welfare would remove at least some of the incentives for producing illegitimate children. While the cycle of poverty might not be broken immediately or inevitably, a noncategorical welfare system holds a greater potential that it will be broken eventually. Requiring extensive counseling and mandatory educational training for women who have one illegitimate child and are receiving AFDC payments as a requirement for continued transfers might lengthen the interval between second and third pregnancies, and possibly even lower AFDC birth rates. Massive sex education programs in the public schools could not only address the issues of unwanted pregnancy, but also the issue of AIDS. Birth control clinics in high schools, and even junior high schools, as the age of initial sexual activity drops, are part of the solution.

Racial minorities, such as blacks and Hispanics, might charge that especially the mandatory counseling and educational requirements are racially motivated, since a higher proportion of those populations depends upon AFDC (23.6 percent of black families in 1983, compared with 2.7 percent of white families). In absolute numbers, however, white recipients outnumber racial minority recipients. In the past, AFDC categorical requirements have forced families confronting economic hardships to split up, so that the mother and children may receive support.

In addition to forcing needy individuals to try to fit into an eligible category, the requirements for categorical assistance are often technical, complex, and in some instances, arbitrary. Consequently, they are difficult for potential recipients to understand, and may exclude persons who otherwise would fall into the deserving category. Unemployment assistance requirements illustrate this point. Applicants for unemployment assistance must have worked a requisite number of weeks in the immediately preceding quarter, arbitrarily defined by the calendar, in order to be eligible.

Applicants who do not have the exact number of weeks of employment in the appropriate time frame are not eligible. A broader measure of eligibility, such as amount of time worked in the past year or the past few years is not relevant. An even broader measure would provide unemployment assistance to all able-bodied adults in the labor force who are unemployed. Anxious to keep down budget deficits, politicians have not embraced this more comprehensive, rational, and humane criterion, preferring to use complex and sometimes arbitrary rules to exclude potential recipients and keep down program costs.

A third problem with the categorical nature of the transfer system in the United States is that payments sometimes go to nonneedy recipients. As an example, the complex agricultural subsidy programs have ballooned to total spending levels approaching $25 billion in the 1980s and primarily reward affluent corporate farm owners, ironically, in a country that values work, for work they do not perform. Created during the Great Depression, these programs have long outlived their usefulness, encourage overproduction, and have not saved the family farm (which, probably should not be saved at public expense, any more than any declining industry should be saved). If categorical aid were abandoned, and transfer payments were based strictly upon poverty and income-based need, most recipients of agricultural subsidies would not (and should not) be eligible.

Social Security payments to the affluent elderly are another example of government transfers to nonneedy recipients. Originally sold to the American people as a pension system, Social Security assumed more and more welfare functions across the years. Today, it is half-pension, half-welfare, and critics would argue, performs neither function well. It does not service all needy elderly, necessitating the creation of an additional program, Supplemental Security Income, to provide a bare subsistence payment to people who fall between the cracks of Social Security eligibility requirements. Nor is it a pension system since payments received are only loosely connected to total lifetime contributions into the system. These functions should be separated, so that the welfare aspect of social security is integrated with other transfer systems and is determined strictly on income-based need. The affluent should not be eligible for such assistance. A separate pension system should allocate payments on the basis of total lifetime contributions, in which payments for high-income recipients are calculated by the same criteria as payments for moderate- and low-income contributors.

A fourth problem with the categorical transfer system is that some needy individuals have no category and do not receive assistance. Unless they are in states that provide minimal general assistance, nonelderly able-bodied men and nonelderly women without children do not fall into a deserving category and are not eligible for public assistance. These individuals may have become unemployed and have exhausted their unemployment benefits without finding work. Their job skills may have become obsolete but they may not know how to apply or may not be eligible for retraining programs. These individuals in need of assistance and eligible by an income-based needs criterion find that the categorical transfer-program safety net in the United States is not woven tightly enough to catch their economic fall.

A fifth and severe criticism of the categorical transfer system is that it frequently discourages work and penalizes recipients who do work. Both AFDC and Social Security curtail benefits when a recipient gets a job and works. The rate at which benefits are curtailed for additional before-tax dollars earned, called the "effective tax rate" for the program, is above 50 percent and in some instances, approaches 100 percent. Nor are before-tax earned dollars, from which taxes and work expenses must be paid, the equivalent of tax-free benefit dollars, making the effective tax rate for working even higher. In short, unless AFDC recipients can earn wages much higher than the minimum wage, which typically they cannot since poor job skills are a source of their economic difficulty in the first place, there are strong financial incentives once they are in the program to eschew work and continue to receive benefits.

Similarly, Social Security work restrictions and benefit reductions also penalize work. For recipients between retirement and the age of 72, earnings from wages result in a 50 percent benefit loss, while earnings from investments do not. Those with small or no investments, who have the greatest need to supplement their Social Security benefits by part-time employment, are penalized for doing so. Those with substantial investment incomes are not penalized for additional earnings. These nonsensical requirements reflect the confused and muddied focus of a program that intertwines welfare and pension purposes. Periodically, Congress has debated eliminating the work restriction but has determined that it would be too costly. Separating these two functions, to create an income-based needs poverty program for the needy elderly, and a pension system based on lifetime contributions for everyone else would remove this arbitrariness and unfairness.

Another related criticism of categorical welfare programs is that they discriminate against the "working poor"—those individuals working at minimum wages (not all jobs are covered by minimum-wage requirements) who barely live above the subsistence level, despite full-time employment. Ironically in a country that values work, individuals on welfare, especially when their in-kind assistance is considered as well as cash payments, are better off financially than the working poor. Welfare, managed by the Department of Health and Human Services is a system and bureaucracy separate from the tax system, which is administered by the Internal Revenue Service. The two are not coordinated, creating inequities in the income range in which the two systems overlap. A negative income tax approach would integrate the two systems into one, with income as the sole criterion of whether individuals gave the government money in taxes or received benefits through transfer payments.

The ambivalence of the U.S. individualist culture toward public assistance has made strong national action in this area difficult, and has produced a patchwork system, in which public assistance is jointly financed by federal and state levels of government. Benefit levels vary greatly, creating incentives for recipients to move to, or at least stay in, high-benefit areas. This penalizes state and local governments that have been more generous in payment levels, adding to the financial burden of many older declining core cities. A more restricted national standards range for benefit payments would eliminate a great deal of this disparity.

The best alternative to public assistance—an alternative that heightens international competitiveness and holds the greatest potential for substantial improvement in income inequality—is full employment. While, as Thurow has pointed out, an expansion in unemployment does not compensate for a decline in productivity, expanding employment to include many of the currently unemployed, while productivity is rising, would reduce inequality.

Yet massive public employment programs have only been attempted in times of great national trauma: the Great Depression. Despite the 1946 Full Employment Act, which directs Congress to develop budgetary policies that maximize employment, Congress has not adopted sufficiently large public employment programs to achieve this purpose. By the final passage of the Humphrey-Hawkins Act in the 1970s, which was public employment legislation proposed in response to the recession brought on by the OPEC cartel and the shock of spiraling energy costs throughout the economy, the act had become a pale version of itself and was too weak to bring about substantial employment gains.

Congress has pursued tax cuts and credits to stimulate private-sector employment programs. Stimulating private-sector employment is felt to be more efficient than public-sector employment programs. Yet tax incentives are not efficient from the government's point of view if the goal is to increase employment. Dollar for dollar, the most effective way to stimulate employment is to hire people for public-sector jobs, since at least part of the dollars granted through tax incentives go to the owners of capital to provide the incentive for them to alter their behavior, rather than to hire the unemployed.

Critics of public-sector employment programs also charge that people hired in those programs would not serve any useful function but would provide "make-work" services. Yet current users of the massive public works projects of the 1930s (dams, public buildings, roads, and parks) know that benefits from those programs are still being derived today. In an era when a great deal of America's infrastructure, from bridges to water and sewer systems to mass transit systems, is in major disrepair, public employment programs could add significantly, not only to the economy but also to the quality of life. Nor would public employment programs necessarily be restricted to capital improvements, since day care, among other functions, remains greatly undersupplied.

On the surface, this strategy coincides with the strong U.S. bias toward capitalism, since no government checks are being issued. Yet real benefits are being transferred through the tax code, no less valuable than the benefits that might have been transferred through direct expenditures. The primary, or at least initial, recipients of tax credits to stimulate private-sector employment are not the unemployed themselves, but rather industry and capital owners who pay reduced income taxes as a result.

Since tax expenditures, as noted, are not subject to the same scrutiny and rigorous evaluation standards as direct expenditures, the impact of these tax incentives on employment levels, and their superior effectiveness over direct expenditures remains unproven. The structurally unemployed—those workers disadvantaged by geographic location or an absence or obsolescence of job skills—have been particularly hard to reach through tax incentives.

Why has Congress been so resistant to public employment programs, despite unemployment levels regularly exceeding 6 percent and occasionally, as in the 1970s recession, hitting double digits? The unemployed have few lobbyists in Washington compared with industry and capital owners who have plenty. Nor do the unemployed belong to PACs and contribute generously to political campaigns. Equally relevant, while the unemployed have an interest in securing employment, industry and capital owners have no interest in maintaining high employment levels. If there is a large pool of unemployed workers, wages can be suppressed through worker competition for scarce jobs, especially if workers are unorganized. High unemployment reallocates resources from labor to capital, and therein lies the stumbling block.

7

THE CRIME DRAIN

Crime is a social cancer on America, draining the economy and the vitality of the labor force. According to the Federal Bureau of Investigation (FBI) crime statistics, in 1986, one crime on the FBI crime index occurred every two seconds, including one violent crime every 21 seconds and one property crime every three seconds. Of violent crimes included, a murder took place every 25 minutes, a forcible rape every six minutes, a robbery every 58 seconds, and an aggravated assault every 38 seconds. Among nonviolent property crimes, a burglary occurred every ten seconds, an act of larceny-theft every four seconds, and a motor vehicle theft every 26 seconds.

Both in number of offenses and in rate per 100,000 inhabitants, all seven major categories of crime used in the Uniform Crime Reporting Program increased in 1986 over 1985 figures. Rates rose 8.9 percent for murder and nonnegligent manslaughter, 2.2 percent for rape, 8.0 percent for robbery, 14.3 percent for aggravated assault, 4.5 percent for burglary, 3.8 percent for larceny-theft, and 9.9 percent for motor vehicle theft (Federal Bureau of Investigation 1986).

But the aforementioned figures, grim as they are, do not tell the whole tale in America. The total costs have an adverse impact on productivity and international competitiveness, and include the following:

—missed days at work for victims resulting from injury and time spent in legal hearings and court;

—lost or destroyed property of victims;

—stolen property of business from burglary, robbery, and employee theft;

—higher insurance costs for businesses to cover theft, arson, and criminally damaged goods;

—higher overhead for businesses that hire private security guards to protect against shoplifting, vandalism, and theft from both employees and nonemployees;

—loss of competitive advantages for businesses subjected to industrial espionage from stolen trade secrets;

—higher overhead for businesses and individuals from legal fees for criminal prosecution;

—financial loss and loss of productivity for consumers from faulty products and other forms of corporate crime;

—loss of tax monies from other purposes to fund a more extensive judicial system;

—high public costs of maintaining one of the most extensive prison systems in the world (behind only South Africa and the Soviet Union in the number of people per capita incarcerated);

—diversion of public monies into the war against illegal drugs; and

—loss of life, work absenteeism, and reduced productivity from drug addiction.

In addition to more traditional crimes against individuals and property, recent years have seen a growth in white-collar crime, ranging from the petty to insider trading on Wall Street netting millions of dollars for the perpetrators. Crime through computers has increased the take of some thefts, exposing the financial nerves of corporate giants.

While crime represents a drain on the productivity and competitiveness of the nation, criminal activity often proves lucrative for the perpetrator. Contrary to myth, crime and punishment are not highly correlated, and crime often pays. The processing of persons accused through the police and judicial system has been likened to a leaky funnel. Many crimes are not reported, leading to significant discrepancies between official FBI crime statistics, and the incidence of crime indicated by unofficial interviews of citizens.

Of 500 serious crimes that are reported, 400 remain unsolved. Of the 100 cases in which a suspect is arrested on felony charges, 35 are juveniles who are sent to juvenile court. Of these 35 juveniles, 30 are either dismissed or placed on probation, and only five are officially confined. Of the 65 adult cases out of the 100 in which a suspect is arrested, 25 are rejected by the prosecutor either for insufficient evidence or from lack of staff to deal with the case compared with other cases in which the crime is viewed as being more serious or heinous. Only 40 cases of the 100 arrested are accepted by the prosecutor. Of these 40, six are dismissed by the judge or jump bail. The remaining 34 adults are sent to trial. Of these 34, two are acquitted. While 32 out of the 100 are arrested are convicted or plead guilty, 12 are placed on probation and 20 adults are imprisoned. Of the 500 original serious offenses, then, 25 people eventually serve time: five juveniles and 20 adults (Burns et al. 1987).

Of those prosecuted and incarcerated, many are recidivists: one out of three persons released from prison is incarcerated again within three years. Crime remains a problem that is both pervasive and persistent. It is a problem with high opportunity costs, draining productive resources from alternative uses.

THE CRIMINAL JUSTICE SYSTEM

The increase in crime in recent years has been attributed to many factors, none quickly remediable:

- Baby boomers passed through the most crime-prone years of 18 to 25, raising the crime rate with their large numbers.

- Mobility within society has undercut community socialization and pressure to conform to laws. The erosion of value education in traditional institutions, such as the family, church, and community, has not been replaced by effective value education in the schools or elsewhere. Value education in schools remains controversial and politically sensitive.

- The disparity in wealth between the rich and poor has increased in the 1980s, leaving the poor further and further behind and increasing incentives to resort to crime.

- One out of four U.S. high school students drops out before graduation, leaving them with few job skills and increasing the attractiveness of illegal activities to rapidly gain wealth.

- Job mobility across companies decreases loyalty to corporations, and diminishes incentives not to commit crime against companies. This lack of loyalty is compounded by the adversarial relationship between management and labor.

- Illegal drugs are readily available from abroad and provide a quick way to get rich.

- American values often place greater emphasis on the possession of great wealth rather than on how it was acquired. Negative attitudes toward government undercut enforcement activities and make criminals antiheros.

Scheingold (1984) notes that fear of crime has had a substantial and conservative impact on American political life over the past 20 years. While in 1965, only 34 percent of respondents to a Gallup poll reported fear of walking alone at night, in 1982, 48 percent reported this unease. One in ten Americans carries a gun for protection at times. Other surveys reveal an increase in general anxiety that, in turn, generates a climate of fear and increases the popularity of politicians who promise to crack down on crime. Scheingold contends that law-and-order candidates divert public attention from fundamental structural problems in the economy and social order that have contributed to the increase in crime, and are, in effect, attacking the symptom rather than the cause.

The growth of a law-and-order culture generates a police subculture, in which police and other law-enforcement officers develop shared values (Manning 1974, p. 175). At the core of this belief system is a cynicism about human nature, perhaps understandable since police must rapidly sort the world into "good guys" and "bad guys." Their job preoccupies them with the bad guys and imposes heavy penalties in the form of administrative sanctions, criminal prosecutions, personal injury, and even death for mistakes in sorting. Among the shared beliefs in the police subculture are:

—"People are often dangerous and cannot be trusted."

—"Experience is better than abstract rules."

—"You must make people respect you."

—"Everyone hates a cop."

—"The legal system is untrustworthy."

—"People who are not controlled will break the laws."

—"Policemen must appear respectable and efficient."

—"Police can most accurately identify crime and criminals."

—"Stronger punishment will deter criminals from repeating errors."

Yet despite the conviction of most police that stronger punishment will reduce crime, there is disagreement across and within states over the proper role of punishment, especially imprisonment, and it is on the state level that most criminal activity is prosecuted. Four different rationales have been offered, and support for the different rationales has varied across time. The first rationale for imprisonment is retribution—that society has the right to punish offenders, and if it is not exercised, people will be tempted to engage in vigilante justice. A second rationale is incapacitation: removing those who commit crimes from other potential victims in society at large. Deterrence, or warning others who might commit crimes that they will be similarly punished, is a third while rehabilitation, or converting criminals through a controlled environment into law-abiding citizens, is a fourth (Burns et al. 1987, p. 642).

Lack of agreement on the primary purpose for incarceration has allowed a recent expansion of the criminal justice system and flurry of prison construction without a clear vision of what the outcome of these substantial public expenditures should be. The increased emphasis on law and order plus continued high recidivism among repeat offenders has diminished the role of rehabilitation in prison programs in recent years. Also undercutting rehabilitation has been the growth of an increasingly widespread feeling that many of the reforms defending criminal rights imposed by the Warren Court during the 1960s (e.g., reading Miranda rights to the accused at the time of arrest, providing publically financed lawyers for indigent defendants, the silver-platter rule making illegally seized evidence inadmissible in court, increased adherence to strict protections of procedural due process, etc.) have tilted the criminal justice system too far toward the criminal and too much away from supporting victims and society at large.

In 1986, 284,000 guards, probation officers, and parole officials monitored the custody of more than one million people on probation and 450,000 prisoners in 800 different prisons. Stricter sentences have caused the prison population to increase by 12 percent a year in recent years, often resulting in prison overcrowding and increasing the total cost of the criminal justice system. Construction costs of each prison cell in 1984 ranged from $75,000 to $100,000, depending upon labor costs and the degree to which inmate labor was employed. Annual costs for feeding and guarding each prisoner were $23,000, more than a year's worth of education at even the most expensive private college (Funke 1984).

Prison overcrowding resulted partially from an increase in the crime rate, which some attributed to the passage of the baby boom generation through the high crime years of 18 to 25. Yet amazingly, little coordination exists between the intake portion of the system—judicial sentencing in state criminal court—and the capacity of the system to house prisoners. Suits initiated by inmates that overcrowding constituted cruel and unusual punishment led to federal court orders in some states to reduce prison populations and improve conditions. Prison overcrowding and court backlogs have increased the incentive for prosecutors to plea bargain, a widely used method of settling cases that reduces the number of cases on court dockets but does little to facilitate justice. If innocent, the accused may be pressured into pleading guilty to a lesser charge that he or she did not commit under fear of conviction of a more heinous crime. If the accused is guilty, society is deprived of the punishment of the criminal for the actual crime committed and must settle instead for punishment for a negotiated lesser crime.

Prison overcrowding has also increased interest in sentencing guidelines for judges, more as a method of reducing prison populations than as an instrument for standardizing sentences for equal or similar offenses. To date, sentencing remains a function of several factors, including:

—the judicial philosophy of the sentencing judge;

—the sentence range allowed by state law for the particular offense (in many instances, quite broad);

—the potential for rehabilitation of the convicted back into the community (usually positively correlated with social class, education; employment potential, and stable family relationships);

—the actual crime committed;

—the intent of the perpetrator at the time of the crime (spontaneous crimes are treated less severely than premeditated crimes with the same impact upon the victim); and

—whether or not deadly force is used.

In the absence of more rigorous and binding sentencing guidelines in most states, the wide variance in punishment for the same crimes contributes to a distrust in the criminal justice system, and a belief that it administers injustice as frequently as justice.

ORGANIZED CRIME

The scope of organized crime is unknown, but has been estimated to exceed the gross sales of the nation's largest multinational companies. The primary organization used against organized crime is the Justice Department's Organized

Crime Strike Force. The 1968 Omnibus Crime and Safe Street Control Act defined organized crime as "the unlawful activities of members of a highly organized, disciplined association engaged in supplying illegal goods and services, including but not limited to gambling, prostitution, loan sharking, narcotics, labor racketeering, and other unlawful activities of such associations" (Alexander and Caiden 1985, p. 22). The 1976 Task Force on Organized Crime of the National Advisory Committee on Criminal Justice Standards and Goals identified these characteristics of organized crime (Alexander and Caiden 1985, p. 9):

- Organized crime is conspiratorial.
- It has profit as its primary goal.
- It is not limited to illegal enterprises or unlawful services, but includes sophisticated activities such as laundering money into legitimate businesses as well.
- It is predatory, using intimidation, violence, corruption, and appeals to greed.
- Organized crime groups are well disciplined and incorrigible.
- Organized crime is not synchronous with the Mafia, and knows no ethnic bounds.
- It excludes political terrorists, and is politically conservative, rather than radical.

Innovatively, organized crime has expanded in recent years into computer fraud in banking, insurance, and real estate; professional sports; male prostitution and pornography; and contracting in hazardous waste disposal, garbage collection, and defense industries. Drug trafficking, however, remains a substantial if not the largest base for organized crime. In addition to violation of drug laws, drug traffickers commit a variety of other offenses, including tax evasion, bribery, obstruction of justice in all forms, and all degrees of bodily assault, including homicide, directed at each other, officials, and potential witnesses.

In drug enforcement, policies have been developed at all levels of activity: source control, interdiction of drugs internationally, high-level domestic distribution; wholesaling or middle-level dealing; and street sales or retailing. None have succeeded in stemming the flow and use of illegal drugs. In 1970, Congress passed two additional pieces of legislation for combatting organized crime and drug trafficking. This represented a sharp break with earlier policy. Both the Racketeer Influenced and Corrupt Organization's (RICO) provisions of Title IX of the Organized Crime Control Act and the Continuing Criminal Enterprise's (CCE) provisions of Title II of the Comprehensive Drug Abuse Prevention and Control Act created a form of asset forfeiture not used in the United States since the Civil War. The strategy of Congress in these provisions was, through seizure of assets purchased with profits from illegal activities, to reduce the profits of criminal activities as well as to cut off offenders from their economic power. Despite these tools, the annual flow of illicit funds from drugs is thought to be more than $79 billion, while theft and fencing may produce $40 billion and gambling another $5 billion annually. Combined with the $100 billion estimated to be earned through white-collar crime, the flows of illegal funds are large enough to threaten the integrity of the entire society. At $79 billion annually, illegal drug expenditures are more than 3.5 times the $20.7 billion Americans spend yearly on tobacco and a little less than twice the yearly $43.7 billion spent on alcoholic beverages. Illegal drug expenditures are even approaching the $89.7 billion spent yearly on motor vehicle and parts, and the $86.3 billion spent yearly on furniture and household equipment.

WHITE-COLLAR CRIME BY INDIVIDUALS

During the 1970s and 1980s, FBI scams snaring congressmen, judges, and other high-ranking officials for accepting bribes and payoffs, as well as Securities and Exchange Commission (SEC) crackdowns on insider trading on Wall Street, renewed interest in white-collar crime. White-collar crime may be occupational, conducted by individuals in business, and includes tax evasion; embezzlement; illegal manipulations of used cars and other products; fraudulent repair of automobiles, television sets, and appliances; check kiting; and violations in sales of securities. Government employees may commit occupational offenses such as the misappropriation of public monies, the illegal acquisition of public funds through padded payrolls, illegally placing relatives on public payrolls, or accepting payoffs from appointees. Some public employees in charge of contracting for goods and services may become involved in kickback schemes in exchange for granting contracts to contractors offering payoffs. Corrupt public officials may also issue fraudulent licenses or certificates, or grant lower tax evaluations or tax exemptions illegally.

Professionals also have ample opportunity to commit occupational offenses. Physicians may prescribe narcotics illegally; make fraudulent reports; make exaggerated or illegal claims from third-party payers including Medicare, Medicaid, Blue Cross and Blue Shield, and private insurers; and give false testimony in accident cases. Lawyers might misappropriate funds in receiverships, abet perjured testimony from witnesses, and engage in ''ambulance chasing'' to the point of litigating claims with no foundation in reality (Clinard 1983).

Corporations and business establishments are often the victims of white-collar crime. The Council of Better Business Bureaus (1985, pp. 12–14) has collected the following data on the extent of white-collar crime, especially that directed against businesses. In 1982, one-fifth of the investigative staff of the Federal Bureau of Investigation (FBI) was directed exclusively toward solving fraud and white-collar crime, resulting in nearly 4,000 convictions, which prevented an estimated $2.6 billion losses in crime. The FBI reports that white-collar crime losses total over $40 billion annually.

The U.S. Congressional Committee of Banking, Finance, and Urban Affairs reports that in the early 1980s, an average of 20,000 credit-card crimes were committed every day. In the bank credit-card industry alone, the fraudulent use of credit cards rose over 1,000 percent in a decade from $11 million in losses in 1972 to over $125 million in 1982. Losses from insurance fraud exceed $4 billion annually and are rapidly increasing (Council of Better Business Bureaus 1985).

The National Office Products Association conservatively estimates annual losses to business due to office supply schemes at $50 million. Shoplifting and internal pilferage by employees add up to 15 percent of retail prices, according to the U.S. Department of Commerce. The International Trade Commission estimates that foreign product counterfeiting was responsible for the loss of over 130,000 U.S. jobs in 1982.

Additional losses result from cargo theft, embezzlement, and coupon fraud. Check fraud, estimated to cost more than $3.4 billion in 1984, can occur in a variety of ways: checks drawn on insufficient funds, completely falsified checks drawn on nonexistent or defunct bank accounts, legitimate checks that have been stolen from the mails, offices, or homes and are forged; and stolen blank checks that are falsified.

Finally, computer fraud is growing in the workplace, resulting in losses that are difficult to estimate, since breaking the security of its computer system is embarrassing for a firm and is often hushed up. A study of the Electronic Data Processing (EDP) Fraud Review Task Force for the American Institute of Certified Public Accountants (1984) of computer fraud in the banking and insurance industries uncovered 119 cases of fraud. Among them were $200 million insurance fraud at Equity Funding, $21 million at Wells Fargo Bank, a $24 million misstatement of revenue at JWT Group, Inc., and a $10 million wire-transfer theft from Security Pacific National Bank.

Computer crime schemes employed in banking included diverting customer funds into the perpetrator's own account, making unauthorized extensions of credit limits and loan due dates, creating fictitious loans, and deferring recording of the perpetrator's own checks and charges. Other banking schemes used were forging customer input documents, such as checks and withdrawals, making automatic-teller-machine extractions, making adjustments to customer deposits, diverting loan payments and customer income into the perpetrator's account, and wire-transfer theft.

Computer schemes employed in insurance included the creation of fictious claims, triggering unauthorized refunds or reductions in premiums, creating unauthorized policy loans, and forging checks. Other strategies employed created unauthorized mortgage loans, reinstated lapsed policies, and invented fictitious pension payments. A wide variety of types of employees engaged in computer crime in both industries, including clerks, managers, date processors, tellers, insurance agents, item processors, and system programers. However, the larger losses occurred in crimes conducted by managers.

CORPORATE CRIME

A second form of white-collar crime is organizational. Not only are corporations the victims of white-collar crime, but they are also perpetrators. One study revealed that nearly two-thirds of the Fortune 500 corporations were charged over a two-year period between 1975 and 1976 with violations of corporate law, and at least one sanction was imposed on 321 of the companies. (Clinard and Yeager 1980). Between 1970 and 1980, 115 of the top Fortune 500 were either convicted of at least one major crime or had paid civil penalties for serious illegal behavior. Furthermore, the largest corporations were the chief violators, receiving a disproportionate share of the sanctions for serious and moderate violations.

Criminal activity by America's largest corporations is perceived as a serious matter by the public and has eroded public confidence in U.S. business. Harris polls showed that public confidence in the heads of large corporations dropped from 21 percent in 1965 to 15 percent ten years later. Eighty percent of U.S. citizens felt that "if left alone, big business would be greedy, selfish, make inordinate profits at public expense, and, if left unchecked, big business would stifle competition" (Clinard 1983, pp. 15–16).

Why are some coporations more ethical than others? In a survey of 51 middle managers from Fortune 500, spanning a variety of industries, half of whom were drawn from the 50 largest companies, 53 percent blamed top management for most corporate violations. Where corporations were perceived as ethical and compliant with the law, government regulations kept top management in line and top management, in turn, issued explicit instructions regarding ethics and compliance with government regulations to middle management. Nine out of ten middle managers in the 1983 Clinard survey felt that top management set the ethical tone for the company, and that top managers should use their influence to speak out against unethical and illegal behavior in the corporate world. Three-fourths of these middle managers felt that top management knew about violations of law and regulations either before they occurred, or shortly thereafter.

Part of the middle-management criticisms of the role of top management in setting corporate ethics might be attributed to middle-management jealousy of the greater success and financial compensation of top managers. However, one-half of middle managers expressed no resentment and one-third expressed only some resentment. Additionally, nine out of ten middle managers felt that pressure from top management on middle management to engage in illegal activities did bring about the intended result.

The second most cited factor contributing to unethical behavior was the pressure of competition, while the type of industry was the third factor cited. In the 1975–76 study, the oil-refining industry was charged in one out of five legal cases brought during that time period, and in one out of every ten serious and moderate violations. Three-fifths of all serious and moderately serious financial violations, almost one-half of all environmental violations, one out of every six trade violations, and one out of seven administrative violations were committed by oil-refining companies. In this industry, 22 of 28 companies violated the law at least once, and 20 had at least one serious violation (Clinard 1983).

The motor vehicle and pharmaceutical industries were also disproportionately charged with corporate crime. The motor vehicle industry was responsible for one-third of the total manufacturing violations, one out of nine labor violations, and one out of eight trade violations. The pharmaceutical industry was responsible for a fifth of the manufacturing violations, and one out of seven administrative violations. All 17 pharmaceutical companies violated the law at least once during the study period.

Other factors included the ethical history of the company, financial difficulties a firm may be experiencing at the time, including a decline in corporate profits, and pressure from unfair competitive practices employed by other firms.

Generally, coprorations violating government regulations and laws do not receive maximum penalties (Clinard and Yeager 1980, p. 122). For the 477 manufacturing companies studied that received a total of 1,529 sanctions in the 1975–76 period, warnings were used twice as much as any other sanction. Of the total number of sanctions, 44 percent were warnings, including recalls. Only 23 percent were monetary penalties. Unilateral orders constituted another 18 percent, while 13 percent were consent orders and decrees. As is the case with recidivism and individuals, the majority of the cases involved a relatively small number of corporations that violated the law repeatedly.

Generally, serious violations receive minor penalties. Only administrative penalties were given in two-thirds of the serious violations. Over two-fifths of the sanctions for serious crimes and violations were warnings; another one-fifth were consent orders. Seventy percent of the consent orders simply directed the charged company to cease the illegal activity in the future, rather than being remedial in nature. Victims of corporate crime may be categorized by party affected and the nature of the effect (Clinard and Yeager 1980, p. 123):

- Consumers experiencing violations affecting product safety, product quality, and health hazards are typically the victim in cases before the Consumer Product Safety Commission (CPSC), the Food and Drug Administration (FDA), and the National Highway and Traffic Safety Administration (NHTSA).

- Consumers whose economic power has been violated through credit violations and misrepresentation in advertising and sales are affected by rulings from the Federal Trade Commission (FTC).

- The entire economic system is the victim in unfair trade practices, including antitrust violations and other infractions of competitive rules, and most financial violations except those related to consumer purchases.

- The physical environment is eroded by environmental violations primarily regulated by the Environmental Protection Agency (EPA), including air and water pollution.

- Violations involving the Occupational Health and Safety Administration (OSHA), the Equal Employment Opportunity Commission (EEOC), the National Labor Relations Board (NLRB), and the Wage and House Division of the Labor Department victimize members of the labor force.

- Violations of administrative or court orders and tax fraud cases victimize the government directly, and the broader public indirectly.

According to a *Harvard Business Review* survey (Baumhart 1961), four out of five executives believed that some generally accepted business practices in their industry were unethical, and four out of seven thought that other executives would violate a code of ethics if they felt they would not be caught. Executives sometimes practice selective adherence to laws, and many believe that laws regulating securities and banking procedures, trade, labor, and environmental pollution are not as formally binding as burglary and robbery laws. Often, corporate executives are insulated from persons with different beliefs, associating almost exclusively with people who are probusiness, conservative, and antigovernment regulation.

Corporate executives, lawyers, and business writers have offered a variety of defenses for law violations. Some contend that most laws, especially those relating to commerce, constitute government interference with the free-enterprise system. Furthermore, government regulations and bureaucratic procedures impose additional costs on business and are unjustified. For example, the *Wall Street Journal* estimated that the combined regulatory costs of EPA, CPSC, and OSHA regulations exceeded $100 billion in 1978. Dow Chemical claimed that the costs of compliance with federal regulations in 1976 cost the company 50 percent of after-tax profits and six percent of sales. Critics charge that many of these compliance costs are highly exaggerated (Alexander and Caiden 1985; Clinard 1983).

Executives rationalizing illegal activity also argue that government regulations are incomprehensible and too complex, and hence, are inherently faulty. Other justifications are that regulation is unnecessary, because the matters being regulated are unimportant (a rationalization particularly applied to environmental regulation violations), and that many corporate violations are mistakes or violations of omission rather than commission.

Additionally, executives argue that competing firms advance their own positions by illegal activities, and that if a violation prevents a loss rather than increases profits, it can't be wrong. While some violations, such as price-fixing cases, involve millions or even billions of dollars, the damage is so diffuse that no single individual or set of individuals is hurt extensively. Some executives claim that their stock is widely held, and hence their illegal and questionable activities to increase profits help the larger public. A final rationale is that violations are caused by economic necessity and are done for desirable reasons, such as protecting the value of the company's stock, ensuring an adequate return for stockholders, and protecting job security for employees by creating financial security for the corporation.

The risk for a corporate executive of a criminal conviction or prison sentence for illegal actions conducted on behalf of the corporation is very low. Only limited use of criminal sanctions against corporate executives has occurred, for a variety of reasons. While bribery of officials, price fixing, and the manufacture and shipment of harmful products are likely to be regarded as criminal, actions related to defective products and harming the environment are less likely to lead to criminal penalties. Corporate officials are usually well educated, have high status, and are visible within their communities. Some feel that the advances made by corporate officials in improving the standard of living and providing employment to workers exceeds any damage done by illegal "mistakes."

Until recently, the same investigatory techniques used against street offenders and organized crime have not been levied at corporate offenders. Pinpointing responsibility for illegal decisions may prove difficult in corporations since tasks and responsibilities are divided. Often the effects of violations are extremely diffuse. Corporate exeuctives charged with illegal activities frequently plead *nolo contendere*, or no contest to the charges, and plea bargain, avoiding lengthy trials and their more likely outcome of imposing full criminal penalties.

How might the incidence of corporate crime be decreased? The solutions involve the development of a stronger business code of ethics, and more active participation by stockholders. Some have suggested the appointment of general members of the public to represent the public interest to corporate boards, a practice similar to that of appointing union representatives to corporate boards (Clinard and Yeager 1980).

Even more widesweeping is federal chartering of corporations in place of the current system in which corporations are chartered by individual states. Federal chartering would result in more even and comprehensive enforcement of laws and regulations, and would more evenly match the size of the regulatory body (the federal government) with the size of the regulatees (increasingly multinational companies whose scope far exceeds that of any single state).

Other suggestions would stiffen the penalties for corporate crime. Among them are strengthening consent decrees to provide for remedial and follow-up action to ascertain compliance, imposing substantial monetary fines after one warning or consent decree, new federal laws imposing stiffer penalties for environmental and health and safety violations, stronger statutes prohibiting corporate violators from receiving federal contracts, publicizing coprorate violations in advertising at the expense of the violating firm, and more extensive use of imprisonment for corporate executives who commit serious violations. Additionally, federal legislation could preempt state laws that allow convicted corporate officials from being indemnified by their corporations, prevent convicted corporate officials from assuming similar positions in other companies for a specified period of time, impose some liability on corporate directors for illegal actions conducted by their companies, and strengthen commercial bribery laws against kickbacks from customers and suppliers.

ADDRESSING THE CRIME PROBLEM

Crime is a problem intertwined with many other economic and social problems. It cannot be successfully addressed in isolation from these other problems. While some observers have contended that crime is primarily a problem among the underclass that is not uniformly spread throughout other social classes, there is little evidence to support this idea. Rather, the type of crime appears to be related to social class. While street crime is more prevalent among the unemployed, the poor, and drug addicts, white-collar crime is more prevalent among the middle and upper classes. Domestic violence and terrorism seem to know no class bounds.

In addition to attacking street crime directly, through more stringent law enforcement, simultaneous efforts to reduce unemployment, improve the educational oppoortunities of the disadvantaged, and reduce the incidence of poverty are crucial to a frontal attack on street crime. Greater emphasis should be placed on values education in the schools for both disadvantaged and middle-class students.

Massive public campaigns against drug addiction directed at the schools and American youth should be undertaken to attempt to reduce drug addiction and the concomitant street and organized crime it fosters. Federal efforts to centralize and coordinate the attacks against drug trafficking and organized crime across different federal agencies and at different levels of government should be continued.

Public funds should be increased to discourage prosecutors from seeking to plea bargain criminal offenses down for the accused to a lesser charge. Sentencing guidelines should be implemented, not only to increase the sense of fairness of the system for those subjected to sentencing, but also to reduce prison overcrowding and to coordinate the intake of the prison system with its capacity to house inmates. Greater emphasis in sentencing should be placed upon the impact of the crime upon the victim and society, rather than upon the intent or condition of the perpetrator at the time that the crime was committed. White-collar crime should be enforced, prosecuted, and penalized as rigorously as street crime. Inmates should be encouraged to develop job skills in prison and should be rewarded for doing so.

Finally, alternatives to prison, an incredibly costly and often ineffective way of dealing with offenders who have committed nonviolent crimes, should be implemented. Among these are electronic surveillance and incarceration within one's home, and to allow the perpetrator to continue working. Social ties that will be needed to reintegrate the offender as a productive member in the economy should be maintained. Financial relief should be provided for each victim or for the victim's relatives. Perpetrators should remain incarcerated or confined through electronic surveillance until they can pay for all this relief for the victim, or for a substantial part of it.

8

MANAGEMENT-LABOR RELATIONS AND EMPLOYEE RIGHTS

In the United States, the three major actors in the economy—management, labor, and government—have typically regarded each other as adversaries. While those postures may have been more appropriate for the closed economy of earlier decades, fierce international competition is making those attitudes archaic. Yet the foundations of distrust, particularly between management and labor, are deep and long-standing. On occasion, especially in the initial attempts to organize auto workers and coal miners, these relations became bloody and violent.

Multiple factors facilitated the growth of adversarial management-labor relations in the past, including deep beliefs in individualism and unfettered markets, massive pools of new immigrant labor that allowed management to ignore worker demands for greater rights, and a trade union movement born out of management-labor strife. Further, the decentralized system of American government allowed labor and management to ''capture'' more favorable responses from different branches of government at different times. In particular, while labor sometimes received a more favorable response in the legislative branch, since Congress was and is sensitive to widespread public opinion and votes, management often received a more favorable response in the courts.

In contrast to other societies with greater ethnic homogeneity, the great ethnic heterogeneity in the United States created additional barriers between management and labor. Members of the laboring class often ate different foods, came from different countries, practiced different customs, went to different churches, and sometimes even looked different from members of the managerial class. In some regions, a tradition of slavery in the eighteenth and much of the nineteenth century is further added to the cultural gap between management and labor in the twentieth.

Many of these factors facilitating adversarial relationships between management and labor in the United States still exist, but the consequence of their impact has grown greater as heightened international competition has sharply increased the need for trust and teamwork at home. While management and labor have typically been viewed as adversarial, continued profitability of the firm is in the interest of both, and increasingly, profitability is linked to cooperation rather than conflict.

THE DEVELOPMENT OF THE MODERN LABOR MOVEMENT AND UNIONS

The classical economic theory of Adam Smith (1776) and the neoclassical theory of Alfred Marshall (1930) are essentially theories of production. Comments and concepts of distribution are scant, offered only when they impinge upon maximizing productive output and the efficient allocation of resources. Marshall, in his neoclassical theory of relative wages, included that workers are paid the value of their marginal products and are employed in the job in which their marginal value product (i.e., their wage) is the highest. If one worker earns more than another, according to Marshall, this is the consequence of a proportionately greater contribution to total output (Marshall 1930). This type of analysis ignores the impact of race, sex, and class discrimination on the distribution of earnings.

Other economists, including Hicks (1932), have qualified Marshall's analysis to accommodate real-world institutions and rigidities, such as long-term contracts, shifts in demand, and labor unions. However, most economists still agree that one group of workers is paid more than another group of workers because it contributes more to total output and therefore deserves higher compensation (Pettengil 1980).

Thus, economists have not generally viewed unions favorably, often arguing that unions create monopoly power and raise wages above competitive levels in the union sector (Hirsch and Addison 1986). The union power to strike is central to this cartelization argument, since the strike makes possible a reduction in industry output so that monopoly prices and profits (higher than competitive prices and profits) can be obtained. Economists of this mindset further argue that society suffers net welfare losses from unionism due to the inefficient factor mix and to a misallocation of resources between union and nonunion sectors. (The union sector is presumed to get too much relative to the nonunion sector.) Pettengil (1980) has developed elaborate analyses incorporating many classical and neoclassical assumptions to prove that unions actually increase rather than decrease inequality of earned income.

Galbraith (1967), however, has pointed out that large power begets countervailing power, and in fact, large unions grew up in response to increasingly concentrated corporate and managerial power. In the early 1900s, few federal laws existed to regulate industry or to prevent monopolistic and cartel practices among owners of capital and management, including many that today are illegal. Concentrated power among capital owners and management against unorganized individual atomized workers left them vulnerable and economically impotent to argue for higher wages or better working conditions. Unions were a natural if not an inevitable response.

The growth of the American labor movement was slow, and until the 1930s, the American Federation of Labor (AFL) represented no more than three million workers (one out of 16 workers). The Great Depression, the New Deal, congressional passage of the 1935 National Labor Relations Act (NLRA, also called the Wagner Act) and the establishment of the Congress of Industrial Organizations (CIO) all provided an impetus to the movement. As a result of the NLRA, workers were given the right to call for a secret vote to determine whether or not they would be represented by a union, and if so, which one. If a union received a majority worker vote, it had exclusive rights to bargain on behalf of that group of workers. Further, the employer was required to negotiate in good faith with the union to arrive at a written agreement. While employers were given the right to present their views to employees, they were prohibited from interfering with union organization.

The Wagner Act protected workers against unfair employer labor practices, as well as guaranteeing them the right to organize and bargain. The National Labor Relations Board (NLRB), created to supervise and administer the act, was empowered to prevent management's attempts to interfere with the right to unionize and bargain, to dominate a union, to discriminate because of union membership, or to impose reprisals on an employee for testifying before the NLRB.

Ironically, a second development that fueled union growth after the Great Depression was good old-fashioned market competition. The AFL proved unresponsive to members' requests to establish units organized along industry lines to represent skilled and unskilled labor. Several members split off to form a rival federation that was organized in this manner and called the Congress of Industrial Organization (CIO). The competition between the two rivals for membership contributed to the spread of union organizations and to general improvements in working conditions and wages. However, the percentage of total workers unionized in the United States remained small compared with that of other countries, never exceeding slightly more than one-third at the peak of union power and, more typically, hovering around one-fourth.

By 1947, after the war period, in which emphasis had shifted from protecting workers to dealing with labor shortages, the pendulum had swung back toward protecting the rights of management. In amendments to the NLRA called the Taft-Hartley Act, unfair union practices were targeted as illegal, and legal protection for workers not wanting union membership was created. This act established penalties for unions forcing employers to engage in unfair hiring practices and for violence while picketing. It outlawed a "closed shop" in which workers were required to belong to a union prior to being employed by a firm, but allowed a "union shop," in which workers may be required to join a union 30 days after being employed, or lose their jobs for nonpayment of union dues. By strengthening the hand of the common adversary—management—the Taft-Hartley Act drove the rival AFL and CIO groups closer together.

The power of the government in management-labor relations is that of a third-party observer who facilitates negotiations and the process of collective bargaining. Except in cases of national emergencies, such as World War II, the Korean War, and a short series of balance-of-payment emergencies during 1971, the government has refrained from dictating or influencing the content of management-labor agreements, except for establishing a minimum wage applicable to larger firms operating in interstate commerce. One of the few decisions actually made by the NLRB affecting negotiations was the determination of the bargaining unit. In the United States, most collective bargaining agreements cover employees of a single enterprise or plant and are negotiated by the management of the plant rather than by an employers' group.

The respective presidents of the ALF and CIO, William Green and Philip Murray, had developed considerable personal animosity across the years. Their deaths, plus a partial refocus of the AFL, allowed the merger of the two federations into the current ALF-CIO in 1955. The issue of corruption was raised early in the union movement and continued to hang over the collective heads of organized workers. The CIO began an internal housecleaning in 1949 by expelling nine affiliated organizations for communist domination. Shortly afterward, the Longshoreman's Association was expelled for corruption. After the AFL-CIO merger, an annual convention, on the recommendation of the executive council, suspended the affiliation of the Teamsters, the Laundry Workers, and the Bakers, for similar reasons.

In 1959, the Labor-Management Reporting and Disclosure Act, strengthened reporting requirements by both. This act reinforced earlier internal union anti-corruption efforts, but also introduced federal regulation in internal union affairs beyond a level that union leadership desired. The law created a bill of rights for union members, regulated internal union election procedures, established limits on the control of national officers over local unions, and began reporting and disclosure requirements. The unions were long plagued by charges of and the reality of racism, and the 1959 law diminished internal racial discrimination.

The issue covered in the average management-labor contract, which is typically quite complex and often with over 100 pages of fine print, include the scope of the bargaining unit, contract duration, strikes and lockouts, union security, management rights, grievance procedures, wages (e.g., rates, incentive systems, job classification, etc.), work rules, hours of work, discipline and discharge, paid and unpaid leave, employee benefit plans, and the role of seniority in layoffs, promotions, and transfers. Additionally, fringe benefits have grown in importance, both in contracts and as a vehicle for worker compensation.

Union responsibilities toward members extend beyond writing and negotiating a contract with management. It goes into the arena of administering the contract and of settling individual and group grievances that arise under it. The grievance procedure—usually lengthy, detailed, and complicated, and involving seven different appeals levels—has become the core of modern contracts. Unions typically employ a large number of full-time workers who move from plant to plant, intervening in the grievance process if the complaint is not settled at a lower level by the elected shop steward. The rank-and-file worker has the most contact with the shop steward and this "international" roving representative. The last appeals stage is typically adjudicated by impartial umpires chosen by both management and labor and paid in equal parts by each. These umpires do not write contracts, but rather decide application and interpretation disputes.

In carrying out contract administration and grievance adjudication, unions have free access to plants and are regarded as the counterpart to management. Although unions are a small part of the total industrial sector, the impact of union negotiations and grievance settlements has extended to much of the rest of the industrial sector. Bargaining in some industries has become almost continuous, allowing the exploration of difficult problems before the expiration of a contract.

THE RECENT LABOR MOVEMENT

With the decline of the industrial sector (the traditional base for U.S. unions) in recent years, American labor unions have fallen on hard times. Large, industrial-based unions have experienced massive membership losses, a trend exacerbated during the recession in the early 1980s. Overall, union membership as a total of the nonfarm labor force declined from 27.3 percent in 1970 to 19 percent in 1984.

Since its peak year of membership in 1942, the United Mine Workers' membership had declined 84 percent by 1985. Similar data for other big membership losers show the United Steelworkers down 45 percent from their 1975 peaks, United Auto Workers down 33 percent from 1969, the American Federation of Government Employees down 32 percent from 1972, and the Hotel Employees and Restaurant Employees also down 32 percent from 1970. The International Ladies' Garment Workers declined 26 percent from 1969, the Teamsters 20 percent from 1974, and the National Education Association 20 percent from 1976 (Pauly et. at. 1985).

Labor has had to retreat on wages and benefits at the bargaining table. While the average annual rate of wage increases negotiated by unions was 7.1 percent in 1980 asnd 7.9 percent in 1981, by 1982 that figure fell to 3.6 percent. Equivalent averages for 1983 and 1984 were 2.8 percent in both years. In 1983, wage increases of nonunion workers actually exceeded those of union workers.

Union political influence waned in the face of the Reagan administration's open hostility to labor concerns (English, "Why Unions Are"). The percent of winning candidates endorsed by the AFL-CIO fell from 71.3 percent in 1976 to 62.7 percent in 1984. Under the Reagan administration, federal agencies that regulate labor law have reversed some earlier decisions favorable to labor. In one important decision, the Reagan-appointee-dominated National Labor Relations Board ruled that an employer may relocate operations to a nonunionized facility during the term of a labor agreement, even if the move is solely designed to escape the higher labor costs of the unionized plant.

Critics of the NLRB charged that its backlog of unresolved cases was so formidable as to discourage unions from seeking redress from the agency. Labor advocates also criticized the Reagan administration for gutting federal enforcement of safety and health standards in the workplace. Conflict between federal agencies newly titled toward management over labor and labor representatives have served to further exacerbate the adversarial nature of management-labor relationships in America.

In the 1980s, management brought renewed vigor to the fight against unions and worker demands. Many companies began to hire labor law experts to help them defeat unions. The AFL-CIO estimated that over 400 firms employing over 6,000 employee-oriented labor law experts have organized at least one union-decertification drive.

By the mid–1980s, employers in major industries were also undertaking a new approach to labor costs by engaging in individual head-to-head contract negotiations with unions (English, ''Why Firms,'' 1984). Companies in trucking, steel, coal, and other industries were electing to negotiate with unions alone, rather than banding together with competing firms in the same industry to achieve the best overall deal with nationwide unions. Such independent bargaining represented a sharp break with the traditional industry-wide united front management had sought to build against unions.

Part of the impetus for this managerial shift in negotiating tactics has been increased global competition in the area of labor costs. When coordinated bargaining was pursued, it resulted in one wage rate for the entire industry, which meant that wages were removed as an element of intercompany economic competition, and no one company had an advantage over any other domestic company in that area. With increased global competition in many sectors of industry, firms are feeling greater pressure to compete both internationally and domestically on wages and have resorted to individual company negotiations to do so. Some companies have concluded that, with declining union membership and increased pressure on labor from plant closings and other symptoms of global competition, they obtain more favorable agreements through the individual strategy.

One consequence of the weakened condition of labor has been the development of a two-tiered wage system, where contracts offering higher wages for workers with greater tenure are honored by management, but newer workers are hired for the same work at lower rates. Two-tier contracts generally specify that workers hired after a certain date will be paid less than employees on the job when the contract is approved. In essence, employed workers, facing pay cuts or layoffs, accept concessions in the pay or benefits of those not yet hired. Managers felt that two-tier plans were easier to sell to unions than other types of concessions.

The trend toward two-tiered contracts has been labeled ''significant'' by proponents, but has been criticized as dividing union leadership from members, damaging productivity (among those paid less for the same work), and permanently lowering the wage structure of many industries (Seaberry 1985). Starting salaries for newly employed workers under this system have averaged about 15 percent less than the previous starting salaries for the same group of workers. A Wharton School report estimated in 1985 that the two-tier system could reduce the annual growth rate of aggregate nonfarm wages betweeen 0.2 and 0.3 percent across five years, with double the impact when fringe benefits and other indirect effects are factored in (Seaberry 1985).

In an adversarial management-labor climate, perhaps nothing demonstrated the weakened condition of labor more than the decline of both the use and success of the strike as the ultimate labor weapon. Work stoppages involving 1,000 or more workers peaked in 1974 at 424. By 1983, the annual number of those work stoppages had dropped to 81. Further, several highly publicized strikes resulted in defeats for labor, including the Professional Air Traffic Controllers' Organization (PATCO) strike of air traffic controllers against the federal government, and the 1987 National Football League players' strike against NFL management. In the PATCO strike, all employees on strike were fired by President Reagan, who ordered the crippled air traffic control system to be run by supervisory and nonstriking personnel. In the case of the players' strike, management hired replacements, all to eager to play, and refused to grant any concessions to the strikers.

Foremost on organized labor's long-term agenda is rebuilding membership, primarily by appealing to previously unorganized segments of the labor force, such as white-collar workers and workers in fields dominated by women. According to an AFL-CIO study, the percentage of white-collar workers who belonged to labor unions doubled between 1970, when 5 million white-collar workers made up 21.8 percent of total union membership, and 1980, when 8.5 million white-collar workers constituted 37.8 percent of total union membership. Over half of these new members were technical and professional employees. As more doctors work for Health Maintenance Organizations and more lawyers work for corporations, even these professions may eventually prove amenable to organizing for collective strength.

The AFL-CIO has also placed renewed emphasis on fields in which women have traditionally been the primary worker. Of those fields, education and teaching have proved to be slightly more amenable to labor organizing than either nursing or secretarial and office work. Progress in all fields has been slow.

In the 1980s, with deregulation of the trucking industry and a growth of independent haulers, Teamsters membership in this area fell. The Teamsters countered this decline in trucking by increasing organizing efforts in other industries, including airlines, government, and health care. By the mid–1980s, the Teamsters were able to restore their membership to 1.9 million and in 1987 rejoined the AFL-CIO, giving that parent organization a much-needed boost in membership, bargaining clout, and political influence. The American Federation of State, County, and Municipal Employees also increased its organizing efforts and experienced some decline during the 1980s, which most likely is a smaller decline than would otherwise have occurred. The 1975 peak figure for organized government workers was 5.8 million in 1975. That number had declined to 5.5 million by 1982. To attract new members, unions may offer increased services in the future, including legal advice and personal counseling, low-cost auto and health insurance, day care centers, literacy training, bargain home loans, and recreation facilities.

Despite these holding actions, however, the long-term prospects for unions, especially in the face of the declining economy of the last half of the 1980s, remained poor. Some sectors have proved resistant to organizing efforts. In 1983, the American Banker's Association reported that only 28 of 14,500 U.S. banks had been organized. High-tech areas, such as California's Silicon Valley, also proved highly resistant to union organizing. The share of representation elections won by unions declined from 55.2 percent in 1970 to 43.7 percent in 1982. Textile companies have also been widely known for vigorous—and labor advocates charge also virulent—efforts to break organizing drives within the U.S. textile industry.

Union corruption is one area in which Reagan administration regulation has remained strong. Labor union leaders charged that administration investigations into wrongdoing bordered on harassment, while administration officials countered that there was nothing political about their probes, contending that labor racketeering remains a serious problem. Regardless of the current reality, even labor advocates acknowledge that their image has been hurt over the years by reports of high-level corruption, gangland-style killings, abuse of pension funds, payroll padding, bribes, and extortions.

Even investigators have admitted that much of the stereotype of unions as a haven for criminals and Mafioso is undeserved (English "Why Unions Are Running Scared" 1984). According to Raymond Maria, the Reagan administration's deputy inspector general in the Labor Department supervising the Office of Organized Crime and Racketeering, the problem is not a corrupt labor movement, but a relatively small, very influential group of criminals who undermine the goals and objectives of legitimate labor organizations.

Most corruption cases have been concentrated in a few unions. Of the 379 indictments obtained by the Office of Organized Crime and Racketeering between 1978 and 1984, only 145 were of union officials, and over half of the indicted union officials were from the Teamsters, which has long been plagued by much more corruption than other labor unions.

The 400,000-member Hotel Employees and Restaurant Employees International Union has also been subjected to criminal probes in recent years, leading the Senate Permanent Subcommittee on Investigations to conclude that the union is under "the substantial influence" of organized crime. Senate investigators found that the union made loans to borrowers with alleged mob conections and that the union president consorted with mobsters. The union responded that the investigation was biased, and no charges of wrongdoing against the president were ever substantiated.

Most labor leaders, especially in the more conservative AFL-CIO, have favored cleaning up corruption and mob connections. In recent years, investigators have changed targets as the nature of corruption has shifted from strong-arm techniques to complex embezzlement schemes and more sophisticated misappropriation of funds. Especially targeted is suspected corruption in employee benefit plans, attractive because of their vast accumulation of assets. While only 37 percent of the racketeering office's probes were directed toward prosecutions involving employee-benefit schemes when the office was created in 1978, over 62 percent of its prosecutorial efforts were in that area by the mid–1980s.

Other criticisms of unions besides corruption are that they have unnecessarily hamstrung management and reduced productivity by insisting on rigid allocation of work and detailed work rules. Unions have fought for job security, even for jobs made obsolescent by technological advances, and in some instances, have resisted the adoption of technological innovations out of fear of job displacement. Unions have also resisted plant closings. At their best, however, they have significantly improved the working conditions and wages of average workers, have prevented management from running roughshod over workers' rights, and have helped to elevate blue-collar workers of the past into the middle class.

Hovering on the horizon is yet another challenge for organized labor: the growing practice of employee leasing. Under this system, leasing companies hire employees who are then leased under contract to private firms, mostly small businesses with fewer than 25 employees. By 1984, as many as 40 companies with a total of more than 25,000 employees were providing leased workers to private firms. Leasing companies charge subscribing firms a fee on top of the total cost of wages, benefits, pensions, and taxes for the employees each subscriber leases.

Advocates of employee leasing contend that fringe benefits for workers are better because leasing companies can use economies of scale and larger numbers to negotiate lower rates for benefits such as health and life insurance. Often-leased employees have attractive pension plans, whereas nonleased employees in the old work setting did not. Such new arrangements diminish the incentives of workers for joining unions.

Despite the current problems of organized labor, it is not likely to disappear from the economic scene. What will the typical U.S. labor union look like as the country moves into the 1990s and the twenty-first century beyond that? While no one knows for sure, experts speculate that those unions which survive will adopt a cooperative rather than a confrontational style.

The union of the future will probably be more flexible on issues of wages and work rules as long as management guarantees jobs and increases cooperativeness. Opposition to new technologies may be dropped in exchange for guarantees of new jobs generated by those new technologies. Nobody, not even professionals, will be regarded as immune to unionization. Finally, as the target groups of unions become more female and minority based, the complexion and sex of union leadership may change accordingly.

UNEMPLOYMENT AND JOB-TRAINING PROGRAMS

A labor policy designed to restore competitiveness must confront several issues. Foremost among these is unemployment. Unlike the Japanese tradition in which the top third of companies have offered lifelong commitment to employees, the adversarial relationship between management and labor in the United States has fostered no such commitment.

Workers in the United States are hired when doing so benefits the firm's bottom line. They are laid off when retaining them is deteriorating the bottom line. Unemployment in America is viewed as the problem of the worker, not the firm. While during economic downturns a few of the larger and more advanced companies attempt to keep workers on the payroll in nontraditional and even make-work positions, that type of commitment to employees is rare.

One consequence of the attitude that unemployment is the employee's problem, is that unions have become concerned about job security and seniority. A second consequence is that, shirked by private firms, responsibility for reducing unemployment and for assisting and retraining unemployed workers has fallen onto the public sector.

Economists distinguish several different types of unemployment by their source and solution. Aggregate demand or Keynesian unemployment occurs when there is too little demand to stimulate enough buying to raise production to full employment. In this case, unemployment is dispersed across different sectors of the economy.

The Keynesian solution was to increase demand by either increasing government spending or cutting taxes, or both. Sometimes called "cyclical unemployment," since unemployment from lack of adequate aggregate demand is tied to the business cycle, one solution has been the funding of countercycle public service employment programs. Conservatives have typically favored tax concessions to industry to provide incentives for expanding the number of jobs and increasing employment as an alternative to public service employment programs.

Frictional unemployment occurs when workers leave one job and are temporarily unemployed before securing another. Economists are rarely concerned with ordinary frictional unemployment and regard it as a necessity of labor mobility, which keeps the employment market running efficiently. Similarly, seasonal unemployment, while regrettable, is not regarded as a major cause for alarm and is viewed as unavoidable as long as some jobs, such as construction and forestry, are tied to seasonal weather patterns.

Structural unemployment, however, has long concerned policy makers. It occurs among disadvantaged workers who lack sufficient skills and training to compete successfully in the modern labor market. Sometimes the structurally unemployed are laid off industry-specific skilled or semiskilled jobs and are not geographically mobile to areas where jobs are more plentiful. Nor are their old skills readily applied to new jobs. Job-training and employment programs are the standard solution to structural unemployment.

The role of the federal government in employment and training programs expanded greatly during the twentieth century, peaking in the two decades between 1960 and 1980. Before 1960, federal action had been limited to establishing and maintaining a network of land grant colleges, providing matching grants for state vocational training programs, providing loans for post-secondary education, and developing temporary public employment programs during the Great Depression (Johnston 1984). In addition to the Federal-State Employment Security System established by the 1935 Wagner Act, legacies of this pre–1960 involvement include the 1935 Social Security Act, the creation in 1937 of the Bureau of Apprenticeship and Training in the U.S. Department of Labor, and the 1946 Full Employment Act expressing support for fiscal policy directed toward the generation of full employment.

Under the Kennedy and Johnson administrations, federal efforts to reduce unemployment through employment and training programs were greatly increased. The 1961 Area Redevelopment Act that introduced federally financed skill training for unemployed workers in distressed areas was short-lived. The 1962 Manpower Development and Training Act and the 1964 Economic Opportunity Act expanded the concepts of direct federal employment and training for the unemployed. A major operating division of the Office of Economic Opportunity was the Job Corps, conceived by OEO director Sargent Shriver, to be not merely a vocational training program, but an educational venture. Up to 100,000 trainees between the ages of 16 and 21 entered the program, and many disadvantaged young men and women graduated to secure steady jobs. Problems of mismanagement plagued the program, which soon fell into disfavor with Congress and then faded away under the Nixon administration. However, the largest federal employment programs occurred during the 1970s.

In 1971, the Emergency Employment Act authorized the first large-scale direct federal employment initiative since the 1930s and cost $2.25 billion over two years. In 1973, the Comprehensive Employment and Training Act (CETA) was passed with bipartisan support. Its purpose was to consolidate more than the dozen separate employment and training programs that had developed in the 1960s into one, and to turn administrative control over to elected state and local officials.

The primary goal of CETA was to provide skill training and other employment-related services to unemployed low-income persons. However, the persistence of cyclical unemployment led to the inclusion of two public service employment programs as well. From 1974, when CETA took effect, to 1979, outlays for all federal employment and training programs tripled to $14.5 billion. Over $9.4 billion of the 1979 expenditures were for CETA, and of those, $5.0 billion resulted from the two public service employment programs (PSEs). In 1978, the highly criticized PSEs were reoriented toward the economically disadvantaged.

In the 1980s, federal outlays for training, employment, and related services stabilized at around $10 billion. In 1982, Congress created the Job Training Partnership Act (JTPA) to replace the highly criticized CETA program. In keeping with the Reagan philosophy to reduce the role of government, public service employment was specifically prohibited under the act. Further, administrative responsibility for the act was assigned to both elected officials and Private Industry Councils (PICs) representing private businesses. Despite these efforts, unemployment in the United States remained stubbornly stuck above 6 percent for most of the 1980s.

The Left and the Right of the political spectrum have clashed not only over the importance of unemployment on the national agenda, but also over the appropriate solution. The Left regards unemployment as a major issue and considers one of several appropriate solutions to be public service employment programs in which the government becomes the employer of last resort. The Right regards unemployment as less important than inflation and maintaining low interest rates, and favors tax incentives as a method of addressing the solution. The concept of "enterprise zones" in depressed urban areas mixes limited public subsidies with substantial tax incentives for businesses providing jobs to the disadvantaged within those areas.

The Right charges that countercyclical public employment programs occur too late, after a recovery has already begun, so that the new public monies are likely to fuel inflation. The Left responds that public service programs should be designed to fight structural unemployment that is not countercyclical, as well as addressing countercyclical unemployment. Further, the Left charges that tax incentives for job creation in the private sector benefit business owners and managers as much as or more than workers, and have not proved to be effective. Even so, federal funds for employment and training remain relatively modest, constituting less than 10 percent of all funds spent for that purpose.

One approach to improving labor market efficiency, reducing frictional unemployment and possibly some fraction of structural unemployment, is to increase job search assistance through the development of a National Job Bank, to match jobs and prospective employees nationwide. Job search assistance could also include vocational counseling, aptitude testing, instruction in proper job search and interviewing techniques, area-market labor analysis, dissemination of labor market information, job development, employer services (e.g., job definition, screening, and recruitment), relocation of unemployed workers, and other placement services.

Since the 1930s, the Employment Service, renamed the Job Service, has been the primary conduit for government support in job search. The Job Service currently operates through affiliated state agencies and about 2,600 local offices nationwide. Any unemployed person legally qualified to work in the United States is entitled to Job Service assistance without charge. However, some groups have been targeted as deserving special attention and assistance, including veterans (who receive first preference in all referrals by law), the poor, welfare and food recipients, the young, the old, minorities, dislocated workers, and migrant and seasonal farmworkers. During the 1960s, the Job Service was criticized by the unemployed as being too oriented toward employers.

Business also criticized the Job Service for focusing on placement for the poor and disadvantaged at the expense of meeting the needs of private employers. Many employers also resented the inspection of migratory housing and other compliance with regulations that the Job Service was mandated to inspect. Consequently, in the early 1980s, the number of employers participating in the Job Service declined, as did the number of individuals seeking Job Service assistance.

The Job Service, while providing needed job placement services, remains regional in focus and falls short of the scope and potential of the proposed National Job Bank (NJB), which could facilitate labor mobility across regions of the country, increase labor market efficiency, and reduce unemployment. All unemployed persons could be required to register with the NJB to be eligible to receive unemployment benefits. If the negative income tax approach were adopted, all recipients of government redistributive payments would register. The more effective approach to ensure employer participation is to require all employers above a minimum size to register. A softer approach, but more costly and less effective, is to provide tax incentives to induce employer participation. The NJB could keep records on the unemployed and on current jobs available. A related data base would provide information on relocation. In a more advanced form, the NJB could employ videotaping, initially of the job seekers, but eventually of supervisors, to minimize travel costs and improve decision efficiency.

Currently, unemployment benefits are a jointly financed federal-state program, underpinned by an employer payroll tax. Benefits are based, in part, on the wages of the currently unemployed worker during the most recent quarter of employment. Unemployed workers must report periodically to their local unemployment offices to secure and maintain eligibility for the allowable 26 weeks. Areas with high rates of unemployment in the past have been eligible for federally financed extended benefits beyond the normal benefit period.

Several criticisms have been levied at the current system of unemployment benefits. Workers who exhaust their benefits but have not found work often become discouraged and drop out of the unemployment statistics (which are collected from local unemployment offices), understanding the true extent of unemployment in the United States.

Second, the unemployment system is not linked to the welfare system. Hence, discouraged but still unemployed or underemployed workers not eligible for benefits because they did not work in covered jobs or the sufficient amount of time within a quarter, receive no benefits. This contrasts with many other Western industrialized democracies where all unemployed persons are eligible for benefits until they find work. A comprehensive income-based transfer program integrating welfare and unemployment transfers with the tax system discussed in Chapter 6 would address many of the current gaps in coverage.

Third, employers criticize the program for not tying the receipt of unemployment benefits to the retraining of the unemployed. Addressing this by providing retraining for the substantial number of now structurally unemployed workers in the U.S. economy would require either large increases in public monies for public-sector retraining efforts or legislation requiring private-sector retraining of workers to be laid off. A combination of these two approaches would hold down public outlays and allow public-sector programs to concentrate on the long-term unemployed and the unemployed who have never worked.

PENSIONS AND SOCIAL SECURITY

Experts estimate that by the year 2030, one-fifth of the population may be 65 and older, resulting in fewer workers relative to the number of retirees. As Americans live longer, they have become increasingly concerned about income security in their old age. The 1935 Social Security Act established the Old Age, Survivors, and Disability Insurance Program in the United States. Most, but not all, American workers receive Social Security benefits. In 1981, out of 118.2 million total workers, 104.6 million, or 88.5 percent, were covered by Social Security (Myers 1985). In 1986, workers reaching the age of 62 must have 35 quarters of coverage in order to be eligible. In 1991, the required minimum work in a covered position will be 40 quarters, or ten years.

Initially sold to the American people as an annuity-based pension program, Social Security has changed immensely in the intervening years. Today it encompasses both welfare and pension functions, performing neither adequately, critics would charge. If Social Security were truly a pension plan, it would operate on the principle of funded liability, in which the contributions of current workers are set aside and invested for the subsequent payment of their benefits. Today, current workers fund current beneficiaries, creating a potential financial crisis as the ratio of workers to beneficiaries continues to decline. A pension-like system would also link benefits with contributions more closely than that which is present in the current system.

Nor is Social Security an adequate welfare system based on need. While it has welfare components, such as payments to survivors of Social Security beneficiaries and disability payments, need is not the only or even primary consideration in benefit levels. Those with substantial incomes from investments and other sources receive payments, even though they are not needy. The affluent often receive the largest payments.

Never intended to become the primary retirement income for citizens, Social Security has come to fill that role for large segments of the currently retired, partially because they lacked an adequate private pension plan and partially because U.S. savings for all functions, including retirement, are so low. The heavy dependence upon Social Security, plus the large number of recipients has made the program almost invulnerable politically. While other programs, for instance, were subject to Gramm-Rudman-Hollings deficit-reduction cuts, Social

Security has been immune. Even Reagan's popularity has not been sufficient to reduce Social Security cost-of-living adjustments (COLAs).

Nor is the system of private pensions adequate to guarantee income security for the retired. Currently a patchwork of private pensions exist. Pension fraud and abuse led to the 1974 Employment Retirement Income Security Act (ERISA), which attempted to regulate and protect private pensions. The act established new requirements in pension administration and funding for private plans, excluding church or church-related plans, as well as public employee plans. ERISA created a Pension Benefit Guaranty Corporation within the Labor Department to protect plan participants through insurance in the event of plan termination. In termination cases, ERISA required full vesting of all accrued benefits (Greenough and King 1976).

As a result of a political compromise, ERISA sets three alternative minimum vesting standards. The first provides for full vesting of all accrued benefits after ten years of recognized service, regardless of the participant's age. The second (the five- to 15-year standards) employs progressive vesting. At least 25 percent of a participant's accrued benefits must be recognized after five years of service, and another 5 percent a year during years six to ten of service, and 10 percent a year during years ten to 15 of service, irrespective of the participant's age. The third standard uses a more complicated point system (McGill 1975). Prior to ERISA, company pension plans often specified that employees could not participate and accrue benefits until reaching some minimum age, typically 30 or 35 years.

Despite ERISA protections, many companies during the boom growth years of the bull market between 1982 and 1987 decided to terminate their pension plans, leaving their workers with no coverage. Part of the reason were the extraordinary returns being earned on pension investments in the market during that time, leaving funds with large surpluses, even after all pension liabilities were funded. While the pension fund was operative, management could not tamper with the surplus. By terminating the pension plan, however, management could gain access to the surpluses, prompting many pension plan terminations.

In recent years 401(k) plans have gained in popularity. Employers have pushed the plans as a way to curb pension costs by encouraging employees to assume a greater role in providing for retirement. In 1985, about 14 million workers used the plans, which allowed pretax dollars to be set aside for retirement purposes (Wiener 1985). Additionally, earnings are tax free, although retirement benefits are taxed. Early withdrawals are limited to hardship cases and are taxed.

The patchwork of pension benefits allows some people to fall through the cracks. It does not promote commitment on the part of employers who can terminate employee pension plans to raid cash surpluses, nor mobility on the part of workers who may be bound to a company after a certain number of years in order to receive pension benefits. An approach to address this is to separate the pension-like and welfare functions of Social Security into two separate national systems.

The welfare component of Social Security would become integrated with a needs-based negative income tax approach to income distribution. The needy elderly and survivors of previous Social Security beneficiaries would be treated in the same fashion as the needy in any other age group. A second system would be the development of a mandatory National Pension System (NPS), to be run on principles of sound pension management, including the annuity concept and funding liabilities from contributions of recipients rather than current contributors.

The National Pension System would not preclude employees from participating in additional private pension plans or making private investments toward retirement. However, that type of plan would allow greater labor mobility and would more closely link benefits to contributions. Persons with irregular unemployment histories of low lifetime earnings, who generate an inadequate flow of retirement income, would receive supplemental government assistance through the negative income tax approach. Finally, the National Pension Plan could invest some of its funds in U.S. Treasury securities, partially easing the increasingly heavy reliance of the Treasury on foreign investment to finance the national debt.

9

COMPETITION AND TECHNOLOGY

TRENDS IN TECHNOLOGY DEVELOPMENT

Technology represents the application of science to production. It depends on both the generation of new scientific knowledge and the development of new and better ways of manufacturing the products that incorporate those discoveries. More than anything else, it is the phenomenon by which humankind improves its material and total well-being. Technology is also the battleground on which the trade wars of advanced industrial nations will be won or lost.

Several trends have affected the development of technology in the twentieth century. Throughout much of the century, the driving force behind the evolution of technology has been increasing efficiency gains from economies of scale, derived both from expanding the scale of production and the scope of markets. However, some experts feel that we have now reached the limits of economies of scale (Brooks 1981; Reich 1983; Toffler 1980).

No recent gains have been realized from expanding the size of electric-generating plants, for instance, while evidence mounts that the reliability of large plants may be less than that of smaller plants. Pollution control costs less as plant size increases, but pollution becomes more visible and subject to attack. Supertankers have become so large that they can enter fewer and fewer ports. Furthermore, many environmental problems are related to the scale on which new technologies are applied, rather than on the technologies themselves (Brooks 1981, p. 43).

Do modern technologies have a centralizing standardizing impact, creating boring repetition and lack of choice in the extreme form, or do they have a decentralizing impact, creating greater heterogeneity and individual choice? Arguments can be made for both centralizing and decentralizing aspects of modern technology since, at times, it does both. The longer-run impact on daily living has been the decentralizing trend. Automobiles, television, personal computers, modern electronics, cable television, and many other technological advances allow greater individual choice.

Yet standardization is occurring in modern technology on a national scale, as well as on a worldwide scale. Standardization not only allows centralization and economies of scale in production, but it also facilitates the development of worldwide markets, allowing consumers to select from both domestic goods and technologically comparable imports when making purchasing decisions.

Over the past 100 years, technology development has saved labor and time rather than materials and resources, making labor more productive. Concerns over conservation of resources in the future and long-run limits to growth may slow down this trend by rechanneling efforts into developments that save resources rather than labor.

Products have become more complex, making it more difficult for average consumers to judge their performance and qualities. In a world of simpler products, consumers were expected to look out for themselves in selecting purchases that matched their expectations and performed as stated. In the modern world of increased product complexity, consumer protection laws, regulations, and consumer groups all help buyers diminish the mismatch between increasingly sophisticated technological products and consumers' abilities to effectively judge them.

High technology also has a dark side, including increased pollution, new man-made hazards, and long-term deleterious health effects from exposure to harmful substances. Interests within the United States have increasingly argued for reconciling the benefits of technological development with the costs, achieving a balance between the two. Concern over the side effects of technology has shaped, if not slowed, the course of growth.

NEW TECHNOLOGIES

In recent years, a technology gap has been widening between the United States and some of its major competitors, reflected by declines in both productivity growth and deteriorating balances of trade. Between 1947 and 1973, services experienced average annual productivity increases of 2.4 percent, while manufacturing averaged 2.9 percent. Between 1973 and 1981, however, the average annual productivity gains for services fell to 0.5 percent, and manufacturing productivity dropped to 1.3 percent. Manufacturing experienced a rebound between 1981 and 1985, growing at more than 4 percent annually, but services, the larger sector of the economy, lagged at 0.7 percent. Poor productivity in services dragged overall U.S. productivity for the 1980s to an annual average of 1.4 percent, a considerably slower growth rate than that during the 1970s and much slower than productivity growth in Japan, Germany, and other major economic competitors.

Cohen and Zysman (1987) have argued against letting the manufacturing sector slide further into decline, contending that ''manufacturing matters'' in achieving economic prosperity. These authors contend that the United States cannot hope to pay for imports by selling services abroad, mostly because it needs too many goods relative to the services it can export. Furthermore, the service sector cannot be effectively separated from the manufacturing sector it was designed to serve. If it does, the manufacturing sector will develop its own capacity to handle needed services.

Nor has America proved competitive in the revolution in manufacturing generated by programmable automation. Japanese plants make greater use of robotics than do U.S. plants. The U.S. share of the world semiconductor market dropped from 57 percent in 1982 to 51 percent in 1985, while the Japanese share gained from 33 percent to 39 percent during that same time frame (Dworkin et al. 1985). By 1987, a Defense Department study produced for the Defense Science Board was recommending that the United States pump hundreds of millions of dollars more into semiconductor research, development, and manufacturing.

Several factors have contributed to slower productivity growth in the United States. The first is a lower growth in the United States of investment in new industrial plant and equipment than in other industrial countries since the 1950s. While of less significance during the 1960s, lower rates of investment in new industrial plants and equipment were particularly important in the 1950s and 1970s. Past U.S. reliance on investment tax credits and the manipulation of capital depreciation allowances have proved inadequate in maintaining competitive productivity levels.

The United States has also lagged behind in relevant research and development (R & D) efforts. Previous analyses have inflated U.S. R & D efforts in several ways. Most of the comparisons of various nations' R & D efforts include expenditures for defense and space, producing a huge bias toward the United States, which is high in these areas relative to civilian R & D. Despite the ''trickle-across'' theory that some defense technologies can be converted to civilian uses, civilian spin-offs have been greatly exaggerated. Defense R & D efforts rarely lead directly to the new technologies suitable for widespread consumption domestically or for exporting.

Research and development expenditures have typically been based on local currencies converted into U.S. dollars by official exchange rates, which, until the fall of the dollar, also produced a bias in U.S. favor. Due to differences in educational systems, even comparisons of qualified scientists and engineers have favored the United States. Baccalaureate holders in the United States are often called engineers, while persons with the equivalent number of years of training elsewhere are called technicians.

CREATING AND PRODUCING NEW TECHNOLOGIES

An entire complex of institutions affects the pace of technological development and the quality of new technology generated, including companies, universities, research institutes, and local, state, and federal governments. In the past, members of government and industry have regarded each other warily and often with hostility. Extremely simplified, the hostile view of industry from one government vantage point was that private businesses had little interest in public concerns and were strictly motivated by money to the point of avarice, ignoring the social costs of their actions. The equally simplified hostile view that business held of government was that it was populated by unproductive paper-pushing bureaucrats concerned with generating needless regulations and maintaining their own power base.

Such adversarial views do not facilitate cooperative ventures to enhance technological development. Yet total innovation is the sum of change in each of the institutions affecting technological development. Increased innovation is possible within each and may occur in a variety of ways. Companies within an industry may coalesce to promote innovation from within. One industry may invade another to apply new technologies developed in the invading industry. Industries, universities, and research institutes may form consortia to promote regional economic development through technology growth (Schon 1981).

Particularly important is the relationship of industry to the federal government. In many other industrialized nations, government has assumed the responsibility of and leadership in introducing new technologies into industry, acting like a partner instead of an adversary. These countries often have national departments of science and technology charged with the responsibility of facilitating joint government-industry collaboration, for example, Britain's Ministry of Technology, as well as similar government institutes in Holland and Germany.

A great deal of the technical innovation in these and other countries is government financed and encouraged. Concomitantly, the central governments also provide a leading role in encouraging exports, dealing with import issues, providing risk capital, developing industrial standards and codes, and testing and certifying innovations.

By contrast, adherence to free-enterprise principles in the United States makes businesses reluctant to embrace government as a partner. A strong belief exists in the United States that all technical innovation should be controlled by and benefit the private sector. Government intervention and initiative is viewed as unwelcome and intrusive. Nonetheless, the federal government still provides many functions for businesses related to technology development and production.

Among these government activities beneficial to business are the collecting and publishing of statistics on industry, such as the GNP and industry-specific statistics; controlling tariffs and quota regulations to protect U.S. businesses from certain forms of foreign competition; and using fiscal and monetary policy to facilitate economic growth and prevent recessions. The federal government also subsidizes various industries, such as the aircraft and maritime industries. A study sponsored by the Executive Office of the President in the late 1970s identified several additional federal activities to stimulate industrial innovation. Increasing the amount of and enhancing the transfer of technical information, improving the patent system, clarifying antitrust policy, improving federal procurement, and upgrading federal regulator systems were among the federal activities the report advocated (Mercer and Philips 1981).

Major technical innovations that require great capital investment in the public interest, such as weapons systems, technology for space exploration, peaceful uses of atomic energy, desalinization of water, and the supersonic transport, are government financed and sponsored. This type of federal involvement sponsoring large-scale capital-intensive projects has a long history, including federal granting of land rights to facilitate the westward expansion of railroads; direct federal support for new transportation and communication systems, ranging from the telegraph to new satellites; and federal support for the development and first models of new technologies such as aircraft, computers, electronics, atomic energy, numerically controlled machine tools, and operations research methods. Despite this, technology development in the United States over the past 50 years has depended more upon interactions among industries than on interactions between industries and the federal government (Schon 1981, p. 152).

Schon argues that industry is highly sensitive to public opinion, so that companies stall the introduction of new equipment that changes labor input until they can forsee a period of growth that will either enable them to move displaced workers elsewhere or facilitate their movement to jobs with other companies. Yet currently, despite concern over the impact of plant closings on the communities in which they are located, the federal government has no systematic plan for coping with technological dislocations.

To date, the federal government has mostly responded to the problems of industries such as railways, shipping, agriculture, and textiles through depressed area programs that concentrate on public works and loans to local corporations. Unemployment insurance and welfare have been the primary government response to assist displaced workers. Schon finds these inadequate for the future, however, and sees the development of a labor mobility policy, with an effective job information system, support for workers moving to new jobs, and improved training and retraining programs as essential to technological development. Firms threatened by new technology should be encouraged to diversify into more profitable areas, and assistance to depressed areas should be targeted to the development of new industry based on new technology.

Throughout much of the twentieth century, the attitude has prevailed that technological development is solely the result of market forces driving firms into innovation through the desire for higher profits. Until World War II, government was a reluctant patron of science and technology development, restricting its support of scientific development to its own laboratories. The massive weapons programs of World War II resulted in an unprecedented amount of federal monies available for research and created an awareness among scientists of the potential that large amounts of federal support could provide.

Despite this early reluctance of government to support scientific and technological development, most federal policies affect innovation indirectly, if not directly. Antitrust, regulatory, patent, and economic policy may all affect innovation positively or negatively. Policies may have uneven impacts, enhancing innovation in one industry and inhibiting it in another. For example, antitrust policy may prevent the concentration necessary for technological innovation in industries in which high capital investment is necessary for the development, dissemination, and production of new technologies. Yet the same policy may stimulate innovation by allowing the continuing formation of new firms based on new technologies in industries in which less capital is required.

More directly, an elaborate system of federal research funding has emerged, with most of the monies allocated through project grants and contracts to universities and industrial firms. The largest stream of research monies continues to focus on issues of national security and defense. Federal research monies remain only a part of the total impact of government on science and technology development.

Despite the difficulty in identifying and directing this total governmental impact, the role that innovation plays in international economic competition and the unintentional ubiquitous impact of government policies both create an incentive for making the impact intentional and positive. Critics contend that the absence of a strong U.S. policy to nurture and promote new technologies does not imply that the nation has no industrial policy. Rather, it has an ad hoc one, built by responding to crises and oriented toward propping up old and declining industries through tax incentives and other subsidies. An inadvertent policy oriented toward "sunset" industries, rather than an aggressive overt one oriented toward "sunrise" industries, may be a luxury that the United States can no longer afford.

THE EXECUTIVE BRANCH AND TECHNOLOGY POLICY

The American Association for the Advancement of Science (AASA) has argued that the federal government's approach to research and development has been more tactical than strategic, placing the greatest emphasis upon tactical, short-run scientific and technical responses to crises (1975). Financing R & D has been perceived as discretionary spending rather than as an investment crucial to achieving national goals. The National Science Foundation, which has emphasized long-term research, remains the exception to this general rule.

The AASA envisioned the federal executive branch as performing three staff support roles, including a science and technology policy advice role, an R & D management and coordination role, and a scientific and engineering advocacy role. The AASA further concluded that the first two roles were best performed within the Executive Office of the President, while the third, the advocacy role, should be more broadly disseminated and carried out primarily, but not exclusively, by the National Science Foundation (NSF), the National Academy of Sciences, the National Academy of Engineering, and the National Institute of Health.

The first, the policy advice role, should include both short-run and strategic planning. Part of the duties of a science and technology policy advisory staff should be to establish working relationships between the Office of Management and Budget (OMB), the Domestic Council, the National Security Council, the Council on Environmental Quality, and operating departments and agencies on matters directly affecting scientific development.

The R & D role of a White-House-based advisory staff would be to fill a gap created by the poor functioning of interagency committees that are designed to achieve coordination but sometimes reflect a collection of agency-based parochial interests. The OMB is primarily concerned with issues of program content, total costs, and cost effectiveness. Partially in response to calls for greater coordination, the Office of Science and Technology (OST) was created within the Executive Office of the President by a reorganization plan in 1962. The director of OST has statutorily defined duties, and therefore is perceived to be more than a presidential advisor. The director is partially relieved of the confidence that would surround a strictly advisory role. The OST director has been called upon to provide frequent testimony to Congress. The OST has subsequently been replaced by the Office of Science and Technology Policy (OSTP).

The AASA does not feel, however, that the OST has adequately met the need for R & D coordination within the executive branch. The AASA continues to push for a larger executive role in scientific management and coordination. Roback (1981) and others have argued for a Department of Science and Technology to meet this need. Not only would that sort of department provide greater policy coordination within the executive branch, it would also force a reorganization of committees and committee assignments within Congress to generate greater coordination there as well. Currently, special committees and subcommittees within Congress that are concerned with science and technology examine cross-cutting issues, but each has its own jurisdictional outlook, work schedules, staffing arrangements, and methods of conducting legislative business. Suggestions to establish a joint committee on research policy along the lines of the Joint Committee on Atomic Energy have not been implemented. They should be if Congress is to play anything but a reactive role in the future.

As part of an expanded presidential role in R & D management and coordination, AASA has called for a new major presidential report to be prepared annually on science, technology, and national policy, accompanied by a major address to Congress. Potentially having the status of a State of the Union message or Budget Message, that type of report would assess the U.S. scientific and technological capabilities. It would identify gaps in current capabilities and provide guidelines for directing scientific research to scientific and engineering communities. Hopefully, some future president will act upon this sensible suggestion soon.

CONGRESS AND TECHNOLOGY POLICY

Policymaking in Congress affecting science and technology is complicated by both decentralization and differing committee jurisdictions between the House and the Senate. While the defense, atomic energy, space, and commerce committees dominate scientific legislation, there are a dozen committees and about 100 subcommittees in each house that have a hand in legislation impacting on science and technology.

Roback argues that given the complex committee structure and varied committee jurisdictions, a small central group of scientific advisors could not hope to respond effectively to recurring requests of legislative advice and information on scientific affairs. However, if the staff were attached to the various committees, they would not operate within a structure that would facilitate sharing information and mutual aid. If the scientific experts became full-time employees, they would be expected to assume numerous responsibilities beyond their scientific skills and could become remote from the scientific community. Yet if they were part-time consultants, they would be too removed from the legislative process to respond effectively to immediate demands and would be no better than witnesses before testimony.

In 1963, the Science Policy Research Division in the Legislative Reference Service of the Library of Congress was created to respond to congressional requests for scientific information. The division is small but fills a much-needed function by collating information, undertaking special studies, and developing background material for legislation.

The Office of Technology Assessment was established in 1972 to provide advice to Congress on matters of science and technology. Until then, Congress was much more reliant upon the executive agencies, precisely those agencies with the most to gain or lose by congressional decisions, for advice on scientific issues. The OTA is governed by a 12-member bipartisan board composed of six senators and six representatives, with an equal number from each political party. The authorizing legislation creating OTA also established a ten-member citizen advisory council, but the duties of the council were not seplled out, and it remains subsidiary to the OTA board.

Yet science policy, as is the case with most national policy, is essentially determined at the committee level. Congressional committees and their subcommittees often develop a close, nonadversarial relationship with the executive agencies they oversee and the industries they regulate, establishing ''iron triangles.'' Casper (1981) found little evidence that advice from the OTA has altered this committee operating style, nor had it diminished the impact of the cozy relationships in the iron triangle on scientific policymaking, especially in the area of military technology.

Casper also found that the choice of assessment topics was strongly linked to the interests of a few dominant board members, and that some of the most significant areas of technology development, particularly strategic weapons, were perceived to be out-of-bounds. The bulk of OTA studies was on short-run issues, and the early warning function had been ignored. With a few exceptions, OTA reports were bland and superficial. Large contracted studies with private think tanks were judged mediocre or worse. The OTA remains a promise only partially fulfilled.

COURTS AND TECHNOLOGY POLICY

Courts also enter into technology management through the role of common law in settling disputes between private parties and in monitoring the actions of executive agencies. Across the past five decades, courts have been increasingly willing to impose civil liability upon companies for the reasonably forseeable consequences of their technological choices (Tribe 1981).

Contract law served the initial basis for this extension of liability to corporations as injured buyers sought damages from sellers for defectively manufactured products under a ''breach-of-warranty'' theory. Courts gradually relaxed the requirements for an explicit warranty or contract. Buyers were allowed to collect damages from the original manufacturer, with whom they had no explicit contract. From remote buyers, this rationale has been extended to include even ''innocent bystanders'' injured accidentally by defective products.

Tort law, which governs wrongdoings other than breach of contract, includes actions not necessarily criminal but for which civil damages may be sought. Manufacturers and other technology users have been found liable in tort cases, even when there is no evidence of intentional wrongdoing or negilgence. Under more recent, looser standards of causation and more liberal standards of injury, firms have increasingly been required to compensate all individuals able to show injury due to a product defect. Tribe sees little probability for reversal of this trend in tort law intended, in part, to induce firms to seek safe technological alternatives.

Property law also affects the ease of technology development and dissemination. Individuals affected adversely by the property use of another may seek relief through the courts. Persons using property in a way that causes ''unreasonable'' injury to the interests of a threatened neighbor may be subject to an injunction ordering a stop to the offending property use. For lesser offenses, a violator may be required to at least compensate the neighbor in lieu of an injunction to cease the action altogether.

Court-developed nuisance doctrine conducive to the relatively free exploitation of property accompanied periods of most vigorous economic growth. More recently, the trend has moved toward limiting the economic exploitation of property to protect neighbor interests in advance. This expansion of neighboring interests has occurred especially in the area of environmental pollution, with courts holding that individuals demonstrably injured in some tangible way by environmental pollution are entitled to money damages. In some instances, courts have also issued orders to the offending company to develop technological solutions to the pollution. This trend emphasizes holding accountable those creating technological harm.

TECHNOLOGY AND STATE GOVERNMENT

Although the federal role in supporting research and development has grown in recent decades, the role of state government has remained relatively static. National defense, space exploration, and basic support of R & D, areas typically attracting large amounts of research dollars, have not been basic state functions. Of total national research and development expenditures for all purposes, state agency expenditures constitute not more than one-half of one percent.

State scientific advisory boards have proliferated, but their advice does not carry the high prestige associated with national sicentific advisory boards. Saplosky (1981) has concluded that states have been relatively unsuccessful in their attempts to incorporate scientific expertise into the policy-making process.

Despite the comparative inactivity of state governments in fostering science and technology, some states have proven notable exceptions in their ability to develop a climate conducive to research and high-level technology development. Among these exceptions are North Carolina with its Research Triangle; Massachusetts's high-tech beltway around Boston; the burgeoning development of technology in Austin, Texas; and Silicon Valley in California.

PATENT RIGHTS AND INTELLECTUAL PROPERTY

To protect capital invested in generating new technologies and therefore to provide a financial incentive for that investment, the U.S. government grants patents giving inventors special privileges. Patents may be granted for both products and manufacturing processes.

In earlier eras, with a patent, an inventor could hope to dominate a field, keeping others out or extracting royalties from those using the invention. Ramo (1980, p. 83), former director of TRW, Inc., notes that the value of obtaining a patent has become much more doubtful in recent years. The complexity of government patent management has increased the cost of acquiring one. Furthermore, the receipt of a patent from the U.S. government does not guarantee that it is valid, a question sometimes answered only after lengthy and expensive court battles. Part of the confusion may arise from the the the fact that an innovation is usually related to or an extension of an existing art. The government cannot afford the detailed, technically based studies necessary to ascertain without a doubt that a patent applicant is the first to have a unique scientific invention.

Others have criticized the patent system for granting monopolies to inventors, thereby retarding the rapid dissemination of new technologies among competing firms within an industry. In lieu of the existing patent system, some have proposed pooled research funding of R & D efforts by all the major firms in an industry, with the resulting inventions to be shared by all immediately. This consortium-funding approach is currently being used on a trial basis by U.S. computer manufacturers to finance research on supercomputers.

More frequently criticized is the common practice of patent piracy, or using a patented invention without informing the inventor or paying the required royalties, and lax U.S. enforcement of patent laws. The International Trade Commission (ITC) has estimated that theft of intellectual property costs U.S. manufacturers between $8 and $20 billion a year. Large losses have been logged especially in the chemical, wearing apparel, automotive parts, records and tapes, and sporting goods industries, although no industry is immune. Under section 337 of the Tariff Act, U.S. companies can seek relief from process-patent infringements before the International Trade Commission as part of its duties to prevent foreign countries from employing unfair trade practices. However, the ITC cannot impose monetary damages upon offenders, and the grievance process is typically lengthy.

The U.S. Congress has considered toughening patent laws by allowing the owner of a U.S. process patent to sue for damages and obtain an injunction in federal court if a company has imported or sold a product in the United States made through the protected patent process. Another amendment would remove the requirement that U.S. firms show that they have suffered economic damage from patent infringement. Biotechnology firms, recently granted the right to patent new life forms, in particular have been advocates of patent reform. As patent piracy has moved up on the national agenda from being a nuisance to becoming a threat to economic vitality, those reforms are long overdue.

TECHNOLOGY AND INDUSTRIAL ORGANIZATION

The expansion of technology has spawned giant, integrated, large-scale enterprises with much in common, whether they are based in the United States, Japan, or Europe. Most of the large integrated firms are located in the same industries across the advanced economies in earlier decades. In the United States, the 200 largest firms in the first half of the century were in the areas of food, chemicals, petroleum, metals, and machinery. Large hierarchical firms achieved economies of scale and were dependent upon modern transportation and communication networks. This pattern was typical of other nations.

By 1973, however, many of these large firms had diversified so much that they could no longer be listed in any single industry. Other changes also accompanied product diversification, including a shift in strategic resources from financial capital in the industrial society to human capital in the information society. Middle management is increasingly being whittled away in the modern corporation, as national companies become transnational ones (Naisbitt and Aburdene 1985).

Behrman (1984) differentiates these new transnational corporations (TNCs) into resource seekers, market seekers, and efficiency seekers. Resource seekers find raw materials and supplies wherever they can, often abroad in host countries. Their investments restructure the location of industrial activities and increase employment in local communities. These companies must integrate the extraction of resources from the host country with U.S. production activities.

Market seekers investing abroad produce in the host country and therefore have little integrating effect. For the host country, the new TNC production is often substituted for imports, reducing international specialization. Such companies also develop new markets within host countries. This type of TNC is most successful when national markets are distinct or highly protected.

Efficiency seekers are oriented toward serving a world market from least-cost sources anywhere in the world. Often called multinational enterprises (MEs), this type of company knows few national bounds or loyalties. Affiliates are integrated not only with the parent headquarters, but also with each other. Centralized corporate policies cover financing, pricing, technologies, R & D, finding sources of components and raw materials, sales and distribution, product design, production layout, site selection, and personnel policies. Examples of this highly integrated, centralized, efficiency-seeking TNC are IBM, Ford-Europe, Inc., and Philips. Altogether, over 400 firms could be classified as MEs.

Transnational corporations are both sought and feared by governments. They are sought for their technological dominance and feared for the same reason. They bring employment and economic growth, and yet national governments remain concerned about heavy economic and political dependence upon TNCs. Another concern is the perceived inequitable distribution of benefits resulting from TNC-based growth. Transnational corporations have been seen as first being loyal to their own financial interests and only secondarily being concerned about the host country, truly transcending nationalism. Yet no effective international government exists to regulate these corporations whose scope increasingly exceeds that of any single nation. If Galbraith (1967) is correct that the accumulation of massive power generates countervailing power, pressures for increasing international cooperation to regulate TNCs cannot be far behind.

As the twentieth century draws to a close and the twenty-first century comes ever closer, there is little doubt that the U.S. supremacy in science and technology is being threatened. As George Packard (1987) notes, "Japan is already challenging the United States with a major new drive toward creativity and leadership in advanced technology." It has announced its intention to build 19 Silicon Valleys or "technopolies" throughout the 16 prefectures of Japan. Their idea is to bring together "new, advanced-technology plants in industrial parks with universities and the needed infrastructure of airports, roads and recreational facilities" (Packard 1987).

The Japanese are increasingly assuming that they have already caught up with Western science and technology and now must forge ahead on the basis of the "creative genius" of the Japanese people and a top-to-bottom overhaul of the educational system. They expect spectacular advances and ever-widening supremacy in such fields as industrial ceramics, lasers, semiconductors, biotechnology, solar energy, robotics, super-conducters and even space exploration.

These outputs are to be used to promote consumer products for export. Given the Japanese record since 1945, there is every reason to suppose that they will make it more difficult for America to compete. The rising fears of "techno-nationalism'' and self-defeating protectionist legislation already worry American bureaucrats and politicians. To avoid this ugly collision, Packard (1987) suggests a Wiseman's Commission of four or five experienced statesmen from both countries who would have five-year renewable terms, a skilled and permanent staff, and would meet once a month to discuss issues and advise their prime minister and president. Hopefully, they would plan for a free-trade agreement between Japan and the United States along the lines of the U.S.-Canadian Agreement of October 1987 and a long-range treaty that would ensure the economic security of both countries by granting Japan guaranteed access to American raw materials, food, and oil and the United States guaranteed access to Japanese markets and leading-edge technologies. The result would be collaboration and cooperation rather than the acrimony and antagonism of prevailing relations.

The Soviet Union too has its own plans for overcoming the historic scientific and technological superiority of the West and the United States. Under the new leadership of Mikhail Gorbachev, whose twin policies of *glasnost* (openness) and *perestroika* (restructuring) promise a new freedom for Soviet scientists and a reorganization of the economy, the Soviet Union may at long last overcome its ambivalent attitude toward science and scientists. According to Gordon Smith, "On the one hand, sience has been accorded a prominent role in Soviet ideology. . . . On the other hand, scientists have often been at odds with official policies in the USSR" (Smith, 1988).

"Organizational fragmentation" had also retarded Soviet developments in science and technology in the past, as had inadequate equipment, instruments, supplies, and a poorly trained labor force working under primitive conditions. Nonetheless, the Soviets have in recent years devoted considerable resources to science and technology, but so far at least, they have not been able to catch up with American scientists in most fields. In fact, as Smith observes, "Soviet performance in engineering and other technical fields has been hampered by the practice of following the lead of Americans, Japanese and Europeans" (1988).

Gorbachev, however, has made it clear that he intends to utilize the potentiality of science and technology to improve economic performance through innovations. This emphasis on applied research will probably continue for the near future. It will no doubt improve the performance of the faltering Soviet economy, but may affect long-run development by downgrading basic research. Yet, according to Loren R. Graham (1987), Soviet science has come a long way from Stalin's time and the heyday of T. D. Lysenko. At least the theories of dialectical materialism are discussed openly and on a high level. This new intellectual freedom cannot but help stimulate thought and ideas in those areas of Soviet science such as genetics, chemistry, quantum mechanics, relativity physics, and psychology.

Gorbachev, if he can remain in power, not only envisions a domestic restructuring of the economy, but also the extention of *perestroika* to the world arena. Security must become multilateral, and capitalism and socialism will have to exist "within a framework of peaceful competition which necessarily envisages cooperation'' (Gorbachev 1987). No longer will class struggle describe the outcome of this competition, but history will decide. Whether this new configuration will in fact occur remains to be seen, but if Gorbachev's policies prevail, they may make the Soviet Union a more, not less, formidable opponent than it is today. In any event, it is becoming increasingly clear that the Soviets, like the Japanese, are determined to challenge the United States in an area long thought to be its main strength. No longer can the United States rest on its laurels. It will only ''rust'' on them if it does. It must adopt, not just acknowledge, the many suggestions that have been put forth in this chapter by leading scientific associations. The United States, like the Soviet Union, must overcome its stalemated bureaucracy, party structure, and iron triangles if it is to successfully compete in this crucial area.

10

INVESTING FOR THE FUTURE

As the twenty-first century rapidly approaches, many and varied challenges will face the United States. We have discussed many of these in previous chapters. Foremost are the challenges of new scientific discoveries and their technological applications, demographic changes at home and abroad, increased international economic competition, and the evolution of the United States from an industrial to an information society. Workers of the twenty-first century will need to be broadly educated in the arts and humanities, as well as in science and computer technology.

According to the Hudson Institute's study, Workforce 2000 (New York *Times*, January 6, 1988, p. 26), jobs will grow for the most skilled workers and shrink for the least skilled. However, if "world deflation" should occur in the long range, then there would be a worldwide glut of labor and U.S. growth rates would drop to 1.6 percent per year. If a technology boom should occur "with coordinated international monetary, fiscal and trade policies smoothing world business cycles and third world countries getting back on the growth path" (Leonard Silk, New York *Times*, January 6, 1988, p. 26) then the growth rate could rise to 4 percent per year. For the U.S. economy to keep growing, it will become even more crucial to keep the world economy growing, according to the authors of Workforce 2000.

By the year 2000, many experts predict that the world will be either one free-trade zone or a crippled collection of protectionist clouds. If the United States wishes to avoid the latter possibility, it must help the world to become more, not less, of a global village. To maintain, let alone improve, its standard of living and continue its role as a great power, the United States must find a way to improve its investment policies in the future, for investments of money, time, energy, labor, and talent are the key to keeping America competetive. Without wise investments of America's material and human resources to enhance productivity, the prospects for the future are clouded indeed.

What are the problems involved? How have we gotten to where we are? How should we proceed? What are the projects of success? These are the questions we address in the concluding chapter.

INCREMENTAL DEVELOPMENT OF INVESTMENT POLICY

Political scientists and policy analysts have observed that most policy made in the decentralized U.S. system is incrementally developed, rather than approached in a manner approximating the rational decision model. Investment policy is no exception. Several different strategies to affect levels and types of capital investment range from a laissez-faire free-market strategy to government-owned corporations. While U.S. investment policy has been incremental, decentralized, and often unplanned, increasingly, the United States is moving from a closed self-contained economy to one integrated with and affected by the international economy. The tension of international economic competition pulls investment decision making toward the rational model, to shield U.S. citizens and firms from external forces.

Yet counterforces strongly mitigate any movement away from incrementally developed investment policy. These include the historical bias in the United States toward tax incentives and the tax structure as the appropriate mechanism for implementing investment policy, the greater potential for redistribution through planned, rationally developed investment strategies, and the decentralized political structure of Congress and the presidency.

Lindblom (1959) has presented the basic distinctions between observed incremental and ideal rational decision making. While optimum decision-making models emphasize a comprehensive rational approach (the root method), decision making more typically resembles an incremental approach (the branch method), in which successive limited comparisons are made. Root decision making is characterized by a clarification of values or objectives that precede an empirical analysis of alternative policies. Goals or ends are established before the means to achieve those ends are evaluated. Policies that achieve the desired ends most effectively are preferred over policies that are less appropriate for achieving the desired end. Analysis is comprehensive, examining a full range of alternatives for future as well as current impact. Theory often guides priority setting and evaluation criteria (Lindblom 1959).

Branch decision making does not always result in clearly established goals whose development precedes the evaluation of alternatives. Rather, goals and analyses of policies to achieve those goals are often blurred and intertwined with little distinction between ends and means. Good policies are those that evoke consensus, especially among policy analysts. Analysis is limited, in that important possible outcomes, potential alternatives, and affected values are all neglected. The role of theory is downplayed.

Juxtaposed between the opposing root and branch models is Etzioni's (1967) mixed scanning model, which meshes the two. Etzioni suggests that root and branch models can coexist. Most of the time, decision making occurs at the operational level through branch methods, where detail and daily problems are addressed incrementally, goals are rarely specified or questioned, a comprehensive range of alternatives is rarely evaluated, and ends and means are blurred. Periodically, major turbulence or rapid change in the environment force decision making to a higher level where goals and premises are reevaluated in a somewhat comprehensive fashion. Once new goals are established or old goals are reaffirmed, a range of alternatives is examined to ascertain which will best achieve the goals.

Economists as well as political scientists have embraced the distinctions of the root and branch approaches. Capitalist markets and free-enterprise theory resemble incremental decision making, where social goals in production, investment, savings, consumption, and distribution are not present, but evolve from market processes, as individual firms, employees, distributors, retailers, and consumers reach consensus on terms of trade. The law of supply and demand, operating through prices and profits, guide production and consumption decisions, rather than goals based on a theory of social need and growth.

Centralized economic planning represents rational planning. While democracies are not prevented from engaging in comprehensive planning resembling the root method, often they do not, largely because democratic consensus on controversial and specific issues is so difficult to obtain. In the United States, the difficulty of achieving consensus is compounded by the multiple veto points in the system at which policy innovations may be stopped by groups with vested interests in the status quo. The third strategy of mixed scanning has its economic counterpart in mixed economies, where extensive public-sector programs and regulation of industry coexist with decentralized private markets.

The United States' investment policy is wedded to an incremental free-enterprise model, a relic of the golden years of a closed economy and superior economic prowess, rather than a mixed scanning approach more appropriate in dealing with international competition. The free-enterprise model assumes that individuals and firms are motivated solely by dollar gains, that the extent of motivation depends upon the elasticities of supply and demand, and that resource mobility is omnipresent. One critical asumption is that of competition; production units (firms) are so small that no single firm can unilaterally affect either the quantity or product or its price. Profits are assumed to be short-run phenomena, occurring only until economic gains guide additional firms into a lucrative industry, driving long-run profits downward to zero.

Critics of the free-enterprise approach to investment and growth contend that many of the theory's assumptions are unrealistic, no longer and often never reflective of the U.S. economy. Individuals and firms have multiple goals and do not always strive to rationally maximize economic gain. Sometimes they satisfice. Prices and wages are often downwardly rigid, in contrast to theory assumptions. Resources are sometimes characterized by immobility rather than mobility, as evidenced by structural unemployment, market arbitrage, and cries for protectionism. More crucially, many markets are oligopolistic with a few firms dominating both price and quantity in the industry, so that true competition is crippled or absent. Yet attempts to employ anti-trust policies to artificially induce competition hinder U.S. firms in exporting and international competition. Nor have profits proved to be ephemeral, often reflecting market imperfections and barriers to market entry rather than serving as a guide to efficiently steer resources.

Perhaps in no arena is the ill-conceived incremental method of policy development more apparent than in the area of energy investment (Goodwin 1981). Policy has ranged from source-specific planning during the Truman administration, with an emphasis on the promise of nuclear fission, to reluctant intervention based on the Truman administration's Paley Report during the Eisenhower years. In piecemeal fashion, the appropriate mix between public and private nuclear power was debated, attempts to regulate the price of natural gas was stalled in Congress, and administrative intervention redirected the signals of oil prices.

From studied inaction in the Kennedy years, policy was developed by various federal agencies in the Johnson years to service the energy needs of their various constituents. With no central executive department coordinating energy policy, responsibility was divided between subcomponents of the Interior Department (the Office of Coal Research and the Office of Oil and Gas); the State Department, particularly when energy issues affected Middle East relations; and the Federal Power Commission. Discussions on energy policy in the Johnson era lacked any notion of impending scarcity or price increases.

Nixon's energy policy consisted of "putting out fires," which has been allowed to spread during earlier administrations (Goodwin 1981; p. 395). A new oil-import policy was developed in 1973. Project Independence attempted to increase energy supplies, conserve energy, and develop alternative sources to fossil fuels. However, the Old Oil Entitlements program, compensating producers with less than the national average access to old crude oil priced lower through federal regulation, encouraged consumption and helped perpetuate U.S. dependence on imports.

Still dependent upon industry data during the Ford era, the federal government focused on divestiture of the vertical integration of the major oil companies, government-sponsored production of energy through an Energy Independence Authority, and a uranium enrichment program. Carter administration officials found it difficult to formulate a National Energy Plan and construct a Department of Energy simultaneously. Achieving the latter, the administration failed to resolve the relationship between public and private participation in long-range development of energy sources. The Reagan administration focused on deregulation rather than investment and development, attempting unsuccessfully to dismember the Department of Energy created by the preceding administration. Without a vision or consensus, and often reflective of public sensitivity to energy prices at the time, U.S. energy policy continues to lurch forward, incrementally, into the 1990s.

U.S. INVESTMENT TRENDS

Investment (capital formation) represents expenditures in plant and equipment, including buildings, and inventories. The level of national investment is developed through national income accounting. Components in gross private domestic investment include new construction, producers' durable equipment, and changes in business inventories, while net investment equals gross investment minus depreciation (Samuelson 1973). Only private-sector investment is measured directly in the national income accounting. Measures exclude all government expenditures, even though some government outlays contribute to capital formation rather than consumption. Nor does the format of the federal budget enhance consideration of direct government capital formation. Unlike state and local government budgets, where capital and operating expenditures are divided into separate budgets, no such distinction is made in the single unified federal budget that intermingles capital and operating expenses. Separating federal expenditures into two budgets—a practice employed by corporations as well as state and local governments—would allow measurement of the role of the federal government in capital formation and facilitate the development of a more rational investment policy.

Popular opinion holds that investment has been declining in the U.S. economy, was inadequate in the 1970s, and is the primary culprit in productivity declines (Bosworth 1982). Yet measurement difficulties compound even that assessment. For several methods of calculating capital formation, investment rose during the period between 1951 and 1980. When gross fixed nonresidential investment as a percent of gross output is examined, that figure, measured in current dollars, rose from 11.4 percent in the 1951–55 period to 14.6 percent in the 1976–80 period. Measured in constant dollars, the same statistic rose from 11.7 to 14.5 percent. The picture of increasing investment across the 30-year period between 1950 and 1980 is retained if the measure is shifted to net fixed nonresidential investment as a percentage of net output, rising between the first and last five-year periods from 3.8 and 4.3 percent in current dollars, and 3.9 and 4.3 percent in constant dollars.

Only the comparison of capital formation to measures of the economy other than output reveals investment declines. The picture is the gloomiest when comparing capital increases to labor, by examining the percentage change in the ratio of net capital stock to total business hours. Using actual hours, this percentage declined from 3.3 to 0.6 percent across the 30-year peiod, while using cyclically adjusted business hours, it shows a drop from 3.3 to 1.3 percent. Slight declines also become apparent when using the measure of net fixed nonresidential investment as a percent of net capital stock, a figure that decreased from 4.1 to 3.8 percent (Bosworth 1982).

By contrast, Vatter (1982) examines investment trends across the longer time frame of a century, comparing various measures of investment for the 25-year periods from 1875–1900 and 1949–1975. All indicators of investment across this longer time frame declined: net fixed investment as a percent of GNP fell from 6.0 to 3.0 percent; gross fixed investment as a percent of NNP (net national product) fell from 15.0 to 10.0 percent; net investment as a percent of gross investment declined from 39.0 to 30.0 percent; and the derived average of the ratio of net stock of fixed capital to NNP fell from 1.3 to 0.86 percent. During the same time period, capital consumption as a percent of GNP rose from 61.0 to 70.0 percent. This is indeed a bleak picture of long-run decline.

INVESTMENT POLICY GOALS

Several goals may be posited for U.S. investment policy.

Investment policy should:

1. Produce a sufficient level of capital formation to ensure a desirable level of economic growth
2. Provide rates of return to capital to induce savings to be used for capital formation
3. Result in efficient uses of capital
4. Produce moderate or low interest rates
5. Not induce or increase inflation

A great deal of the public debate over appropriate investment strategies has assumed a neoclassical model of the U.S. economy, yet neoclassical theory has only partially addressed these investment policy goals.

1. Investment policy should produce a sufficient level of capital formation to ensure a desirable economic growth rate.

Some economists have argued that the decline in investment, when measured as a percentage of labor hours, has contributed to productivity declines and decreases in the rate of growth of output. Vatter (1982), for example, found that across the past century, the annual compound growth rate in NNP (GNP minus depreciation, sometimes called the "capital consumption allowance"), has declined from 4.6 percent in the 1875 to 1900 period to 3.5 percent in the 1949 to 1974 period.

Confounding this, and all measures of output growth that use NNP rather than GNP, however, is the measure of depreciation. Depreciation schedules and consequently total depreciation in the economy are at least partially politically determined, since depreciation allowances greatly affect tax liabilities for individual firms. Rapid or accelerated depreciation schedules allow for more rapid tax write-offs of capital purchases, for lower before-tax incomes, and consequently for lower tax liabilities, especially in the early years of the life of an asset. Simultaneously, rapid depreciation schedules lower the measure of NNP by increasing the capital consumption allowance. At any point in time, the measure of NNP is sensitive to the method of determining depreciation, which may bear only loose resemblance to the true life of capital assets.

Ascertaining the relationship of investment trends to overall economic growth is further complicated by the need to develop an index of the flow of services generated by new capital formation, yet currently, no consensus exists among economists about the appropriate method to use (Bosworth 1982). Bosworth finds that assessments of capital growth's contribution to output growth are sensitive to the economic sector that is being examined and to the assumptions made vis-à-vis capital services. One assumption is that each unit of capital yields a constant flow of service throughout its lifetime, as does a light bulb (straight-line depreciation). A second assumption is that the efficiency of capital declines in a straight line over its lifetime (single-declining depreciation). A third assumption is that capital efficiency declines at a geometric rate (double-declining balance depreciation), losing most of its efficiency in the early years of its lifetime.

How much capital formation is enough? Two competing schools have developed concerning the optimal capital stock. The neoclassical school has dominated. In an early version, the optimal capital stock is derived from a model assuming constant returns to scale (e.g., there are no increasing or decreasing returns to scale as the amount of capital formation increases), and exogenously given output (the level of output is set outside the model and, presumably, is predetermined for the economy) (Hayashi 1982).

The assumption of exogenously determined output is incompatible with the neoclassical assumption of perfect competition and assumes away the problem of examining the relationship between investment and output. Nor does neoclassical theory have the capability to determine the rate of investment. Tobin suggested an alternative approach of assuming that the rate of investment is a function of q, where q is the ratio of market value of new additional investment goods to their replacement costs. Many studies then explored the impact of q in an attempt to ascertain the optimal rate of investment, but all were limited in verification by the fact that q is not directly observable. Consequently, hypotheses about the impact of q were not directly testable, and the bottom line is that economists do not know the optimal rate of investment, nor the strength of the relationship between investment and economic growth. Ultimately, the rate of investment is a political decision.

2. Investment policy should provide rates of return to capital to induce savings to be used for capital formation.

Traditional economic wisdom holds that saving and investing are done by different individuals for different reasons (Samuelson 1973). Primarily individuals, families, and households save, often to reduce uncertainty about future income. Capital is created by businesses and corporations. Incentives for savings do not have to be the same as incentives for investment. Investment incentives would reward new capital formation (by rapid depreciation schedules lowering taxable income in the early years of the life of an asset), while savings incentives would reward personal savings (by exempting from taxation part of interest from savings).

Classical Keynesians argue that savings and investment must be appropriately regulated by macroeconomic fiscal policies, since a laissez-faire economy cannot guarantee enough investment to ensure full employment. Samuelson (1973) has noted: "As far as total investment . . . is concerned, the laissez-faire system is without a good thermostat." By contrast, neoclassical economists, wedded to their model of perfect markets functioning within a closed economy, have attempted to demonstrate that various government interventions to affect investment and savings are deleterious. The corporate income tax is regarded by neoclassical economists as particularly distortionary with the impact of reducing growth.

3. Investment policy should result in efficient uses of capital.

Efficient uses of capital involve implicit trade-offs between current and future consumption, since invested funds are not available for consumption, as well as trade-offs between various investment alternatives at any single point in time. Common assumptions about economic development and growth are that current consumption must be foregone to allow for present investment if future growth is to occur. The larger the desired future output and the more rapid the desired rate of growth, the greater the amount of current consumption that must be foregone to current investment. Yet neoclassical economic theory has little to say about the trade-offs between consumption and investment, since it is non-dynamic and is particularly ill equippped to examine trends across time. The best neoclassical theory can do within its assumptions of perfect markets and closed economies is to engage in comparative static analysis (comparison of "snapshots" of the economy at different points in time, rather than the theoretical equivalent of a motion picture) (Thurow 1983).

Application of neoclassical theory to the second investment problem of how to allocate capital at any point in time leads to the standard neoclassical conclusion that government intervention is bad. Under the neoclassical assumption of perfect markets, efficient allocation of capital between competing uses in the same time period becomes a moot point, since perfect markets imply that factors of production (e.g., capital, labor, etc.) are rewarded proportionately to their contribution to total output. Given that assumption, government becomes the only distortionary force reducing efficiency, a common neoclassical conclusion.

4. Investment policy should produce moderate or low interest rates.

Raising interest rates may increase the cost of capital to businesses, retarding the development of new plant and equipment. Additionally, the dollar is strengthened vis-à-vis foreign countries, may become overvalued, and retard the sale of U.S. exports as the purchasing power of foreign currencies to buy those exports declines. The typical relationship examined by neoclassical economists, however, is not the impact of investment policy on interest rates, but rather the impact of interest rates on capital markets. The major force raising interest rates is assumed to be rising government deficits, financed by borrowing in the private capital markets and using up increasingly greater shares of funds available for (private) capital formation.

A tool used to examine the relationship of investment to interest rates and levels of income is the *IS-LM* curves. The IS curve shows the relationship between interest rates and income when savings and investment have been kept equal. The LM curve shows the liquidity preference between money and income, taking into account the dependence of holding money on interest rates and on income. The intersection of the IS and LM curves represents the equilibrium level of GNP for a given M (M represents the supply of money, which is assumed to be fixed). Only at equilibrium will the existing amount of money produce a just sufficiently low interest rate and a just sufficiently high amount of investment to lead to a maintainable level of income (Samuelson 1973). This elaborate *IS-LM*-curve equilibrium analysis, however, provides little useful information to policymakers attempting to fashion an investment policy to foster economic growth and competitiveness in international markets.

5. Investment policy should not induce nor increase inflation.

Most studies examining the relationship between market interest rates and inflation begin with the Fisher hypothesis that the real rate of interest is independent of the level of anticipated inflation. A leading neoclassical economist, Feldstein (1980) has examined ways of increasing capital intensity without increasing the rate of inflation. He concludes that, contrary to Tobin's theory, a higher rate of inflation may not succeed in increasing the willingness of investors to hold real capital. Using a monetary growth model that distinguishes between money and interest-bearing government bonds, he identifies and uses a concept called the "safety preference" for government bonds, arguing that it may be as important as the traditional liquidity preference (LM curve) for holding money. Feldstein (1980) makes the traditional neoclassical assumption of full employment.

Feldstein concludes for a fully employed economy, an increase in the government deficit must increase the rate of inflation, which decreases capital intensity and production. He argues that, in some instances, an increase in savings can increase unemployment rather than increase investment (the problem of "excess savings") if the return (yield) on capital becomes so low that individuals prefer to hold government bonds rather than more risky capital. There is no problem with excess savings, however, if investors are willing to hold real capital even though capital yields less than bonds (e.g., the classical assumption that individuals are motivated by economic gains is incorrect), or if the government lowers the rate on government bonds by increasing the money supply more rapidly than the stock of bonds. Under either condition, an increase in savings will increase capital intensity without changes in either inflation or the government deficit.

To increase the savings rate and consequently investment, Feldstein argues that the private savings rate must be increased by either raising the Social Security retirement age (so people save for their old age rather than rely on Social Security), or by reforming the personal income tax to resemble a consumption tax. Feldstein's conclusion is congruent with the normal neoclassical finding that social programs represent government intervention into otherwise perfectly functioning competitive markets and therefore have deleterious effects.

INVESTMENT POLICY STRATEGIES

Five strategies are available for investment policy formulation:

1. A laissez-faire approach of no government intervention
2. Tax incentives to the private sector
3. Credit incentives to the private sector
4. Budget subsidies to the private sector
5. Government-owned and controlled public investment

These investment policies may be conceptualized as lying along an incremental-rational decision-making continuum. They are listed above in an order going from the most incremental to the most rational. While incremental policies are decentralized with little emphasis on national planning, rational policies are centralized with emphasis on national planning. Incremental policies require little clarification of goals, failing to distinguish between means and ends. Rational policies require clarification of goals, which are clearly distinguishable from strategies to achieve those goals.

1. A laissez-faire approach of no government intervention.

This approach, commonly assumed by classical free-enterprise theory, provides little useful assistance to the development of an investment policy to foster international competitiveness. Under this approach, investment is induced and determined by market incentives alone. Interest rates are set within capital markets by supply and demand for money. When the economy is in equilibrium, the amount of money individuals and households wish to save equals the amount of money firms wish to invest. The approach typically assumes a fixed money supply, full employment, and a closed economy with no intervention from international economic forces or from government. Keynesian and neoclassical economists have modified their model of this approach to include government taxes and spending, but neoclassical economists have typically retained many of the restrictive and unrealistic assumptions of classical theory. This approach is the most incremental of the five possible strategies. Decision making is decentralized to individuals, households, and firms. Policy goals are not articulated. Strategies to achieve goals are not evaluated independent of deriving consensus about the goals. Ends and means are intertwined.

2. Tax incentives to the private sector.

Current U.S.investment policy can be described as predominantly using private-sector tax incentives to induce investment. Tax incentives used in the past as inducements to capital formation have included tax credits, rapid depreciation schedules, depletion allowances, preferential capital gains tax rates, and deductions of interest payments. Sometimes these tax incentives have been called tax expenditures—a term used when an individual or firm is taxed at a rate different from the rate that would normally apply by virtue of income alone. Prior to the 1986 tax reforms, tax expenditures had grown to a size approaching one-third the size of the total government budget (Ellwood 1982). The 1986 federal income tax reforms eliminated some tax expenditures for owners of capital, including the capital gains tax, yet others, such as depletion allowances, remain.

Tax incentives are on the incremental side of the incremental-rational continuum. They require some public debate and collective decision making to pass legislation authorizing the incentives, although the goals may not be explicitly designated in legislative hearings. Periodic and unsystematic revisions of the tax code provide for occasional mixed scanning. However, committee specialization within Congress reduces the likelihood that any tax incentive will be compared with the entire range of investment policy options. Once in place, tax incentives are perpetuated indefinitely and are not subject to annual or even periodic review. Until the 1974 Congressional Budget and Impoundment Control Act mandated the Congressional Budget Office to prepare a tax expenditure budget, the volume of financial benefits being transferred through the tax structure was systematically measured. Decision making is decentralized to the individual and firm level once a tax incentive is in place, allowing firms and individuals the option of ignoring the incentive.

3. Credit incentives to the private sector.

Extending government credit is a rapidly growing tool available for investment policy. Government credit may be used to stimulate and target capital formation. Three types of credit mechanisms are direct lending, loan guarantees, and federally sponsored credit enterprises. Direct lending involves the loan of government monies directly to individuals, businesses, and nonprofit organizations. Among on-budget agencies (included in the federal budget) making direct loans are the Commodity Credit Corporation, the Small Busines Administration, the Economic Development Administration, and the Export-Import Bank. Among off-budget agencies (not included in the federal budget) making direct loans are the Railway Association, the Rural Electrification Administration, and the Federal Financing Bank (CBO 1979). Direct loans rose from zero in 1971 to $16.3 billion in 1981, with an annual rate of increase of 19.8 percent between 1976 and 1981 (Ellwood 1982).

A loan guarantee implies that the federal government has removed or lowered the lender's risk on a loan or security by pledging to repay the principal and interest in case of default by the borrower (CBO 1978). Loan guarantees have been made to Lockheed, Amtrak, Conrail, and Chrysler partially for the purpose of inducing capital formation to replace outdated plant and equipment. Loan guarantees rose from $16.1 billion to $76.5 billion between 1971 and 1981, increasing at an annual rate of 54.5 percent between 1976 and 1981 (Ellwood 1982).

Various federally sponsored credit enterprises include the Farm Credit System, the Federal Home Loan Bank System, and the Federal National Mortgage Association, all examples of federally sponsored lending. While the government no longer owns stock in many of these agencies, they are still subject to federal regulation. They consult with the Treasury Department on key decisions, are given special tax preferences, and can borrow in capital markets at rates only slightly above the Teasury borrowing rate. Outlays for federally sponsored lending rose from zero in 1971 to $33.4 billion in 1981, increasing at an annual rate of 60 percent between 1976 and 1981.

Federal credit mechanisms lie in the middle of the incremental-rational continuum. Credit incentives are rational in that legislative hearings allow for the articulation of investment policy goals. In contrast to tax incentives, where decision making is totally decentralized to the firm or individual, credit programs may require active participation on the part of agencies granting the benefit. Also unlike tax incentives, which are often broad sweeping, credit incentives are typically targeted to a particular industry or purpose.

4. Budget subsidies to the private sector.

Direct government financing of private-sector investment involves any government funding of private-sector capital formation. At various points, many agricultural subsidies have stimulated capital formation in the agricultural sector. A great deal of the defense outlay is for capital formation. Federal funds in health care through the Hull-Burton Act and other legislative programs have stimulated investment in hospitals and nursing homes. The Highway Trust Fund has been used to finance interstate highways, as well as capital equipment of private contractors who build and maintain those highways.

Budget outlays are incremental, insofar as the budget base is not closely scrutinized and the annual budget debate, especially prior to the Gramm-Rudman-Hollings Act, focused upon the increment. Yet budget outlays are more rational than the previously discussed investment policy mechanisms. Budget documents require an articulation of goals and program objectives. The 1974 budget reforms required multiyear costing for all proposed programs to facilitate current versus future year trade-offs. The 1974 reforms also required a structure with the potential (not fully realized) to examine trade-offs between current alternatives. Decisions must be reviewed annually.

5. Government-owned and controlled public investment.

A rarely used investment strategy in the United States is government-owned and controlled public investment. The federal government not only would finance capital formation in selected areas, but also would retain ownership and control of the capital it formulates. A few examples in the United States exist: the U.S. Post Office, the Tennessee Valley Authority, some Corps of Engineers' projects, the air traffic control system, the space program and space shuttle, the VA hospital system, and military bases. This strategy has been used in the United States when research and development costs have proved prohibitive to the private sector, or when insufficient profits failed to stimulate businesses to engage in socially desirable investment.

This approach is the most rational of investment policy options, providing the government with greater control and ability to manipulate the newly formed capital. Many possibilities for expanding public-sector development of capital formation exist, including the creation of a National Investment Bank (NIB) to fund "sunrise" industries and projects such as the development of supercomputers and research into superconductivity. The NIB could "buy into" consortium projects conducted by industry, ensuring that citizen interests would be reflected in investment decisions. The consortium board of directors would consist of industry members and NIB-designated public members. The NIB could be funded by a VAT (value-added tax). Unlike many proposals for a VAT, however, the revenues would be earmarked for NIB and, through the NIB, would be returned to the industries from which they originated in the form of incentives for capital formulation and improvements.

Two broad avenues are open for government investment policy: the Japanese strategy of backing "winners" (new technologies or sunrise industries), or the British strategy of backing "losers" (old technologies or "sunset" industries) without the requirement of adopting technological innovations. To back losers is to respond to crises in incremental fashion, choosing between the undesirable option of inefficient uses of capital and the less desirable option of allowing large firms employing many people and affecting whole economic sectors to fail. To back winners requires rationally articulated investment policy goals, deriving some national consensus about those goals, evaluating strategies, and pursuing goal-enhancing policies. This is a difficult task in a political system as decentralized as that of the United States, but Japan also has a democratic government that must cope with and coalesce conflicting views. International economic pressures make the development of a national investment policy all the more urgent.

THE ECLIPSE OF "PAX AMERICANA"

Domestic U.S. investment policy is tied to the stability of the international order, the growth of the world economy, and the U.S. role in the world. Yet, how tightly interwoven is the economic future of the United States with world economic growth? Can the United States continue to provide the leadership required to keep the world economic system stable and growing? These questions have been raised by Leonard Silk of the New York *Times* (1987) in considering the costs to the United States of the burdens of leadership.

Two contradictory answers were posed by Mr. Silk in response to these questions. One answer, pessimistic in nature, was provided by Paul Streeten of Oxford University, who postulates that for the world to remain stable and orderly the dominant country must have four attributes: an export surplus, the ability to supply long-term capital to developing countries, industrial and technological supremacy, and the military strength to secure peace as a precondition for political stability and economic development (Silk 1987). He contends that the United States as the "unscarred victor" possessed all four of these requirements after World War II, but as the postwar period passed, U.S. dominance waned.

First of all, the trade surplus turned into a deficit. Capital outflow converted to a large capital inflow, turning the United States from the world's largest creditor nation to the world's largest debtor nation. Japan and West Germany challenged U.S. industrial leadership. While U.S. military might has remained strong in the NATO alliance, the challenge of the Soviet Union has heavily burdened the American taxpayer to maintain U.S. hegemonic power.

Professor Streeten raises the question of whether the costs of playing "hegemon" outweigh the benefits. He concludes that the costs have indeed exceeded benefits, the old U.S.-dominated system has broken down, and the United States should gracefully make way for a new international order. As Leonard Silk astutely observes, even if the United States were willing to get out of the way, there is no one on the Western horizon rushing in to take its place. Neither Japan nor West Germany is willing to pay the costs of leading the world.

A more salutary view of the ability of the United States to provide future world leadership is presented by Masahiro Sakamoto, a leading Japanese economist (Silk 1987). His thesis is that, while the United States has been weakened economically, its role as the leader of a "Pax Americana" has not disappeared. He insists that Pax Americana is still alive and well, as compared with "Pax Britannica" in the early twentieth century. Mr. Sakamoto argues that, despite concerns about the loss of competitiveness by the United States, its economy is still "the largest and strongest" in the world. Its dynamism is demonstrated by a large and steady increase in population, labor force, immigration between the states, and large national product markets. For these reasons, Japan and other foreign countries want to invest in the United States and participate in its buoyant economy. He also maintains that the United States was the least hurt by violent shocks to the international economic system during the 1970s and 1980s, and argues that it still retains the ability to change the rules of the game, especially in military affairs.

Whether one is pessimistic or optimistic about the role of the United States in the world economy, it is clear that both views see the United States as confronting severe and continuing economic problems at home. Its ability to successfully address these problems will greatly influence its role in world leadership and whether it will continue to decline or maintain its hegemony. One of the implications of this debate is that the historic "low" policy of international trade and commerce has moved to a place of parity with, if not yet supremacy over, traditional, "high," great-power policies of strategic and military affairs. Great-power politics will increasingly reflect a direct correlation with international economic well-being. Foreign policy is becoming inextricably intertwined, if not synonymous with international economic policy.

POLITICS VERSUS ECONOMICS IN FOREIGN POLICY

The elevation of economic concerns to a level equivalent to that of military and strategic concerns represents a significant reversal in traditional emphases of U.S. foreign policy, although economics has always played some role in U.S. foreign policy. The Marshall Plan, which economically restored a devastated Europe after World War II, was partially motivated by U.S. need to restore its major trading partners to economic health. The Alliance for Progress, John F. Kennedy's proposal, was passed to facilitate the economic development of Latin America. Some authors, such as William Appleman Williams (1962), G. William Domhoff (1971), Harry Magdoff (1969), and Gabriel Kolko (1969), have even argued that foreign policy is economically driven, contending that the United States has acted imperialistically to establish and protect foreign markets, to obtain access to raw materials and critical fuels, and to protect U.S. companies and commerce abroad. In the view of economic determinists, the goal of U.S. foreign policy was to make the world safe for American capitalism.

The consensual view among foreign policy experts, however, was that concerns about the balance of military forces, global political strategy, the growth of communism, and protecting the free world were dominant. The cold war, East-West relations, the arms race, the missile gap, and the propaganda war between the United States and Soviet Union were the leading foreign policy issues until recently. As supervisors, the United States and the Soviet Union performed an intricate dance of maintaining peace through the threat of nuclear terror, and engaged in worldwide competition for allies, allegiances, and supremacy in "the correlation of forces." Central to the philosophy of cold-war U.S. foreign policy was the idea of deterrence aned containment. Adherents contended that the United States must deter Soviet power and adventuresomeness with threat of massive retaliation, as well as contain Soviet expansion through U.S. alliances such as the North Atlantic Treaty Organization (NATO), Southeast Asia Treaty Organization (SEATO), and Organization of American States (OAS).

In a triumph of politics and ideology over economic concerns, manifesting this great-power-struggle philosophy, President Jimmy Carter announced a boycott of farm exports to the Soviet Union when the Soviet Union invaded Afghanistan in 1978. In addition to imposing a grain embargo, he suspended high-technology sales and implemented a boycott of the 1980 summer Olympics in Moscow. Despite the public affront, the harm inflicted on the Soviet Union, which secured these high-tech products and argicultural goods from other countries, was questionable. However, U.S. manufacturers and farmers were clearly hurt.

Only since the mid–1980s have America's economic problems been pushed to the top of the foreign policy agenda. There are few observers today who would deny the increased importance of the economic factor in the determination of U.S. foreign policy. While many might still resist called economics the dominant factor, few would argue with its central role in recent times. The annualization of summit conferences of the seven leading industrialized democracies—the United States, Japan, Canada, Great Britain, France, West Germany, and Italy—to address common economic concerns testifies to the increased importance of international economic and trade issues.

The growing role of econmics in U.S. foreign policy abroad has been prompted by the declining state of the economy at home. By 1981, the United States had been the world's leading creditor nation for more than 60 years with a national debt of less than $1 trillion. Six years later, in 1987, the United States was the world's leading borrower and debtor. The national debt trebled during the Reagan administration. The budget deficit became the central core problem affecting all other economic problems.

THE INTERDEPENDENCY OF THE WORLD ECONOMY

The economies of various nations are becoming interwoven into a fabric of world economic growth. The United States is not immune to this trend, but is also increasingly dependent upon world economic conditions and interactions with other countries. According to the Atlantic Council (1987), a prestigious bipartisan group for the formulation of policy recommendations on problems shared by Western Europe, Japan, Australia, and New Zealand, in the last quarter-century U.S. foreign trade expanded 10 percent to more than 25 percent of the GNP. Twenty percent of U.S. industrial output is for export. One in six production workers is directly involved in foreign trade. Forty percent of U.S. farms produce for export. About a third of U.S. corporate profits stem from international activities, and U.S. commercial banks have $130 billion in loans outstanding to developing countries.

Nor do activities abroad always promote U.S. economic growth. In 1979 and 1980, the United States ran an agricultural trade surplus of more than $30 billion, but by 1986, this surplus had dropped to $4 billion. According to Thurow and Tyson (1987), this drop was caused by the "green revolution," which transformed agricultural production to allow China, India, and Pakistan to largely feed themselves and for the Common Market countries to move from importing 25 million tons of grain to exporting 16 million.

One ramification of America's interdependency is its eroding debt position. Since the beginning of the decade of the 1980s, the United States has grown increasingly dependent on foreign borrowing. Up to 25 percent of investable funds in some years have come from abroad and have permitted the United States to consume more than it produces. In 1986, this imbalance of consumption that foreign lending allowed the United States, which was not paid for by exports, approached $166 billion.

Tax cuts and government-spending increases in the 1980s refueled the U.S. economy at the same time that other major industrial countries pursued no-growth or slow-growth policies. Developing countries experienced declining growth rates due to a lack of capital. With economic growth in the United States, demand for private investment rose. At the same time, growing federal deficits increased government borrowing. Both of thee demands on capital markets exceeded U.S. savings, increasing interest rates and creating a need to attract capital from abroad. Foreign investors were attracted to the United States because of high U.S. interest rates, as well as deregulation of several major U.S. industries and tax incentives. Additionally, slow growth in other advanced countries and unstable political conditions in third world countries made U.S. investments relatively attractive. Foreign demand pushed up the price of the dollar, which made U.S. products less price competitive, and worsened the trade deficit.

The interdependencies among the national economies of various countries have interfered with ordinary adjustments in trade imbalances and currency exchange rates. Thurow and Tyson contend that the international economic system ordinarily would have been self-correcting since U.S. long-term productivity and technological leadership were declining. This decline should have caused the U.S. dollar to fall. Instead, the inward flow of foreign capital drove up exchange rates, keeping the dollar high, despite the deterioration in U.S. competitiveness.

Nor is the interdependency a one-way street. Other countries, especially Latin American nations, are becoming increasingly dependent on the United States. Thurow and Tyson (1987) argue that for these nations, the United States is becoming "the buyer of last resort" rather than "the lender of last resort." Between 1981 and 1984, the United States bought 85 percent of the increase of these countries' exports. Total U.S. imports from developing countries doubled to $70 billion, while Japanese imports from developing nations grew by only $2 billion and European imports from those countries decreased. In addition to increasing Latin American dependency upon U.S. markets, this one-sided growth in U.S. imports from Latin countries has had a negative impact upon the U.S. balance of trade. In 1984, one-fourth of the deterioration in the U.S. balance of trade resulted from the Latin American imports not offset by exports to those countries due to the debt crisis there.

UNDERINVESTMENT IN FOREIGN AFFAIRS

The Atlantic Council contends that the United States has consistently under-invested in foreign affairs, diplomacy, and economic and cultural relations with the rest of the world for the last quarter of a century (1987). The underinvestment is both relative and absolute. The Council argues that the government investment in nonmilitary international activities was smaller in 1987 than two years before that. In terms of GNP, key components of our investment fall below levels maintained by our adversaries and principal allies. The council further contends that such frugality has made no appreciable impact on our annual budget deficits. Instead, it has eroded U.S. capability for world leadership and diminished U.S. prospects for security and prosperity.

Among the specific examples of underinvestment cited by the council is the size of the U.S. Foreign Service, which is both understaffed and underpaid. In spite of the fact that the United States maintains relations with 146 countries and 47 organizations, and the demand for political, economic, and scientific reporting and analysis has substantially increased in the past two decades, the Foreign Service increased by only 116 positions between 1960 and 1983. According to a House Foreign Affairs Committee report, the State Department was the only cabinet department having virtually no position increases since 1957 (Atlantic Council 1987).

Nor has the Foriegn Service been able to attract top applicants in recent years since many of those who excel in liberal arts and foreign languages have been turning down Foreign Service careers. Reasons cited include worsening trends in pay and promotion, which caused the beginning Foreign Service salaries in 1983 of $20,000 to $22,000 to compare unfavorably with starting salaries of $30,000 to $34,000 offered to top graduates by commercial banks. Increasing work loads are also cited, since consular work alone between 1960 and 1983 increased by 1,000 percent, with only marginal increases in the number of positions.

A second area of underinvestment is public diplomacy, which includes international communication, cultural, and educational relations involving U.S. and foreign publics. Among those activities are cultural exchanges, radio and television broadcasting, publishing, film distribution, conferences, libraries, and English language instruction. These are managed chiefly by the U.S. Information Agency (USIA) and also involve the State and Defense Departments, the Agency for International Development (AID), Radio Free Europe/Radio Liberty, and the Peace Corps. Traditionally, the United States is outspent in absolute amounts in these areas by France, the Soviet Union, Great Britain, Japan, and West Germany. When expenditures for these areas are considered as a proportion of GNP, the United States lags even further behind, since the U.S. GNP is twice that of the Soviet Union, three times those of West Germany and Japan, five times that of France, and more than seven times that of Britain. Britain and Japan sent about as many or more of their nationals abroad as the United States and brought in more foreign grantees.

Despite high-level endorsements by elites, foreign aid has been traditionally susceptible to the lack of any major constituency, the argument that it is "money down a rat hole," and the fallacious belief that the United States is a big spender in this area. Whereas at the height of the Marshall Plan in the late 1940s and early 1950s, foreign economic assistance constituted approximately 11 percent of the federal budget, in 1987 the combined programs of development assistance, economic support funds, Food for Peace, and the Peace Corps comprised less than 1 percent of total federal spending. According to the 1983 Carlucci Commission Report to the Secretary of State addressing security and economic assistance concerns, the level of total real assistance in constant 1982 dollars declined by 18 percent from an annual average of $16.5 billion dollars during 1968 to 1972 to $13.6 billion in 1983. For the 1987 fiscal year, Congress set foreign aid spending at $13.5 billion. This was $2.64 billion less than the president requested. Under Gramm-Rudman-Hollings, the program faced deeper cuts in subsequent years (Atlantic Council 1987).

Since President John F. Kennedy established the Peace Corps in 1961, more than 120,000 men and women have spent two or more years living and working in 93 third world countries. The potential of the Peace Corps has begun to be realized, but even the present low level of operations has been threatened by budgetary cuts. In spite of the fact that the 1985 Foreign Aid Authorization Act recommended that the Peace Corps should grow from 5,800 to 10,000 volunteers by 1989, the Peace Corps placed 800 fewer new volunteers overseas in 1986 than in the previous year, and faced likely further reductions in the future.

INTERACTION WITH THE SOVIET UNION

Investment policy is integrally tied to foreign policy and the arms race between the United States and the Soviet Union. The arms race not only increases the potential for world war and annihilation, but also consumes capital that might otherwise be used in the nondefense sector to increase exports and improve the standard of living. If Mikhail Gorbachev's efforts to modernize the economy of the Soviet Union are successful in the coming decades, then economic competition from this quarter will undoubtfully increase. Soviet expert Jerry Hough of Duke University expects that by the end of the century, Eastern Europe will be communist in name only and the Soviet Union will dismantle its system of central state control over production, to open their economies to Western investment and to seek Western technology ("Economic Revolution," 1988). Unless the Soviet Union modernizes its economy, it will remain a military giant, but not a competitive force in the evolving world economy. Soviet success in *perestroika* or restructuring its economy may add to the economic tensions among Western countries, but at the same time reduce the political tensions of a nuclear arms race. In any event, a modernized Soviet Union will offer the United States new challenges to develop a successful investment strategy.

Despite powerful international economic forces pushing investment policy debate toward a more rational comprehensive examination of strategies and alternatives, other forces work against movement in this direction. These include the historical bias in the United States toward tax incentives, the greater potential for redistribution with less incremental policies, and the decentralized political structure of Congress and the presidency. Yet more rational approaches to capital formulation must be forthcoming if the United States is to embrace new crosscutting technologies whose development is too costly for any single firm. Funding of new technology development desperately needs to be accompanied by reinvestment in the U.S. foreign policy structure abroad. The neoclassical closed economy of homogenous markets on which U.S. economic strength was built is dead. The demise of U.S. economic strength, however, does not have to be imminent nor even automatic. With reinvestment in new technologies and a foreign policy tailored to facilitate U.S. economic competition, the United States can surmount current trade and productivity problems and compete strongly, impressively, and forcefully, again.

CONCLUSION

Almost as if Americans were not looking, economic competition has shifted from the national level to the international level. Early in the post-World War II period, Americans competed primarily with each other, in a series of adversarial dyads:

—labor fought with management for a bigger share of national output;

—management fought with labor to reduce demands for wages, improved working conditions, and greater job security;

—labor pressured government to erect tariff barriers and programs to protect domestic jobs;

—management lobbied government against redistributive taxes, programs, and regulatory efforts, aided with the increasingly outdated economic gospels of classical and neoclassical free-enterprise theory; and

—government pressured management to act socially responsible toward workers, consumers, and the environment, unsually in a rear-guard action responding to, rather than anticipating, crises.

In all this domestic posturing, pushing, and prodding, however, the long-run national view often was lost. National needs evolved, while national thinking remained wedded to a theory and series of economic relationships two centuries old. Other nations were building powerful partnerships between government and industry, with cooperative rather than adversarial relationships between management and labor, while Americans continued to quarrel among themselves. After all, the United States was the richest and most powerful nation in the world.

Since industry perceived government as a problem rather than a partner, rational planning was not implemented. To plan implied that government would and should have a continuing role as a significant economic actor. To fail to plan was to beg the question. Yet begging the question has not made it a moot issue. Policy development, especially in key areas such as investment and education, has remained crisis driven and ad hoc.

As the economy staggers from the weight of incrementally accumulated excesses—each relatively small but large in total impact—the solutions appear painful. As with excess pounds added by an aging world-class athlete through small daily indulgences to a once sleek and agile body, the U.S. economy has become bloated, a caricature of the fine production machine it once was or could be again.

However, quick fixes and crash diets will not work for the U.S. economy any more than they will prove successful for the aging athlete. Just as the athlete must modify his exercise routine to accommodate changed capacities (some improved from greater practice and experience; some lessened from reduced responsiveness), the United States must modify its major economic relationships to accommodate its greater maturity and the shift from national to international competition. The cocky individualism that served the United States so well in its youth is less appropriate two centuries later in a technologically complex, interdependent economy and world.

The economic game has shifted from one of individual to team competition. The cultural shift from the rugged individual cowboy, confronting the elements and enemies alone, to the highly tuned and practiced team player has not been an easy one. Nor is the transition complete, for ultimately, issues of production are intimately tied to issues of distribution, or who gets what—issues about which classical economic theory is amazingly silent. Even the U.S. political system has encountered great difficulty dealing with questions of distribution and redistribution. Yet, if major actors in the U.S. economy continue to focus primarily upon aggrandizing their own share of the economic pie, the pie will shrink, for no one is taking responsibility for the economy's overall growth. Management and labor have blamed government for economic woes, when, in reality, blame rests with all three major economic actors.

Nor is establishing blame particularly fruitful, but redefining relationships between the major economic actors from adversarial to cooperative ones is. Clearly, adversaries do not become friends, interested in the welfare of each other overnight. No single action cements cooperation. It results from a long series of smaller actions that build trust. We can procrastinate in undertaking this task of trust building, but the lesson of competing nations is clear: united we stand; divided we fall into reduced productivity, lower living standards, and increased debt.

The key question of the future is how to build cooperation and trust between government, management, and labor, without stifling the individual initiative and creativity that has long been a strength of the U.S. economy. Individual initiative must be translated into organizational innovation and action to compete internationally.

No single suggestion for improved competitiveness made here or elsewhere will do the trick. There are no tricks to restoring competitiveness. Rather, long-term shifts in the attitudes of management, labor, and government; gradual reshaping of major social institutions; developing some discipline required for long-range planning to supplement the ''twinkie'' high of crisis management and policy development; and more directly confronting distributional issues are part of the solution. We should have begun yesterday. We can begin now.

REFERENCES

Aaron, Henry J., and Schwartz, William. *The Painful Prescription: Rationing Hospital Care*. Washington, D.C.: Brookings Institution, 1984.

Alexander, Herbert E., and Caiden, Gerald E., eds. *The Politics and Economics of Organized Crime*. Lexington, Mass.: Lexington Books, 1985.

American Association for the Advancement of Science. "Organization for Science and Technology in the Executive Branch." *Science* 187 (1975): 810–14.

"Americans' Satisfaction with Their Health Care Is on the Decline." *Washington Post*, June 10, 1985, p. 38.

Aronson, J. Richard, and Hilley, John L. *Financing State and Local Governments*. 4th ed. Washington, D.C.: The Brookings Institution, 1986.

"As Businesses Turn Offices into Classrooms." *U.S. News & World Report* (April 1, 1985): 70.

The Atlantic Council of the United States. *U.S. International Leadership for the 21st Century: Building a National Foreign Affairs Constituency*. Washington, D.C.: Atlantic Council, 1987.

Baker, James N. "Med Schools Learn Humility." *Newsweek* (June 29, 1987): 61–62.

Baumhart, Raymond C. "How Ethical Are Businessmen?" *Harvard Business Review* 39 (1961): 5–176.

Behrman, Jack N. *Industrial Policies: International Restructuring and Transnationals*. Lexington, Mass.: Lexington Books, 1984.

Bell, Daniel, and Thurow, Lester. *The Deficits: How Big? How Long? How Dangerous?* New York: New York University Press, 1985.

Blaustein, Saul J. *Job and Income Security for Unemployed Workers: Some New Directions*. Kalamazoo, Mich.: W. E. Upjohn Institute for Employment Research, 1981.

Boffey, Philip M. "U.S. Study Finds Fraud in Top Researcher's Work on Mentally Retarded." New York *Times*, May 24, 1987, p. A–16.

Boretsky, Michael. "Trends in U.S. Technology." *Science, Technology, and National Policy*. Edited by Thomas J. Kuehn and Alan L. Porter, pp. 161–188. Ithaca: Cornell University Press, 1981.

Bosworth, Barry. "Capital Formation and Economic Policy." *Brookings Papers on Economic Activity* 2.: 273–326. Washington, D.C.: Brookings, 1982.

Boulding, Kenneth E. 1981. *Ecodynamics*. Beverly Hills, Calif.: Sage Publishers, 1981a.

Boulding, Kenneth E. *Evolutionary Economics*. Beverly Hills, Calif.: Sage Publishers, 1981b.

"The Brain Battle." *U.S. News & World Report*. (January 19, 1987): 58–64.

"Bridging the Gaps in Medicare." *U.S. News & World Report* (May 14, 1984): 93.

Brooks, Harvey. "Technology, Evolution, and Purpose." *Science, Technology, and National Policy*. Edited by Thomas J. Kuehn and Alan L. Porter, pp. 35–36. Ithaca: Cornell University Press, 1981.

Brown, Francis C. III. "Recruiting Drive: Shortage of Teachers Prompts Talent Hunt by Education Officials." *Wall Street Journal*, January 15, 1987, p. 1.

Burke, Edmund. *Burke's Politics*. Edited by Ross J. S. Hoffman and Paul Levack. New York: Alfred A. Knopf, Inc., 1949.

Burns, James MacGregor; Peltason, J. W.; and Cronin, Thomas E. *Government by the People*. 13th ed. Englewood Cliffs, N.J.: Prentice-Hall, Inc., 1987.

Carey, John. "Failing in Fitness." *Newsweek*. (April 1, 1985): 84–87.

Carey, William D. and Schribner, Richard. "Organization for Science and Technology in the Executive Branch" (white paper for the American Association for the Advancement of Science). *Science* 187 (1975): 810–14.

Casper, Barry M. "The Rhetoric and Reality of Congressional Technology Asessment." *Science, Technology, and National Policy*. Edited by Thomas J. Kuehn and Alan L. Porter, pp. 327–45. Ithaca: Cornell University Press, 1981.

Chandler, Alfred D., Jr. "Technology and Industrial Organization." *Technology, the Economy, and Society*. Edited by Joel Colton and Stuart Bruchey. New York: Columbia University Press, 1987.

Clark, Matt. "Nurses: Few and Fatigued." *Newsweek*. (June 29, 1987): 59–61.

Clark, Matt. "Trauma in the Emergency Room." *Newsweek*. (February 16, 1987): 76–77.

Clinard, Marshall B. *Corporate Ethics and Crime: The Role of Middle Management*. Beverly Hills, Calif.: Sage Publications, 1983.

Clinard, Marshall B., and Yeager, P. C. *Corporate Crime*. New York: Free Press, 1980.

Cohen, Stephen, and Zysman, John. *Manufacturing Matters: The Myth of the Post-Industrial Society*. New York: Basic Books, 1987.

"Colleges Urged to Alter Tests for Benefit of Minority-Group Students." *Chronicle of High School Education*. February 3, 1982, p. 11.

Congressional Budget Office. *Loan Guarantees: Current Concerns and Alternatives for Control*. Washington, D.C.: U.S. Government Printing Office, 1978.

Congressional Budget Office. *Loan Guarantees: Current Concerns and Alternatives for Control—A Compilation of Staff Working Papers*. Washington, D.C.: U.S. Government Printing Office, 1979.

Council of Better Business Bureaus. *How to Protect Your Business*. Englewood Cliffs, N.J.: Prentice-Hall, Inc., in association with Benjamin Co., 1985.

"Cutting the Cost of Depression." *The Columbia Record*, May 23, 1985, p. 3–B.

Darwin, Charles. *The Origin of Species*. New York: New American Library, 1958.

Davidson, Joe. "States Strive to Get Medical Care for the Poor in the Wake of Reagan Administration Budget Cuts." *Wall Street Journal*, April 30, 1985, p. 64.

Dedek, John F. *Contemporary Medical Ethics*. New York: Sheed and Ward, Inc., 1975.

Dentzer, Susan; Thomas, Rich; and Borger, Gloria. "The Tax Maze." *Newsweek*. (April 16, 1984): 62–69.

Destler, I. M., and Sato, Hideo. *Coping with U.S.-Japanese Economic Conflicts*. Lexington, Mass.: Lexington Books, 1982.

"Doctors Who Lose Licenses often Start Practices in Other States, Probe Shows." *Raleigh News and Observer*, April 1984.

"Does College Cost Too Much?" *U.S. News & World Report*. (March 9, 1987): 54–55.

Domhoff, G. William. *The Higher Circles: The Governing Class in America*. New York: Vintage Books, 1971.

Donovan, L. "Survey of Nursing Incomes. Part 2. What Increases Income the Most?" *RN* 43 (1980): 27–30.

Dworkin, Peter; Schiffres, Manuel, and Black, Robert F. "Silicon Chips: U.S. Gets Set for a Comeback." *U.S. News & World Report*. (November 25, 1985): 80.

Dye, Thomas R. *Understanding Public Policy*. 5th ed. Englewood Cliffs, N.J.: Prentice-Hall, Inc., 1984.

Easterbrook, Gregg. "The Revolution in Medicine." *Newsweek* (January 26, 1987): 40–74.

"Economic Revolution Seen As Text." *Knight-Ridder Newspaper*, January 7, 1988.

EDP Fraud Review Task Force. *Report on the Study of EDP-Related Fraud in the Banking and Insurance Industries*. New York: American Institute of Certified Public Accountants, 1984.

Eisner, Robert. *How Real Is the Federal Debt?*. New York: The Free Press, 1986.

Ellwood, John W. *Reductions in U.S. Domestic Spending: How They Affect State and Local Government*. New Brunswick, N.J.: Transaction Books, 1982.

English, Carey W. "Why Unions Are Running Scared." *U.S. News & World Report*. (September 10, 1984): 62–65.

English, Carey W. "Bruised Unions Dig In for an Uphill Fight." *U.S. News & World Report*. (November 19, 1984): 98.

English, Carey W. "Why Firms Are Going One-On-One with Unions." *U.S. News & World Report*. (November 26, 1984): 85–86.

English, Carey W. "Who'll Pay for Retirees' Health Plans?" *U.S. News & World Report*. (October 21, 1985): 72.

"Enrollment of Minorities in Colleges Stagnating." New York *Times*, April 19, 1987, p. A–1.

Etzioni, Amitai. "Mixed-Scanning: A 'Third' Approach to Decision Making." *Public Administrtion Review* 27 (1967): 385–92.

Federal Bureau of Investigation, U.S. Department of Justice. *The Uniform Crime Reports for the United States*. Washington,D.C.: U.S. Government Printing Office, 1986.

Feistritzer, C. Emily. "One Reason Why Poor College Kids Aren't Getting Federal Loans." *Washington Post*, August 12, 1985, p. 25.

Feldstein, Martin. "Fiscal Policies, Inflation, and Capital Formation." *American Economic Review* 70 (1980): 636–50.

Friedman, Milton. *Capitalism and Freedom*. Chicago: University of Chicago Press, 1962.

Friedrich, Otto. "One Miracle, Many Doubts." *Time*. (December 10, 1984): 70–80.

"Fuming Over College Costs." *Newsweek*. (May 18, 1987): 66–72.

Funke, Gail S. "How Much Justice Can States Afford?" *State Legislatures*. (July 1984): 26–27.

Galbraith, John Kenneth. *The Affluent Society*. New York: New American Library, 1959.

Galbraith, John Kenneth. *The New Industrial State*. New York: New American Library, 1967.

Goodwin, Crawford D., ed. *Energy Policy in Perspective*. Washington, D.C.: Brookings, 1981.

Gorbachev, Mikhail. *Peace Has No Alternatives*. New York: Advent Books, 1987.

Gould, Frank. "The Growth of Public Expenditures: Theory and Evidence from Six Advanced Democracies." *Why Governments Grow*. Edited by Charles Lewis Taylor. Beverly Hills, Calif.: Sage Publications, 1983.

Graham, Loren R. *Science, Philosophy and Human Behavior in the Soviet Union*. New York: Columbia University Press, 1987.

Greenough, William C., and King, Francis P. *Pension Plans and Public Policy*. New York: Columbia University Press, 1976.

Guthrie, James W., ed. *School Finance Policies and Practices: The 1980s: A Decade of Conflict*. Cambridge, Mass.: Ballinger Publishing Co., 1980.

" 'Gypsy' Faculty Stirs Debate At U.S. Colleges." *Wall Street Journal*, September 25, 1986, p. 33.

Hall, Trish. "What Americans Eat Hasn't Changed Much Despite Healthy Image." *Wall Street Journal*, September 12, 1985, p. 1.

Hayashi, Fumio. "Tobin's Marginal Q and Average Q: A Neoclassical Interpretation." *Econometrica* 50 (1982): 213–224.

Heilbroner, Robert L. *The Worldly Philosophers*. New York: Simon and Schuster, 1967.

Heilbroner, Robert, and Thurow, Lester. *Five Economic Challenges*. Englewood Cliffs, N.J.: Prentice-Hall, Inc., 1981.

Hicks, John R. *The Theory of Wages*. London: Macmillan & Co., 1932.

Hirsch, Barry T., and Addison, John T. *The Economic Analysis of Unions: New Approaches and Evidence*. Boston: Allen & Unwin, 1986.

Hoadley, John F. "Health Care in the United States: Access, Costs, and Quality." *PS* 20 (1987): 197–201.

Hodgson, John S., and Herander, Mark G. *International Economic Relations*. Englewood Cliffs, N.J.: Prentice-Hall, Inc., 1983.

Hough, J. R., ed. *Educational Policy: An International Survey*. New York: St. Martin's Press, 1984.

Ippolito, Dennis S. *Hidden Spending: The Politics of Federal Credit Programs*. Chapel Hill, N.C.: University of North Carolina Press, 1984.

Johns, Roe L. Morphet, Edgar L., and Alexander, Kern. *The Economics and Financing of Education*. 4th ed. Englewood Cliffs, N.J.: Prentice-Hall, Inc., 1983.

Johnston, Janet Wegner. "An Overview of U.S. Federal Employment and Training Programmes." *Unemployment: Policy Responses of Western Democracies*. Edited by Jeremy Richardson and Roger Henning, pp. 57–115. Beverly Hills, Calif.: Sage Publications, 1984.

Jones, Landon Y. *Great Expectations*. New York: Ballantine Books, 1980.

Karatncky, Adrian, Motyl, Alexander J.; and Sturmthal, Adolph. *Workers' Rights, East and West*. New Brunswick, N.J.: Transaction Books, 1980.

Kenwood, A. G., and Lougheed, A. L. *The Growth of the International Economy: 1820–1980*. London and Boston: George Allen & Unwin, 1983.

Keynes, John Maynard. *The General Theory of Employment Interest and Money*. London: Macmillan, 1936.

Koepp, Stephen; Branegan, Jay; Malkin, Lawrence; and Reingold, Edwin M. "Please, Somebody Help Me." *Time*. (February 2, 1987): 48–55.

Kolko, Gabriel. *The Roots of American Foreign Policy*. Boston: Beacon Press, 1969.

Kronenfeld, Jennie J., and Whicker, Marcia Lynn. *U.S. National Health Care Policy*. New York: Praeger, 1984.

Lamont, Douglas F. *Forcing Our Hand: America's Trade Wars in the 1980s*. Lexington, Mass.: Lexington Books, 1986.

Larson, Calvin. *Crime—Justice and Society*. New York: General Hall, Inc., 1984.

Lekachman, Robert. *Greed is Not Enough: Reaganomics*. New York: Pantheon Books, 1982.

Leo, John. "Polling for Mental Health." *Time*. (October 15, 1984): 80.

Levine, Art. "Taking on Teen Pregnancy." *U.S. News & World Report*. (March 23, 1987): 67–68.

Lindblom, Charles E. "The Science of Muddling Through." *Public Administration Review* 19 (1959): 79–88.

"Living with Strokes." *Newsweek*. (June 17, 1985): 83–86.

Lowi, Theodore J. *The End of Liberalism*. New York: W. W. Norton, 1969.

Magdoff, Harry. *The Age of Imperialism: The Economics of U.S. Foreign Policy*. New York: Modern Reader Paperbacks, 1969.

Maloney, Lawrence D. "Take Mental Patients Off Streets, Back to Hospitals?" *U.S. News & World Report*. (July 1, 1985): 55–57.

"The Malpractice Mess." *Newsweek*. (February 17, 1986): 74–75.

Malthus, Robert. *The Principles of Political Economy*. London: Wiliam Pickering, 1836.

Manning, Peter K. "The Police: Mandate, Strategies, and Appearances." *Criminal Justice in America*. Edited by Richard Quinney. Boston: Little, Brown & Co., 1974.

Marshall, Alfred. *Principles of Economics*. 8th ed. London: Macmillan & Co., 1930.

Marx, Karl. *Capital*. Moscow: Foreign Languages Publishing House, 1961.

Maslow, Abraham H. *Motivation and Personality*. 2d ed. New York: Harper and Row, 1970.

Mathews, Jay. "The New 'Values' Curriculum." *The Washington Post*, April 22, 1985, p. 33.

McGill, Dan M. *Fundamentals of Private Pensions*. 3d ed. Homewood, Ill.: Richard D. Irwin, Inc., 1975.

Mechanic, David, and Aiken, Linda H. "A Cooperative Agenda for Medicine and Nursing." *New England Journal of Medicine* 307: 747–50, 1982.

Mercer, James L., and Philips, Ronald J. *Public Technology: Key to Improved Government Productivity*. New York: AMACON, 1981.

Meyer, Chrles W. *Social Security: A Critique of Radical Proposals*. Lexington, Mass.: Lexington Books, 1987.

Moore, W. S., and Penner, Rudolph G., eds. *The Constitution and the Budget: Are Constitutional Limits on Tax, Spending and Budget Powers Desirable at the Federal Level?* Washington, D.C.: American Enterprise Institute, 1980.

"More Gains for Women." *Time*. (September 14, 1987): 64.

Morganthau, Tom. "Abandoned." *Newsweek*. (January 6, 1986): 14–19.

"Most Americans Covered by Health Insurance." *The State*. February 15, 1985, p. 7–A.

Musgrave, Richard A., and Musgrave, Peggy B. *Public Finance in Theory and Practice*. New York: McGraw-Hill Book Co., Inc., 1984.

Myers, Robert J. *Social Security.* 3d ed. Homewood, Ill.: Richard D. Irwin, Inc., 1985.

Naisbitt, John, and Aburdene, Patricia. *Re-investing the Corporation.* New York: Warner Books, 1985.

"A Nation At Risk." *National Commission on Excellence in Education Report to the U.S. Department of Education.* Washington, D.C.: U.S. Govt. Printing Office, 1983.

New York *Times*, April 8, 1987.

New York *Times*, January 6, 1988, pp. 20, 26.

"Opinion Roundup: Demands on Government: Class Differences but No Class Divide." *Public Opinion* (May/June 1987): 23–38.

Otten, Alan L. "Parents and Newborns Win New Legal Rights to Sue for Malpractice." *Wall Street Journal*, June 7, 1985, p. 1.

Packard, George R. "The Coming U.S.-Japan Crisis." *Foreign Affairs* (Winter 1987): 348–67.

Pascal, Glenn. *The Trillion Dollar Budget: How to Stop the Bankrupting of America.* Seattle: University of Washington Press, 1985.

Pauly, David; Hughey, Ann; Ganzalez, David; and Cohn, Bob. "2001: A Union Odyssey." *Newsweek.* (August 5, 1985): 40–42.

Pechman, Joseph A. *The Rich, the Poor, and the Taxes They Pay.* Washington, D.C.: The Brookings Institution, 1986.

Pettengil, John S. *Labor Unions and the Inequality of Earned Income.* New York: North-Holland Publishing Co., 1980.

Phillips, Carolyn. "Medicare's New Limits on Hospital Payments Force Wide Cost Cuts." *Wall Street Journal*, May 2, 1984, p. 1.

Powell, Stewart. "Veterans' Care: Condition Critical." *U.S. News & World Report.* (June 2, 1986): 20–22.

"Question: Who Will Play God?" *Time.* (April 9, 1984): 68.

Raffel, Marshall W., ed. *Comparative Health Systems.* University Park: Pennsylvania State University Press, 1984.

Ramo, Simon. *America's Technology Slip.* New York: John Wiley and Sons, Inc., 1980.

Reich, Robert B. *The Next American Frontier.* New York: New York Times Book Co., 1983.

"Report Says Pupils Lack 'Real Literacy.' " *Richmond Times-Dispatch*, March 13, 1987, p. A–12.

Reston, James. New York *Times*, October 12, 1987, p. 21.

Rich, Spencer. "Reagan Targets Medicaid for Additional Reductions." *Washington Post*, January 7, 1985, p. 37.

Roback, Herbert. "Congress and the Science Budget." *Science, Technology, and National Policy.* Edited by Thomas J. Kuehn and Alan L. Porter, pp. 297–314. Ithaca: Cornell University Press, 1981.

Ross, Austin, Williams, Stephen J.; and Schafer, Eldon L. *Ambulatory Care Organization and Management.* New York: John Wiley and Sons, Inc., 1984.

Russell, George. "Socking It to Imports." *Time.* (February 9, 1987): 48–49.

Samuelson, Paul A. *Economics.* New York: McGraw Hill Book Co., 1973.

Samuelson, Robert J. "Balancing the Budget." *Newsweek.* (January 28, 1985): 58.

Samuelson, Robert J. "Competitive Confusion." *Newsweek.* (January 26, 1986): 39.

Sapolsky, Harvey. "Science Policy in American State Government." *Science, Tech-*

nology, and National Policy. Edited by Thomas J. Kuehn and Alan L. Porter, pp. 367–97. Ithaca: Cornell University Press, 1981.

Scheingold, Stuart A. *The Politics of Law and Order: Street Crime and Public Policy.* New York: Longman, Inc., 1984.

Schon, Donald. "The National Climate for Technological Innovation." *Science, Technology, and National Policy.* Edited by Thomas J. Kuehn and Alan L. Porter, pp. 148–60. Ithaca: Cornell University Press, 1981.

Schwartz, William. "U.S. Medicine Cannot Do Everything for Everybody." *U.S. News & World Report.* (June 25, 1984): 71–72.

Seaberry, Jane. "The Rise of Two-Tier Wages." *Washington Post,* April 22, 1985, p. 22.

Sheler, Jeffrey L., and Black, Robert F. "Is Congress for Sale?" *U.S. News and World Report.* (May 28, 1984): 47–50.

Shuman, Howard E. *Politics and the Budget.* Englewood Cliffs, N.J.: Prentice-Hall, Inc., 1984.

Silk, Leonard. *The Economists.* New York: Basic Books, 1976.

Silk, Leonard. "Costs to U.S. of Leadership." New York *Times,* May 6, 1987, p. 38.

Silk, Leonard. New York *Times,* January 6, 1988, p. 26.

Smith, Adam. *The Wealth of Nations.* New York: Modern Library, Inc., 1937 edition.

Smith, James D., ed. *Modeling the Distribution and Intergenerational Transmission of Wealth.* Chicago: University of Chicago Press, 1980.

Smith, Gordon B. *Soviet Politics.* New York: St. Martin's Press, 1988.

Solomon, Steven. "Will Old Machines Kill New Ideas?" New York *Times,* May 24, 1987, p. F–4.

Solorzano, Lucia. "Rights, Wrongs: Now Schools Teach Them." *U.S. News & World Report.* (May 13, 1985): 51.

Solorzano, Lucia. "A Second Look at Bilingual Education." *U.S. News and World Report.* (June 11, 1984).

Spolar, Chris. "Warning: Military Hospitals May be Hazardous to Your Health." *Washington Post,* March 4, 1985, p. 31.

Sraffra, Piero. Editor. *The Works and Correspondence of David Ricardo.* Cambridge: Cambridge University Press, 1962.

Stevens, Charles W. "Dollar Falls as Bearish Factors Lessen the Impact of Intervention Expectations." *Wall Street Journal,* February 26, 1987, p. 26.

"Study Finds Costly Care Not Needed." *The State,* May 2, 1985, p. 6–A.

Sumner, William G. *Folkways: A Study of the Sociological Importance of Usages, Manners, Customs, Mores and Morals.* Boston: Ginn, 1906.

"Taxation Attitudes Show Little Change." *PA Times,* November 15, 1985, p. 3.

Thompson, Margaret C., ed. *Trade: U.S. Policy since 1945.* Washington, D.C.: Congressional Quarterly Press, 1984.

Thurow, Lester C. *The Zero-Sum Society: Distribution and the Possibilities for Economic Change.* New York: Basic Books, 1980.

Thurow, Lester C. 1983. *Dangerous Currents: The State of Economics.* New York: Random House, 1983.

Thurow, Lester C. *The Zero-Sum Solution.* New York: Simon and Schuster, 1985.

Thurow, Lester C. "A Surge in Inequality." *Scientific American* 256 (1987): 30–37.

Thurow, Lester C., and Tyson, Laura D'Andrea. "The Economic Black Hole." *Foreign Policy* 67 (Summer): 3–21.

Toffler, Alvin. *Future Shock*. New York: Bantam Books, 1970.

Toffler, Alvin. *The Third Wave*. New York: Bantam Books, 1980.

Trafford, Abigail, and Dworkin, Peter. "The New World of Health Care." *U.S. News & World Report*. (April 14, 1986): 60.

Tribe, Laurence H. "Towards a New Technology Ethic: The Role of Legal Liability." *Science, Technology, and National Policy*. Edited by Thomas J. Kuehn and Alan L. Porter, pp. 347–56. Ithaca: Cornell University Press, 1981.

"Trouble in the Groves of Academe." *U.S. News and World Report*. (April 20, 1987): 67–68.

"VA's Goal: 'Model Care' for 9 Million Older Veterans." *U.S. News & World Report*. (June 4, 1984): 93–94.

Vatter, Harold G. "The Atrophy of Net Investment and the Consequences for the U.S. Mixed Economy." *Journal of Economics* 11 (Autumn 1982): 745–48.

Volcker, Paul. New York *Times*. April 8, 1987.

Wallis, Claudia. "Children Having Children." *Time*. (December 9, 1985): 78–90.

Wallis, Claudia. "Gauging the Fat of the Land." *Time*. (February 25, 1985): 72.

Whicker, Marcia Lynn, ed. *Bobbin* 24 (1983): 34–66.

Whicker, Marcia Lynn, and Kronenfeld, Jennie J. *Sex Role Changes: Technology, Politics, and Policy*. New York: Praeger, 1986.

Wiener, Leonard. "For Both Young and Old, A New Retirement Plan." *U.S. News & World Report*. (August 5, 1985): 56–57.

Williams, William Appleman. *The Tragedy of American Diplomacy*. New York: Dell Publishing Co., 1962.

Wohl, Stanley. *The Medical Industrial Complex*. New York: Harmony Books, 1984.

Work, Clemens P., and Walsh, Maureen. "It's Fever Time for Doctors." *U.S. News & World Report*. (January 26, 1987): 44–46.

Woronoff, Jon. *World Trade War*. New York: Praeger, 1984.

Zanker, Alfred. "U.S. Taxpayers Get No Sympathy in Europe." *U.S. News and World Report*. (August 27, 1984): 65–66.

NAME INDEX

SUBJECT INDEX

ABOUT THE AUTHORS

MARCIA LYNN WHICKER is a professor in the Department of Public Administration, School of Community and Public Affairs, Virginia Commonwealth University. She holds six degrees: a Ph.D. (1976) in political science, an M.A. (1974) in political science, and an M.S. (1974) in economics from the University of Kentucky; an M.P.A. (1971) from the University of Tennessee; a B.A. (1970) in political science and economics from the University of North Carolina, and an A.E.T. (1986) in electronic engineering technology from Midlands Technical College, Columbia, South Carolina. Prior to coming to Virginia, she held faculty positions at Wayne State University in Detroit, Temple University in Philadelphia, and the University of South Carolina in Columbia.

Dr. Whicker has worked for a variety of government agencies, including the U.S. Comptroller of the Currency; the Department of Health, Education, and Welfare; the Tennessee Valley Authority; the U.S. Congress; the N.C. Department of Public Instruction; and the Pennsylvania and South Carolina state legislatures. She has published in political science, history, sociology, public policy, and public administration journals. In addition to her coauthored books with Professor Moore, she has coauthored two books with Jennie J. Kronenfeld on U.S. national health policy, and the impact of technology on sex role changes.

RAYMOND A. MOORE is a professor in the Department of Government and International Studies at the University of South Carolina. In addition to the University of South Carolina, he has taught at Upsala Colege in New Jersey, Columbia University in New York, the University of Panjab in Pakistan, the Universities of Sydney and Tasmania in Australia, San Francisco State University, SUNY at Fredonia, and the U.S. Army War College.

Dr. Moore holds a Ph.D. (1961) and a M.A. (1952) in political science from Columbia University, and a B.A. (1950) from the New School for Social Research. He has lectured widely and held numerous administrative posts. He has taught frequently in the areas of American government, U.S. foreign policy, and the American presidency. Dr. Moore has contributed extensively to journals and has published one edited and one single-authored book, besides contributing chapters to several other volumes, including a recent one on the Carter years. He is currently the editor of a forthcoming volume on the Reagan administration, to appear in both the United States and England at the close of Reagan's second term.

Whicker and Moore together have critically examined a range of factors having an impact on the performance of the U.S. political system and economy. While Whicker was at the University of South Carolina, the two jointly wrote a newspaper column on politics and public policy distributed throughout the southeast. *Making America Competitive: Policies for a Global Future* will be their third coauthored book. The first was *The U.S. Constitution: A Time for Change?* (Praeger, 1987), while the second was *When Presidents are Great*.